Insightful, historically accurate, and fascinating, Molineux's narrative brings the events of the 1700s alive. Cam Molineux weaves the who, what, when, where, and whys into a spellbinding story that unfolds like a big-screen, epic adventure. If books like this had been available when I was a student, I would have loved history instead of hating it. As a veteran homeschool educator, I appreciate the book's historical accuracy. As a book lover, I appreciate how the author has lifted the familiar characters out of the graveyard of history books, stood them on their feet, and breathed life into them.

—Lori Hatcher, speaker, editor, author, and
veteran homeschool educator

Cam Molineux weaves together accurate historical context in ways you won't realize you're reading history—unless you already know it. Read it for the story, but also gain insight into history.

—Warren A. Johnson, US Navy veteran

Stepping into the world of William Molineux was both a pleasant and an intriguing journey! The author captured the feel of prerevolutionary anticipation and tension. Through William Molineux's eyes, I experienced what the political, community, and family environments were like during this period of turmoil. I highly recommend this insightful look into one of our country's most significant periods.

—Carol Davidson, mom, grandmother, and patriot

The Spanish philosopher George Santayana said, "Those who cannot remember the past are condemned to repeat it." In her book, Cam Molineux reminds us that our founding fathers fought against regents to establish rule by representative—to place power in the hands of the people, not potentates. In these turbulent times, may we never forget the message of this book.

—Bill Kendall, former high school civics and US history teacher

Cam Molineux captures the reader with a suspenseful plot and beautifully weaves themes of courage and fighting for justice throughout the book. I highly recommend this exciting and historically accurate story that will both entertain and inspire people of all ages!

—Allison Jones, homeschool graduate

The author has lovingly lifted the spirit of William Molineux and woven him back into the homespun fabric of colonial Boston. She folds him back into the everyday lives of his friends and colleagues: John Hancock, Samuel Adams, and Paul Revere. She allows us to listen in on their conversations and lets us walk the streets of Boston with these men of destiny. You can practically feel the cobblestones beneath your feet!

Born of painstaking research, this time-lined story provides an equitable treatment of both patriots and Loyalists. Cam's impartiality is admirable. But, in the end, her love of God and country shines through as the true inspiration in her writings, and we are the ones blessed by her wonderful invention.

—Dottie Molineaux, Mx genealogist

THE *Spirit* OF A
Revolution

THE *Spirit* OF A
Revolution

BOSTON: LIBERTY'S CRADLE

CAM MOLINEUX

MOUNTAIN VIEW PRESS

Published by Mountain View Press, PO Box 427, Enumclaw, WA 98022.

Toll-Free (844) 2REDEEM (273-3336)

Mountain View Press is honored to present this title in partnership with the author. The views expressed or implied in this work are those of the author. Mountain View Press provides our imprint seal representing design excellence, creative content, and high quality production.

The author has tried to recreate events, locales, and conversations based on extensive research. In order to create a story, details may have been changed, such as adding minor characters, creating dialogue, etc.

ISBN 13: 978-1-64645-386-3 (Paperback)
978-1-64645-495-2 (ePub)
978-1-64645-387-0 (Mobi)

Library of Congress Catalog Card Number: 2021907910

Dedication

To my husband, the wind in my sails,
to my ancestors who sacrificed so that I might live in freedom, and
to my posterity for whom I seek to preserve that freedom.

It does not take a majority to prevail . . .
but rather an irate, tireless minority,
keen on setting brushfires of freedom in the minds of men.
—Samuel Adams

Do right . . .
no matter the cost!

Cam mx

Contents

Author's Note

You pronounce the protagonist's last name ma-li-no—with a short a, short i, and long o. William Molineux was a real person, and most of what you will read here is true. I have added just enough fiction to make the narrative flow.

As you may have guessed by looking at my name, evidence indicates the story's protagonist and I are related. Although Molineux's exact heritage is somewhat elusive, distant cousins and I continue to work to solve the mystery. I have woven bits and pieces of Molineux's ancestry into these pages based on my interpretation of the clues we have already uncovered.

William Molineux lived in Boston in the years leading up to the Revolutionary War. His circumstances were not very different from those found in America during the early decades of the twenty-first century. God-given freedoms were under attack, and Molineux had to grapple with whether issues affecting his daily life warranted his time and attention.

As you read, I trust you will come to understand the fight for freedom was by real people with hopes, dreams, and families—like yours. As with those mentioned in this novel—Samuel Adams, John Hancock, William Molineux, and others—each of us has a unique role to play in preserving liberties for which others have already sacrificed so much. I pray you will draw inspiration from those who have gone before and will respond with *The Spirit of a Revolution*.

CHAPTER ONE

The Game
Summer 1764

Seafoam clung to William Molineux's boots as he and Junior hoisted another chest of tea from the small boat into the wagon. The horse at the other end neighed. "Easy, Delilah," Molineux said, "or you will give us away."

Junior wiped sweat from his brow. It seemed Molineux's eldest son had grown another inch overnight, bringing him closer to his father's six-foot frame. "At least we have no need for a lantern tonight," he said, looking across the glistening ocean beneath the moonlit sky.

"And we are far enough from Boston to go undetected." Molineux rubbed his shoulder, grimacing at the pain. His body responded less favorably to physical labor these days compared with his younger years.

He and Junior stepped back into the boat to retrieve another crate, careful to avoid creating a racket or even engaging in conversation with the sailor who had made the delivery. An hour's worth of work had been enough to create a rhythm. Step into the boat. Bend. Lift. Navigate legs over the upper edge of the vessel using eye contact and head nods to prevent an accident. Take a few steps away from the shoreline then heave the crate into the wagon. Repeat.

John, his younger son, patted the mare's neck. "Pa, it's too bad we must do this at night."

Molineux motioned to Junior for a break then leaned against the side of the wagon before replying to his eleven-year-old. "Yes, but the authorities refuse to let us do this openly." Molineux rubbed his brow. His sons were old enough to deserve an explanation for all the secrecy so he plunged in. "Many years ago Parliament passed a law designed to put us out of business. It seems they wanted to keep all the profits from the West Indies for themselves, so they slapped a tax on us."

Molineux straightened and placed one hand on his hip. "We had better finish up so the seaman can return to his ship." The wet sand crunched as he led Junior back to the remaining crates.

"It's like a game," Molineux said to John as he and Junior transferred the last of the tea.

"A game?"

"Like chess, there are rules that anyone who plays the game would follow. But sometimes, like at home, we make new rules. Together, we decide what they are and do it for fun. With Parliament, the rules are unspoken, but we merchants know what they are and act accordingly."

John stroked the horse's mane. "I think I understand."

"We all realized how absurd the tax was because paying it would lead to our starvation. Ignoring it became the accepted protocol. No one on either side of the great pond seems to mind, so we simply pretend to obey."

Molineux threw a rope from the wagon onto the cargo. "You boys use these to tie 'em down while I finish up with the sailor."

Junior grabbed the rope and hurled one end to the other side of the wagon. "The game sounds ludicrous to me."

Molineux walked over and chatted with the man in the boat, then they pushed the vessel away from the sandbar. As it hit water, the sailor jumped in.

"I will be in touch about next spring's shipment," Molineux said.

The sailor nodded and rowed away.

Molineux checked the ropes on the wagon. "Good job, boys." He walked to the front, lifted John into it, and pointed to the alcove behind the seat. "There's the nook we set up for you."

"Thank you, Pa." John settled into the boy-sized spot. "What language was that man speaking?"

Molineux grinned. "It was part English and part Dutch."

"Dutch?"

Junior climbed onto the bench seat. "The language they speak in Holland, featherbrain."

Molineux cast a stern glance at Junior.

John held out his hand. "Can you toss me the sack of hay? I need it for my head if I am going to sleep."

Junior rolled his eyes and shoved the bag at his brother.

"That is quite enough, Junior." Molineux pulled himself up and grabbed the reins. "We all have our weaknesses. Heaven knows I have mine."

John crinkled his nose. "But sleeping isn't a weakness. Is it, Pa?"

Molineux released the brake and clicked his tongue. The horse began to move, causing the wagon wheels to groan. "I guess you're right. We all *need* sleep—whether we get it or not."

John arranged the sack against the tea chests. "I will be glad to get back to my own bed."

"I am afraid it will be a few hours, as we must first unload at the warehouse before we can head home. Cargo at our house come dawn would destroy the illusion we are trying to create." Molineux's body fell into rhythm with the movement of the wagon. "And that, my son, would be the ruin of us all."

The morning sun filtered into the Beacon Hill home as Molineux made a noisy descent down the grand staircase. No need for light from the chandelier today. Sunbeams played with the reds in the carpet and danced with the fresh flowers on the sideboard.

The love of his life stood in the parlor doorway shaking her head. A summer breeze blew in from the open window in the room behind her. "You amuse me, Will."

"Delighted, madam," he said with a bow, "that I am doing my job." After sixteen years of marriage, he still managed to charm her.

A sheepish grin betrayed Maryann's amusement at his juvenile behavior. "Careful, or our fine china may express its displeasure."

"Ah, my dear, but what good are possessions if they restrain the owner?"

"Unless our neighbors begin loosening their purse strings, you may find yourself eating porridge out of something less suitable for your extravagant tastes." Maryann's eyes widened, and she held up her hand. "Watch out—"

Molineux caught sight of their little girl seconds before she ran into him. "Whoa," he howled as he attempted to catch himself. He hit the floor with a thud.

Maryann rushed to his side. "We know from whom she learned her antics."

Molineux chuckled as Elizabeth helped push him back to his feet. "You are mighty strong for a six-year-old." He scooped her up then strode toward a side room where he grabbed the leather pouch from his desk before returning to the entrance hall. "More fun and games later, my dear Elizabeth." He set her down, glancing around. "Where are the others?"

Maryann opened the front door. "Junior and John wanted to stop by the Allens' on their way to the store, and I sent Anne on an errand."

"Then it is to the two of you, I bid adieu." A pat on Elizabeth's head and playful hug and kiss for Maryann, then he was out the door. How he longed to stay and enjoy time with the family, but concerns of the day pulled him away from their hilltop haven.

Molineux stood on the front porch of his home and breathed deeply. Ah, salt air. The morning's golden sun reflected off rooftops in the distance, and ships in the harbor appeared to be a mere extension of the town. His store beckoned from Merchants Row. He practiced another jig on the long flight of stone steps and began his descent to the town.

At the foot of Beacon Hill, flies swarmed around the cows on the fifty acres to his right. Molineux turned onto Long Acre, tipping his hat to each passerby. The female image on the western wall of the Manufactory House across the street, with distaff in hand, reminded him of better days. "Your spinning wheels have lain silent far too long," Molineux said aloud to the inanimate object. "Worry not, madame, we will set them into motion once again—before the year is out, if I have my way." Molineux winked and continued on.

The prior boom years had allowed Molineux to provide a comfortable life for himself and his family. Recently, however, Bostonians were making do with their old saddles, braziery, and cutlery rather than buying new from him. Surely the economic slump would end and business would pick up again. Without the watchful eyes of wartime British cruisers, strains on trade had lessened.

A side trip to check on the new construction would not lengthen the path to his store by much, so he altered his course. Ahead, brick and stone houses and shops rose from the ashes left by the dreadful fire four years earlier. Several of them would soon be in need of his wares. The sound of laborers at work was music to his ears. The diversion made him forget the news recently arrived from Britain. Almost. Molineux turned onto the cobblestone street. Sight of the harbor reminded him of the challenges he and other merchants now faced. With so much at stake, he circled back to the *Gazette* to find out whether Benjamin Edes or John Gill had received any new information and to discover what opinions might be forming.

The pungent smell of ink greeted him as he entered the print shop. The press, whose mechanical motion often entertained Molineux's boys, filled much of the room. Drying newsprint hung from the ceiling while nearby stacks of sheets awaited imprint. Molineux ducked to avoid getting ink on his wig. Those shorter than he held an advantage on printing day.

John Hancock was among a handful already gathered in the cramped space. When Molineux moved from the South End to the North's more prestigious neighborhood a few years earlier, he had acquired Hancock's uncle and surrogate father as a neighbor. Their homes sat atop the summit watching over the town. Molineux had watched the younger Hancock grow into a young man with whom he now stood eyeball to eyeball. The elder Hancock was among the wealthiest merchants in Boston, and like Molineux, carried on illicit trade with Holland, which supplied smugglers with one of the colony's favorite commodities—tea.

"How is your uncle, Mr. Hancock?" Molineux asked. "I haven't seen him about lately."

"Feeling his age," Hancock said. "I am afraid the recent changes have gotten to him."

"London had no right to enforce what we have ignored for decades," Molineux said. "The high duty on sweeteners has always been unreasonable. They should know that."

Hancock let out a feeble moan. "It leaves all of us merchants feeling a bit unsettled."

An apprentice looked up from his place in the corner where he was setting type. "Some are expressing concerns over the legality of Parliament's involvement at all."

Molineux shook his head. "It is the threat of seizures and confiscations of my vessels for suspected smuggling that worries me. And the thought of a juryless trial in Britain-friendly Nova Scotia adds to my discomfort."

"Ah, but if you are targeted," Hancock said, "wouldn't your family and business connections there be able to get you out of any hot water?" He made his way to the door, keeping his fine clothes away from anything laden with ink.

"Mr. Edes will be back soon," the apprentice said. "Mr. Adams was here earlier but left. Said he had other places to be."

"He cannot be too happy, and none of us will be if folks are unable to get molasses for their rum. His father, bless his soul, would have had a thing or two to say about that."

"I will be the one who's disappointed," Molineux said, "if good news has not arrived in time for the fall festivities."

"You live for excitement, don't you, Mr. Molineux?"

"Live for it?" someone else chimed in. "He is at the center of it."

Molineux smiled. "There is never enough for my satisfaction. Pope's Day keeps me going for the rest of the year. If it gets canceled, none of you will want to be in my company."

"All we can do is wait," Hancock said, "and pray for good news, lest we all have to live with a very unpleasant Mr. Molineux."

CHAPTER TWO

Dark Clouds
November 5, 1764–August 12, 1765

Molineux's feet hit the cool hardwood floors early. He beat a fist into his hand. Today he would return "favors." Last year's black eye deserved a response. His grimace faded into a smirk and then a smile. "The fifth of November is finally here. Exhilarating."

"Promise me you'll be careful," Maryann said, brushing her hair at the vanity.

"Not to worry, my dear. We have no plans to blow up the king or Parliament today. Mr. Otis says this is merely an annual frolic, undertaken without malice, and conducted without substantial injury."

Molineux's red cape flashed through his mind. Still in fine shape when he departed Ireland, it had gone out of fashion before he disembarked in the New World. He would find a use for it, but not today. He grabbed his hunting shirt and breeches. They would be more appropriate for the occasion. He perused his hat collection then snatched the felt one. "This will add the flair I want."

Maryann pivoted to face him. "More flair than practicality, to be sure. It does suit you."

Molineux gave one last, glorious bow to the looking glass then dashed into the hall as if the world were awaiting his arrival. Maryann followed.

Sight of their son's closed door stopped his forward progress. He knocked. "Junior, are you ready? Junior?" He opened the door and watched the boy pull the covers over his head.

Molineux's forehead furrowed. "Fifteen. Was I ever that age?"

"Run along, Will." Maryann gestured toward the stairs. "I will send Junior along shortly."

Molineux descended into the main living area two steps at a time.

John sat at a table in the parlor studying the page in front of him. Molineux sized up his son's attire. More suited for church than a scuffle, but perfect for his role today.

John held up a moneybag.

"I knew I could count on you, boy," Molineux said.

John grinned. "I have the recitation memorized."

"Let's hear it."

John stood, straightened his clothing, then began. "Don't you remember the fifth of November, the gunpowder treason and plot?" The lad cast a timid glance toward his father, who motioned for him to continue. "I see no reason why gunpowder treason should ever be forgot. From Rome to Rome the pope is come, amid ten thousand fears, with fiery serpents to be seen at eyes, nose, mouth, and ears. Don't you hear my little bell go chink, chink, chink. Please to give me a little money to buy my pope some drink."

Molineux clapped. "Bravo, as they would say in Italy. Very good indeed."

John returned to his chair. "I shan't be long, Papa. I should be able to complete my task and be there before the festivities begin."

The autumn air tickled Molineux's face as he ran down the hill, whooping all the way. He was anxious to rally the North End men for the friendly—and sometimes not-so-friendly—brawl. For those who cared about its historical significance, Pope's Day was about showing displeasure for religious or political scapegoats through their treatment of feather-stuffed effigies. For Molineux, it was all about the festive atmosphere and abundant interaction. It also gave him the opportunity to scuffle with men from the other end of town and to demonstrate he was not quite as decrepit as some believed.

He spotted the South End's leader circulating among his clan. Their commander flailed his arms.

"Huh, he will need to do more than that," Molineux mumbled, "to ready himself for my North End clan."

Men and boys mulled around their respective floats, eying the other gang's effigy of the pope. Capturing it was the goal. Bumps and bruises, the means. Horses neighed amid the excitement. A few snorted.

"I see your boy is big enough to be one of the puppeteers this year," Molineux said to one of the men.

"Aye. And quite proud to be."

Each float's comically dressed straw pontiff took center stage while each devil—with lantern and pitchfork in hand—lurked closely behind. The boys would manipulate the effigies' heads using poles.

"And where are your boys?" the man asked.

"Junior should arrive soon, and John is going house to house soliciting funds for the victor's bonfire and supper sure to follow." Molineux scanned the crowd. The women and children were ready to cheer on their respective clans. "There's Junior now." Molineux waved to get the boy's attention. What a thrill to have his eldest son join in the Pope's Day action this year.

Men from the North End signaled their readiness. Each float paraded toward the other. North converged with South, and they became indistinguishable.

"North End forever!"

"Nay, South End!" the rivals countered.

Molineux searched the crowd for John. He wanted to ensure his younger son was learning from his father's example. He spotted John, eyes wide and watching, then planted a right punch on a South-ender. Junior howled and did the same.

"Don't stop until you see blood," Molineux yelled.

"Huzzah! Huzzah! Huzzah!" the crowd shouted.

Molineux felt a blow to his back. "Show me your face, ye coward." He whirled to get revenge.

A shriek came from the direction of the South End's float—then shouts of confusion. "Stop! Someone's been hurt."

Molineux stood with his fist frozen in midair. "Your trickery won't work on me." The man with whom he had been fighting ran toward the float. Molineux glanced about. It was apparently not a ploy, so he joined others running toward the commotion.

Gasps rippled throughout the horde of people.

"What? What is it?" Molineux strained to see.

A man made his way through the crowd, motioning toward the float. "A small child has been crushed beneath the wheels of the wagon. His body is as lifeless as an effigy without a master."

Mothers clung to their little ones and frantically scanned the crowd for their older children caught up in the fray. Some staggered about, bewildered. Others tended to the casualty and put their arms around the family. Little ones wept. Many left in a solemn daze.

Unable to locate his own family, Molineux started home. What a disappointing end to an otherwise magnificent day. Surely the new year would bring with it signs of hope.

Molineux sat at the desk in his Merchants Row store and warehouse. Despite two months of passage, a dark cloud still lingered over the town as a result of November's tragedy. With so little activity around town, it was as if time had come to a screeching halt.

He tapped the pen on his ledger. Nothing he tried would make it balance. He stared at the fireplace against the back wall. It was too late in the day to stoke it.

He stood and paced the room then walked to the window and pulled back a bit of the curtain. The harbor and half-mile wharf, Boston's lifeblood, sat eerily silent. January's colder-than-usual winds added to the number of unemployed and to depression among the town's merchants—a far cry from the bustling town that had welcomed him and his adolescent brother in 1742. Their father's passing, coupled with reports Boston was "the most flourishing town for trade and commerce in English America," had made their decision clear. Boston. Now.

Ancestral ties to iron-rich Staffordshire, England, had given Molineux the expertise needed to open a hardware store, and relatives in port cities throughout the empire had placed odds in his favor. Although lessons learned from artisan and merchant kinfolk had increased his chances for success, venturing to the New World had been no small feat. As a young man of twenty-five, he had not realized how much he would one day feel the distance. At least his international trade gave him some continued sense of connection.

Displeasure now mingled with congenial thoughts of home as Britain struggled with her North American colonies. Business slowed to a crawl, adding to the somber mood. Bankruptcy was on the rise, and several shops had closed. The crackdown imposed by the Sugar Act threatened to bring down additional merchants. How ironic the "sweet" act of Parliament left colonists feeling so bitter.

Molineux returned to his desk and picked up the quill. His shoulders drooped more than usual these days. Maybe the position as Mr. Apthorp's power of attorney would come through. Meanwhile, he would prepare to share his thoughts regarding the new tariff with the committee in February.

A gentle rap on the door caused Molineux to drop his pen. John Hancock's head appeared around the door. "May I have a moment of your time?"

"Come in. No shutters or bars on my place—yet." Molineux smiled as much from the pleasure of having a visitor as for still being in business.

Hancock shut the door behind him and moved closer to the coals, even though the shop's smoldering fire gave off more smoke than warmth.

"Better than that," Molineux said. "Will you do me the pleasure of sharing the walk home?"

"I had hoped this would be well-timed for you," Hancock said.

Molineux grabbed his cloak and gathered a few things. "You are looking mighty pale."

"I have been less than well this winter. I needed to check on my warehouses, but the trip has taken much out of me."

Molineux threw on a hat then extended his arm toward the door. "After you."

Outside, the two began their journey toward Beacon Hill.

"What's on your mind, boy?" Molineux said.

"I feel in need of some fatherly advice."

"Missing your uncle, I take it."

"I had hoped for more time with him after returning from London. I apologize if I have neglected my neighborly duties to you. Becoming his business partner left me little time for anything else."

"No offense has been taken, lad. Please continue."

Hancock's eyes stayed downcast as the two made their way up King Street. Molineux provided polite nods to shop keepers sprinkled across their path who were also closing their places of business for the day.

"I am under the impression," Hancock said, "Mr. Adams is encouraging the town to elect me as one of its selectmen at the annual meeting."

"Your uncle held that position for a number of years—and with distinction."

Hancock pulled his collar tight against the wind whipping off the harbor. "I believe he mentioned you were a constable at the time."

Molineux chuckled above the sound of the snow beneath their feet. "'Tis true. That was soon after I arrived." He pursed his lips and squinted. Condensation left his mouth without words then he spoke. "And I believe the elder Mr. Adams was a selectman around the same time."

"How can I live up to such lofty expectations?"

Molineux stopped, reached for Hancock's arm, and faced his protégé. "Do not forget, Mr. Hancock, your uncle was once a young man like you. And I was in my twenties when I served." Sweet aromas emitting from the coffeehouse pulled his attention away from the conversation for a moment.

The two resumed their walk. "I suppose you are right, and I do want to be of service."

"I am sure you do. And if, after a year, the town decides they would be better served by another, then so be it. At least they are not asking you to be a representative. I hear those fellows argued for days over whether to use the word 'privileges' or 'rights.'"

"An important distinction, is it not?" Hancock asked.

"Maybe. But I would be unable to spend hours haggling over the point."

Hancock finally smiled.

"But you, my lad"—Molineux raised his hand for emphasis—"you may be cut out of the proper cloth for those kinds of battles." The two men had reached the two-story Town House at the head of King Street. "More conflicts than I care to know about have taken place inside this building's brick walls. Maybe your initiation would be less rocky than your uncle's. It was quite a brawl between him and Mr. Adams. Helping to keep the town rid of smallpox as a selectman may not be the easiest task in the world, but it is certainly better than what he went through." Molineux turned to Hancock as they moved along. "But that is long past, and there are better days ahead. Mr. Otis says his tract will help Parliament see the error of her ways."

"Do you believe it will?"

"His words, whether written or spoken, are always powerful. He can hold his own—we saw that in the writs case. But as then, he may not care so much if he wins, so long as he has clearly stated what he believes to be true."

"I was in London, but understand it was a disturbing time."

Molineux nodded. "I was among the fifty or so he represented. Alarming to have customs officials search our ships or buildings upon a whim—it was indeed. Mr. Otis's presentation to the court was quite impressive."

"He certainly waxes eloquent when writing about our natural and God-given rights. Do you believe he and Mr. Hutchinson will ever get along?"

Molineux laughed. "Good question. It did take Mr. Otis some time to settle down after Mr. Hutchinson stole the chief justice job from his father." Molineux brought his hands to his mouth, blew, then rubbed them together. "With the state of our economy, we might want to consider trading our lot as merchants for their place in the legal profession."

"The business failures of some of our more notable colleagues have given us all great anxiety. No one appears to be safe."

Molineux sighed at the thought of merchants losing their estates. "The whole world seems to be falling apart. Even my church is facing a messy lawsuit."

"I trust the hard times will come to an end, but it is difficult to say under our present circumstances."

Molineux and Hancock turned onto Beacon Street. "Enough about the bad times," Molineux said. "Tell me about the coronation. It must have been a sight to behold. King George is about your age, is he not?" Molineux stopped and raised an eyebrow. "And your brother—I hear he is leaving your firm to become my competition. Should I assume he has dipped into your pockets to do so?"

Hancock smiled. "I am happy to assist him. Only time will tell if he will succeed. You already have quite the advantage over him, so I would not fret too much over it."

They arrived in front of their homes where Hancock delighted Molineux with tales of his London adventures before they parted ways.

Molineux walked up the long flight of steps to his abode then pivoted, surveying the town. His eyes scanned to the left and settled on the three buildings closest to his home—structures the town had set up for the poor and those for whom their minds or deeds required minor correction. The lives sheltered there stood in stark contrast to his own. Past choices had set him on a different path. Yet even as the master of his own destiny, winds of fate had, at times, blown into the sails of his life. Now was such a time.

Beyond the three buildings sat the Manufactory House, as silent as the harbor. He was sure it would bustle as much as the poor house did now . . . someday.

Molineux spent much of the next few months at home. No need to go to a store without customers. Melodious humming came from the next room. Black cherry trees, his wife's favorite, basked in the sunshine, and she wanted the world to know spring was in the air. Molineux jerked the curtains closed to counter the fragrance wafting in through the open window. Pleasantries had no place in his world. Not today.

He frowned at the newspaper sitting on his desk. "I refuse to believe it."

"Is that you, Will?" Maryann said from the parlor.

"Just talking to the handsome man who put on my shoes this morning." His face turned sour, and a slight growl escaped from his lips. Surely Parliament would not be so bold as to tax every piece of paper in town—newspapers, pamphlets, and property deeds. And, most importantly, his ships' clearance papers. The documents would require a stamp to indicate taxes had been paid.

Molineux thrummed his fingers on his desk. Could it get any worse? Certainly the town would not allow it—neither would those living in the country, for they would also be affected. Their lieutenant governor must have had a hand in this. Molineux's jaw tightened. At times, Hutchinson's blind loyalty to the homeland was maddening.

"Parliament, the demonstration of your authority over us is impressive." Molineux folded the paper. "And there are those among us who shudder to think where it might lead."

Spring blossoms transitioned into summer green. Molineux's family had scattered about the house. After nearly five years in the Beacon Hill home, it felt like a saddle that had finally been broken in—the right furniture in the right place, comfortable, and full of familiar smells.

Junior sat cross-legged in his stocking feet on the parlor floor, fiddling with scrap pieces of leather and a knife.

Molineux settled into his favorite chair. "Still wanting to learn to make shoes, I see."

Junior grunted.

Molineux opened the paper and smiled as he read about recent events in the more cautious colony to their south. He felt a kindred spirit with the new member of the House of Burgess. "It is about time somebody shook up things down there."

"Who?" Junior asked.

"Patrick Henry. He's a bright, young lawyer in Virginia. Maybe his current stand will provide courage for those who have been less bold about our response to the Motherland."

"But aren't we loyal subjects?"

"Yes, indeed, but Mr. Otis says that without representation, Parliament has no right to tax its subjects. And we have none."

Maryann entered the room with a platter of fresh bread and imported cheese. "Anyone in need of nourishment?"

Junior threw his project aside and jumped to his feet. "Always."

"Careful with that knife, son," Maryann said.

Molineux thumped the front page of the newspaper with his finger. "Edes and Gill refuse to place the stamp on their periodical. Instead, they are going to put the skull and crossbones."

"Skull and crossbones?" Maryann set the food on the sideboard.

"A symbol of death. Some say freedom is dying."

"What do you believe?"

Molineux set down the paper. "The jury is still out, but I am proud Edes and Gill will not only refuse to pay the tax but will also use what they have—the printed word—to fight back. 'Good for them,' I say!" His eyes squinted and his hands tightened into fists. "And, who knows? If words are not enough, I may express dissatisfaction using my own set of tactics."

In the coming months, Molineux watched as small groups of activists sprang up to combat what some believed to be illegal policies being forced upon them. Against his character, he held back. Maryann's amiable nature acted as a govern for his volatility.

The evening of August 12 found him at the coffeehouse with James Otis and a half dozen others to discuss the rumblings around town. Something was afoot, and a restlessness stirred within Molineux's soul.

"You were correct, Mr. Otis, in what you wrote," Molineux said. "The Stamp Act has the whole town, including me, thinking more than ever before."

"And rightly so," Otis said.

Everything about the forty-year-old attorney seemed round. Round torso, round lips, and even round curls that stopped halfway down his round face. Even though a few years Molineux's junior, Otis's knowledge of matters related to the law surpassed that of the merchant by decades.

"Do you believe legal documents without a stamp will be worth the paper they are written on?" Molineux stared at his mug then looked up. The heat from within him began to crawl up his neck. "Do you believe they will be honored—or considered null and void? And will my ships be seized if they set sail without the proper papers?"

"Those are some of the questions we need to ponder," Otis said. "And, unfortunately, we will need to do so over a meal of lobsters. For with the economy as it is, it is all we poor Bostonians can afford."

Evening hues filled the sky as Molineux marched down King Street to the harbor then proceeded to the end of the wharf. "Can you hear me?" he shouted at England, saltwater spraying in his face. He spit back. It mattered not to him whether anyone watched. He reared back and cupped his hands around his mouth. "Keep your fingers out of my purse." Then he lifted his arms and waved both fists in the air.

The merchant strode back to shore, shaking his head and mumbling all the way. "What should concern me—slavery, arbitrary power, or my dying trade?" For Molineux, the lines blurred. "Parliament needs to mind its own business while I take care of my own."

He trudged home. With the Stamp Act set to take effect November 1, only two months remained in which to plan their response. He sucked in his upper lip. Based on the pulse of the town, their reaction might astound Britain beyond what it could have ever imagined.

CHAPTER THREE

○‿○

Hutchinson

August 14–27, 1765

*E*vening shadows filtered through the second-story windows of the Town House. Thomas Hutchinson, Massachusetts Bay's lieutenant governor, motioned for the sheriff to enter the council chambers. As the stamp commissioner's brother-in-law, the lieutenant governor was eager to get a report. His focus, and that of the entire advisory board, turned toward their provincial leader, seated at the head of the table.

"You have returned with good news, I trust," Governor Bernard said.

"I am afraid not, your Excellency," the sheriff said. "The crowd threatened to hang me and my men if we attempted to remove the display, so it remains untouched."

The lieutenant governor sat deep in thought. A seven-foot-tall wooden lion and unicorn, symbols of the British monarchy, graced the building's pinnacle. They apparently held no meaning for the lower and middling parts of society who had gathered to mock their own, feather-stuffed symbols of the Crown's authority—effigies swaying in the branches of the great elm tree on the south side of town.

Hutchinson shook images from his mind generated by news of the scene, then he placed both hands on the table in front of him. "The people are demonstrating against the Crown." The notion of a stuffed likeness of Boston's Parliament-appointed stamp official, Andrew Oliver, troubled him. Worse, a large boot hung alongside, representing the Brit who people held responsible for the Stamp Act. A devil-like figure peered out from the oversize shoe, appearing to wave the Stamp Act at those who had gathered.

"Leave the effigies alone," one council member said, "and the situation will die a natural death. Otherwise, your actions will turn this into a serious affair."

"More serious than it has already become?" Hutchinson asked.

The sheriff shifted his weight. "The people claimed, if left alone, they would give the effigies a proper burial."

Governor Bernard placed his fist on his chin. "Against my desires, so be it."

"No record should be made of our advice," someone said.

Bernard frowned. "I insist that you present me with an answer that I may enter into the council book."

"Then order the sheriff to send his officers to preserve the peace."

"Such an act would be one of form more than substance, would it not?"

The sheriff began to light the candles along the exterior wall. He moved closer to the window and looked out. "Your decision may be a bit too late."

Hutchinson joined him. "Oh, dear." He ducked to stay out of sight of the mob filling the street below. "There must be two thousand of them." The Town House rumbled. Hutchinson caught his breath. "They have entered the building." He hastened back to the table.

Heavy footsteps pounded on the steps leading from the ground floor to where they sat above. All eyes shifted to the chamber doors.

Several men carrying effigies entered. Forty to fifty tradesmen followed and paraded around the room. Chair legs dragged across the floor as councilmen jostled to get out of the way. No longer certain if the trembling came from the movement of the floor or from within his own soul, Hutchinson grabbed the edge of the table. Then as quickly as they had appeared, the men filed out of the room and rejoined their comrades in the street.

Hutchinson returned to the window and motioned for someone to raise it slightly.

The mob shouted as they marched down King Street. "Liberty, property, and no stamps! Huzzah! Huzzah! Huzzah!"

The sheriff excused himself, and a few of the councilmen made their way onto the balcony facing the harbor.

Hutchinson said, "They have turned toward Mr. Oliver's dock."

Ten minutes later the mass of humanity spilled back onto King Street. Hutchinson gasped. "Are they carrying lumber from the commissioner's new building?"

"I have seen enough," one of the councilmen said as they all filed back into the chamber.

Soon the sound of shattering glass from a block away broke the silence. Hutchinson hurried onto the balcony then quickly stepped back inside. "I must go."

Hutchinson shuddered at the sight of the beheaded effigy in Oliver's front yard. More smoke than usual filled the night air. Had the mob used their newly acquired lumber for a bonfire? They were too far away to tell, but the noise grew louder, so he quickened his pace to Oliver's home where he found the family huddled together with friends. The stamp commissioner's arms spread wide around his family.

Hutchinson grabbed Oliver's hand. "You and the others must escape out the back. There is no time to spare."

Moments later, the throng forced its way past the fence in the front yard. Hutchinson took two steps back to avoid being trampled as the horde entered the house.

"He is not here," Hutchinson said in a voice less certain than he would have liked.

"We will see for ourselves." Their leader rushed toward the stairs then spun around. Hatred filled his eyes. "Then we will show him what we think of him and his stamps."

Time stood still as the mob ransacked the house. Unable to find Oliver, they left.

Hutchinson sank into a chair. Pieces of dishware clinked beneath his feet, and a portrait lay on the floor. He rose and returned it to its proper place on the wall. The house sat in shambles. What kind of people would do such a thing? And who would be their next victim?

Two weeks later, Hutchinson sat at the dining table with his children for a late evening meal. The stifled singing from outside intensified. A trip to the front door confirmed his greatest fear—a drunken mob was heading toward his home.

He returned to the table, stoic. "Children, prepare the lanterns quickly. You must flee to the neighbor's house."

Martha, his fourteen-year-old, refused to budge. "But Father—"

Hutchinson clutched her shoulder. "Do as I say and assist your younger siblings."

She rose and left with the other children out the back door.

Hutchinson stood for several moments, listening, then he moved toward the front window. A noise from the back of the house startled him.

Martha stood in the doorway. "I have come back for you and will not leave alone."

Loud singing and men's footsteps came up the front steps.

Hutchinson grabbed his daughter's hand. As they fled out the back, an ax came crashing through the front door—then shattering glass.

Hutchinson and his daughter hurried until they reached shadows of the trees in the distant part of his garden, beyond the glow of the moonlight.

Curses from the hellish crew tormented them. "He is upstairs. We will have him!" Seconds later, a chair crashed through an upper window. A lampstand and other small items followed.

Then, the unthinkable. Papers. Hutchinson placed a hand over his mouth. The history of Massachusetts Bay had taken him years to record. Apart from his children, it was his most prized possession. The papers floated to the ground. Household furnishings tossed from the house pressed the pages into the mud. Every bone in Hutchinson's body screamed for him to sink to the ground in agony, yet something within propelled him forward to rescue his labor of love. A hand pulled him back. He fought back tears then left with his daughter to join the others.

What had become of his beloved town?

Several hours later, a tattered Hutchinson stood before the superior court. Four justices sat in their wigs and robes while their chief stood before them in neither. He tugged at the borrowed jacket to cover the wrinkles in the shirt he had escaped in the night before. Nothing could hide the unkempt breeches. "I would like to declare my innocence amid the things for which I have been accused and for which I have been attacked. It is why I stand before you in such inappropriate attire." His spirit wilted. He had appeared to provide the court with a quorum on its opening day and to address the situation at hand.

He straightened to full stature then continued. "Although I am not obligated to give an answer to all the questions asked by every lawless person—God as my witness—I never aided, assisted, or supported, or in the least encouraged what is commonly referred to as the Stamp Act. On the contrary, I did all in my power and strove with all my might to prevent it."

He wiped a tear from his cheek and scanned the bench. "This is not declared through timidity, for I have nothing to fear. They can only take away my life, which is of little value when deprived of all its comforts and all that is dear to me."

Hutchinson took his seat, and the session ended.

CHAPTER FOUR

Resistance

October 7, 1765–May 19, 1766

The smoldering logs in the fireplace kept the chill of the October evening at bay as members of Molineux's family busied themselves with various activities.

Molineux sat at the small game table in his parlor with Elizabeth. "Your turn, Elizabeth." Molineux pointed to the backgammon board.

She rolled the die then her eyes brightened. "Doubles."

Molineux threw up his hands. "Oh, my."

Elizabeth giggled at her father's expressive ways then moved two checkers to her home board.

John adjusted the lantern and the newspaper that lay before him. "What does 'posterity' mean, Papa?"

"You and Elizabeth are my posterity."

"And Junior and Anne," Maryann added, her rocker finding a rhythm as she knit.

"What about Uncle Robert and Uncle John?"

"Their children are also my posterity." Molineux turned toward John. "And the little ones expected next year. And their children and their children's children. Why do you ask?"

"The newspaper mentions it."

"Won't you read it to us?" Maryann asked.

John sat up and adjusted the light once again. He smoothed out the pages and began. "'My Dear Countrymen, Awake!—Awake, my countrymen, and by a regular and legal opposition, defeat the designs of those who enslave us and our posterity. This is your burden, your indispensable duty. Ages remote, mortals yet unborn, will bless your generous efforts, and revere the memory of the saviors of their country.'"

He set the paper aside. "Papa, do you believe we are enslaved?"

"Some believe so."

"But what about you?"

"Parliament's actions have certainly added frustration to my business. Enslaved?" Molineux shrugged. "Could be. But I will withhold judgment for now."

Elizabeth tapped on the backgammon board. "Your turn, Papa."

Molineux spun around to his daughter and grinned.

John stood and walked over. "And Mr. Hancock? What does he believe?"

Molineux looked up at his son. "Like me, he is quite disturbed by how the whole matter could affect trade. Does he believe we are enslaved? I do not know." He rolled his die, moved a checker, then stared thoughtfully at his audience. "I have heard one of our delegates to New York went rogue, and I would like to find out if Mr. Hancock knows any more about it. I shall pay him a visit soon to discuss that—and the matter of slavery. Others seem to be influenced by his leanings so he must continue to stand firm, regardless of the cost."

Two weeks later, Molineux stood in the office of the Hancock home. The young man sat at his desk with quill in hand. His tailored and notably elegant clothing worked well with his fragile frame.

Molineux cut straight to the heart of his concerns—the stamps.

Hancock set down his quill. "It is the most disagreeable commodity ever imported into this country."

"None of us are the happier for their arrival."

"To be sure, the execution of the stamps will stagnate any trade that remains."

Molineux peered out the window, across the tops of the trees punctuated with colors of autumn. "The harbor already sits empty. No merchant with whom I speak will allow a stamp to be placed on his papers."

"The authorities will find a way to make it happen," Hancock said, "and I dread the event."

"I do beg your pardon for having come uninvited and unannounced, but"—Molineux meandered over to Hancock's desk—"a letter to London?"

Hancock stared at the pages before him. "I concluded with, 'Your Sincere Friend but an Enemy to the Stamps.'" He picked them up. "I want this letter to be a standing monument to posterity—and to my children in particular—a statement that I, by no means, agreed to submit to this cruel act."

"Children?"

"When they come." Hancock smiled. "As you know, I must first wed, and there are no plans for that anytime soon, much to Aunt Lydia's dismay."

Molineux motioned. "Back to the letter."

"I have written several in recent days. This one shares my desire with agents that my outgoing vessel return in the spring loaded with goods." Hancock raised his hand as if to stave off an expected objection. "Of course, it is under the condition Parliament has a change of heart and makes the Stamp Act null and void."

Molineux's muscles relaxed while Hancock continued.

"If not repealed, I told them they could bid adieu to remittances for past goods."

"A good plan since, without stamps, our courts will remain closed and would be unable to collect what we owe them."

Hancock waved his hand toward the letter. "Included herein." He stood, moving toward the window. "The people of this country will never suffer themselves to be made slaves. It is cruel and unconstitutional. As for myself, I am resolved not to send one more ship to sea if a stamp must be attached to my papers to do so."

"A bold move for which I commend you."

"I would rather subject myself to the hardest labor than carry on business under so great a burden. If they insist on making slaves of us, I will sell my stock in trade and shut my warehouse doors." Hancock returned to his desk. "I will not be made a slave without my consent."

"Hear, hear."

Hancock's countenance fell. "'Tis a sad time for us all. We are a people worth saving"—he tapped the letter—"for their sakes as much as for our own." Hancock took the pen from its well and signed his name to the letter, then sat quietly for a moment.

"At least attorneys and newspapermen have joined us merchants in the fight."

"And do not forget the ministers. Several are proclaiming the importance of liberty from their pulpits," Hancock said.

"One declared liberty was about to depart from America, leaving Satan's child behind."

Hancock nodded. "Yes, his child, slavery. And another claimed if human efforts should fail, a host of angels would be sent to support it—liberty, of course, not Satan's child."

Hancock stood once again. "With so many factions in play, I trust our combined efforts will help Britain see the error of her ways."

"Any word from Mr. Otis?"

Hancock shook his head.

"I trust two dozen of the colonies' finest will be able to produce a solution," Molineux said.

"The meeting in New York has raised more than a few eyebrows, as it is only the second time such a gathering—a congress, if you will—has taken place."

"I heard one of our delegates weakened his resolve," Molineux said. "But I did not hear the details."

"Ah, yes. He refused to sign the petitions to our superiors in England. It is of concern because it weakens the united front we had wished to present to them."

Hancock walked over to Molineux. "Have we addressed why you came?"

"What else is there to speak of these days besides the stamps?"

Hancock saw Molineux to the door and opened it. "Please do me the favor of relaying any information you receive from New York."

"And you as well."

"With each passing day," Hancock said, "it appears less and less likely we will be ready with a response."

"Don't you fret," Molineux said. "There are those here who are preparing their own demonstration. It will clearly make our frustrations known to those on the other side of the pond." The corner of his mouth lifted. "You will see."

The Stamp Act execution date finally arrived. It almost had the aura of Pope's Day. But something was different. Molineux had no idea how it would play out, and experiencing it as it unfolded was the only option the day afforded.

He chatted with men of the North End clan as they marched behind the cart carrying the handmade effigies they had cut from the limbs of the large elm on the south side of town. Those from the opposing gang blended in. The parade had crept past buildings draped in black and flags flying at half-mast in the harbor. Back in town, church bells tolled sounds of death.

The party crossed onto Boston's Neck, the narrow piece of land with water on either side, which connected the town to the rest of the province. The clacking wagon wheels in front ceased, and the men circled around to get the best view of the gallows. A gust of November wind from the sea brushed the sweat on Molineux's face.

The traditional leaders of the Pope's Day clans removed the stuffed figures from the cart and hauled them to the scaffolding beneath nooses swaying in the breeze.

"These men," one of the commanders said from the stage, "will receive their just due for the role they played in providing us with the hated Stamp Act."

The crowd hissed.

Several of the men tightened ropes around the figures and strung them up. The leader gave the command, and the others carried out the sentence. They removed the effigies from the gallows and threw them into the crowd.

Molineux grabbed the leg of one. Other men tugged and pulled on the remaining limbs. Feathers scattered everywhere. Molineux chuckled. He hadn't had this much fun since he was a child.

"We stand together against the schemes of the homeland," the head of the South End clan proclaimed.

"Hear, hear!" Molineux said.

The chief of the North End jumped onto the base of the gallows. "No longer rivals. From now on, we stand united. Follow me for the signing of the treaty that will make it official."

Molineux fell in line with the others.

A treaty between the North and South Ends sounded good. But would it hold?

At noon a few days later, Molineux and his boys mingled with the North End clan at the head of King Street. The elder Molineux clenched his fists as he surveyed the scene. Men from the South End had gathered at the foot of the street. Ships in the bay beyond them had never looked more majestic. The float of each clan held its usual pageantry, the pope and the devil. New effigies—representing tyranny, oppression, and slavery—had joined them. The leader of the South End, dressed in a blue-and-gold uniform and a hat laced in gold, carried a rattan cane on his left arm. Several thousand spectators watched in anticipation.

How would this Pope's Day unfold? Molineux blinked then squinted. Was that the militia's colonel standing between the two clans? The one to whom the governor had given orders to watch over the town during these uncertain days? The onset of loud music coming from each group interrupted Molineux's pondering, and each tribe began to march ceremoniously toward the other. Molineux glanced down at John whose eyes grew bigger with every step.

With mere feet separating the two gangs, one of the leaders cried out. "Far enough, men."

The other chief echoed the command, then the two men each took an arm of the colonel. Now Molineux's eyes widened.

The three commanding officers motioned for others to follow their lead. The two clans merged and someone from the South End reached out to him. Instead of exchanging blows on this normally turbulent day, the opposing factions locked arms in a show of unity. Unbelievable.

Guns fired from the ships in the harbor, and the town's fortress—a few miles away—responded.

"Huzzah! Huzzah! Huzzah!" the crowd cheered.

Molineux and his sons joined the parade to the Liberty Tree on the south side of town. There they sealed their union with a feast. Merchants and politicians mingled with the town's rabble, and Otis, who had returned from New York a few days before, favored them with a speech.

"The Stamp Act Congress produced a document," Otis said from the platform, "which expresses our concern over privileges we believe essential to freedom—taxation only by consent and trials by jury. These are freedoms which Parliament's recent legislation would deny us."

Hisses slithered up from the assembly.

"I am proud to say the Massachusetts Bay House, now under the watchful eye of Samuel Adams," Otis smiled at the new clerk, "has followed suit with its own document."

"Huzzah!"

Otis's raised hands quieted the men. "To our dismay, local representatives of the Crown, including our own Governor Bernard—"

Someone from the crowd interrupted. "He can stay at the castle, for all we care."

"Indeed—a prisoner in his own fortress," another proclaimed.

A roar of laughter soared through the air.

Otis continued. "Our governor has provided no support for the cause. Instead, he has encouraged the people to submit to Parliament's supreme authority rather than take control of their own destiny."

"We won't have it!" someone shouted.

"Then do what you must in order to regain what is rightfully yours." Otis nodded to the clan leaders then took his seat.

As the sun made its way toward the horizon, the newly formed union proceeded to Copp's Hill on the north side of town where they committed the pageantry to flames.

The sheer energy of the day satisfied Molineux. No need for bloody noses this year. If gangs from the town's North and South Ends could march together in a show of unity for a common cause on the traditionally rambunctious Pope's Day, anything was possible. With pressures from all sides, surely the colonists' oppressor would renege, the clouds would part, and the sun would shine again.

Molineux beat the mud from his boots outside Hancock's counting house located on Long Wharf. One of the bookkeepers eased past Molineux as the merchant entered. "Will this rain never cease?" He shook the drizzle from his jacket before hanging it by the fire and surveying the men sitting in a circle of chairs a few feet away.

Hancock walked over. "But, Mr. Molineux, 'tis the season of cheer and goodwill toward men."

"Not for Mr. Oliver." Molineux snickered. "Or maybe it is—maybe a burden has lifted after today's public resignation."

"We would accept no less, would we?"

"It is the only reason he made an appearance," someone from the small group said.

Molineux managed a smile. "Good to see you, Mr. Otis. Where is Samuel Adams?"

"He will be here shortly."

"You must be pleased, Mr. Molineux," Hancock said as the two men made their way toward the others. "The harbor has reopened, and you and Mr. Rowe managed to do the same for the Custom House."

"The governor should never have closed them to begin with," Molineux said.

Thunder rumbled in the distance.

Hancock picked up a coffee pot and held it in Molineux's direction. "But without the stamps—"

Molineux glared at Hancock. "Open or not, with the act still in place, the port is quieter than it ought to be—even for this time of year."

"Though I have not heard directly from our agents in England, many claim the nonimportation agreement is having the desired effect. And since burying my uncle last year, people of our town have forgone many of the British-produced garbs of mourning. Very few wore black, gloves, or rings at the last funeral I attended."

Molineux took a deep breath. "Only with the help of the port cities of New York and Philadelphia has nonimportation worked. Had they refused to join us, Britain would not have flinched."

A few minutes later Mr. Adams arrived, settled into a chair, and the meeting began.

"As you know," Adams said, "with no one to distribute the stamps, we plan to request of the governor that our legal counsel be heard regarding the reopening of the courts. Mr. Otis has agreed to be part of that counsel, and I believe my cousin John will be ready and willing when the time comes."

"How can you be so certain?" one of the men asked.

"When I last spoke with him, Providence seemed to have stirred his soul. He celebrated his thirtieth birthday a few weeks ago. Times of transition tend to impact the direction of one's life."

"From what you have told me, he has a sense of humor about our present situation."

Adams nodded. "He claims our citizens refuse to postpone death simply because the doors of the probate court are locked."

Several smiled.

Molineux rose from his chair to stoke the fire.

"What of the Stamp Act itself?" someone asked. "The closures have merely been the fruit produced by the act. Does the tree not need to be pulled up at its roots and repealed in order to prevent further unpleasantries?"

"That will come in time," Adams said. "And you are right. My cousin said once Parliament's authority has been established, the ruin of America is inevitable."

"If the Stamp Act is not repealed soon," Otis said, "this country may require more than the pen and the tongue of a lawyer."

Adams removed a paper from his pocket. "Then let us make final preparations for tomorrow's town meeting. Here is the proposed memorial. We need to discuss it so that we can be ready."

On a snowy twenty-sixth of December, the governor and the town came to terms. Molineux reported to the town meeting his certainty the inferior court would proceed with business as usual at their next term. In mid-January, the Massachusetts Bay House voted to reopen the lower courts while the superior court would remain closed. Hutchinson had stepped down as the judge of the probate court for Boston's county, making way for those courts to open as well.

Word came that throughout the colonies, amid threats of violence, Stamp Act agents had resigned their posts and many royal governors were running scared. Boston prepared to conduct its own style of intimidation.

Molineux loved market day for it produced more people in town than usual, both familiar and not so familiar. Men and women from the countryside poured in to buy and sell their wares. Additional wagons and schoolboys in the streets provided an air of organized chaos. It brought sheer joy to a town ready to return to a sense of normalcy.

On this day, the large elm tree on the south side of town became the center point of activity. It had become a place to express displeasure for what many considered mistreatment by those on the other side of the Big Pond. Midmorning sun filtered through the Liberty Tree's winter-bare branches onto Molineux's face, causing him to blink.

John, now thirteen, read aloud the sign men had affixed to the tree a few days before. "This tree was planted in the year 1646 and pruned by order of the Sons of Liberty, February 14, 1766." Without moving, John added, "Pa, that's old."

Molineux chuckled then put his hand on his son's shoulder. "We had better stake out our spot." He pointed to a place across the street. "How about over there? That should give us a good view. Save me a place. I have a few folks I want to talk to before this gets underway."

Molineux shouted a greeting across the way to an old acquaintance. He mingled throughout the crowd as it grew to hundreds then to two or three thousand. One of the Sons of Liberty called for their attention.

"Hear ye, hear ye. This court is now in session."

Molineux scurried back to his place beside John.

A devil-like creature appeared on the stage, ready to hang the Stamp Act if the mock trial proceeded as planned. Chains secured the prisoner, portrayed as a man, to the gallows.

"A most detestable object has been lately transported to the shores of America. The said prisoner did on the first of November last endeavor to make its appearance in a forcible manner and in defiance of the known and established laws of the British constitution."

The crowd hissed.

"A jury has been summoned, so let the trial begin."

As evidence was presented during the two-hour trial, concerns that had been expressed began to make sense. Molineux was glad he had brought John along. The two watched as the jury pronounced the prisoner guilty of a breach of Magna Carta and a design to subvert the British constitution.

"Shall we as one man condone its demise?"

"Huzzah! Huzzah! Huzzah!"

The execution proceeded, then, as the clocks struck noon, the Sons removed the cursed object and committed it to the flames along with the effigies of its authors.

"May all the friends of the Stamp Act be as these, while the friends of liberty thrive and flourish," the moderator said.

The arguments Molineux had heard turned over in his mind, then he felt a tug.

"Papa? Are you all right?"

Molineux caught his breath as he became aware of his surroundings. "Shall we return home?"

"There is no one with whom you want to speak?" John asked.

"Not now." Still lost in his own thoughts, he and John found a path out of the masses. Maybe it *was* about more than how many shillings were in his pocket. The Stamp Act must go. But would the Motherland be willing to loosen her grip on her colonies without a fight?

The curtains of Molineux's bedroom window fluttered in the spring breeze. The cool air against his face added to the sense of elation. Town officials had declared today, Monday, as a day of rejoicing. The Sabbath had barely been able to contain its excitement, as church bells had expressed glee soon after midnight. Molineux smiled at the flags going up around town—from seagoing vessels and church steeples and homes. It was going to be a glorious day.

As winter had loosened its grip on New England, rumors of the impending repeal of the Stamp Act had made their way across the Atlantic, and late on a Friday morning in mid-May, one of Hancock's vessels brought official word. Boston had burst into jubilation.

Molineux rummaged through the wardrobe looking for something appropriate to wear for the occasion. Once dressed, he grabbed his fiddle then hurried outside. He did not want to miss a single minute of the celebration. The family could join him later.

The fifty-acre meadow at the foot of Beacon Hill would provide a perfect setting for the evening's main event. There, on the Common, the Sons of Liberty had set up two stages from which they would release fireworks. One hundred yards away, they had erected a huge obelisk for the occasion. Molineux moved closer to the four-sided structure and the clanging emitting from it.

"Who goes there?" Molineux asked.

The question was greeted with sounds of amusement. "'Tis I, Paul Revere. Could that be Mr. Molineux who inquires?"

Molineux squinted to see Revere through the engravings carved into the monument. "Indeed it is. You have outdone yourself this time, Mr. Revere."

Molineux set down his fiddle to admire the work. He walked to another side, took a deep breath, then proceeded to read aloud what Revere had engraved. "'O thou whom next to heaven we most revere, Fair Liberty!'" Molineux lifted one hand high. "'Thou lovely goddess hear!'"

He rounded another corner and continued to read. "'Our faith approved, our liberty restored, our hearts bend gratefully to our sovereign Lord.'"

Revere crawled out from the tower and gave Molineux a tour around the outside. The top four stories of the obelisk demonstrated the engraver's skills with figures of the Majesties, along with more than a dozen worthy patriots credited with the love of liberty. Sequential scenes at the bottom showed the king saving America from Parliament's monstrous decree.

"You are withholding something," Molineux said. "What is it?"

"Tonight, two hundred and eighty lamps will light her up," Revere said.

"That will be a sight to behold." Molineux picked up his fiddle. "I must carry on and let you be about your work."

Molineux spent the next few hours tickling the strings of his fiddle all about town. Church bells continued to ring, ships in the harbor displayed their colors, and celebratory guns discharged in various parts of town. Two dozen gentlemen dined at the Bunch of Grapes Tavern where they toasted their loyalty to the Crown. Celebration extended as far as the gaol where patriots generously provided funds, so debtors could go free.

Thousands poured in from the countryside. This was no mob but a festival of the free. The Liberty Tree greeted those strolling through the southern part of town. Lanterns and banners hung from its boughs until they could hold no more.

At dusk, a dozen rockets from the two stages illuminated the sky to commence the day's closing activities. Reflections from the fireworks scampered across the field and up the slope to the homes that adorned the pinnacle.

Hancock, Otis, and others who lived near the Common opened their homes to the multitudes who drifted throughout the festivities. It was a day beyond compare.

Molineux had never seen so many smiles around town, and the salt air tingled his senses more than usual. His family seemed to be enjoying the day as much as he. Elizabeth squealed and twirled, her frock swirling. The boys sampled the roasted ox while Anne left with friends. Molineux fraternized with the crowds and enjoyed the free-flowing Madeira wine Hancock had generously provided.

Beacon Hill buzzed with excitement as Molineux made his way back to the area in front of his own home.

Elizabeth and her half-pint friends joined him. She tugged on his cloak. "Tell us the mutt story again, Papa."

Molineux set down his fiddle, and a smile spread across his face. "Weeeell, that is a good story indeed."

The girls settled onto the blankets the womenfolk had provided and Molineux began.

"If ever there was a mutt, 'twas I." Molineux's eyes twinkled. "Well bred, yet a mutt through and through."

"Many in Boston have pedigrees for which they can be proud. Take the Revere clan, for instance. Deborah here"—Molineux motioned with both hands in the direction of the little girl—"her father comes from a line of French Spaniels."

The girl's eyes lit up like the fireflies appearing with the dusk.

"Then there is Hannah," Molineux said. "Her father, Mr. Samuel Adams, is a Tibetan Mastiff. Quiet and unassuming, yet hard-working."

"And Mr. Hancock?" someone asked, pointing to his home.

"Ah, Mr. Hancock is no canine. He is a stallion," Molineux said without hesitation. "Not as strong and healthy, but certainly a sight to behold."

The girls beamed with excitement but tried to contain their less-than-polite giggles. "Tell us more about the mutt."

"I, I am a mutt." Molineux raised his head and placed an arm across his chest. "Born and bred in Ireland but with an English pedigree. My English forbearer hailed from—"

The hiss of another rocket startled the girls. Molineux, playing off the sound, produced a rapid and spontaneous dance culminating with his arms open wide toward the heavens—just in time for the crackles and pops. The girls, no longer able to contain their laughter, spun around to see the explosion of color against the night sky.

As Molineux's eyes adjusted, he caught sight of Maryann and the other mothers walking up the hill. "Ah, it appears the rest of the mutt story will have to wait. 'Tis the unfortunate time of day when little ones must be tucked in."

Sad faces were followed by a round of thank-yous and a good-night hug from Elizabeth. As his wife and daughter made their way home, Molineux looked around for others he might entertain for the remainder of the evening. In no time, his fiddle had the young men on their feet. Molineux reveled to watch each beau attempt to charm his lady of choice with an impressive jig.

Several hours passed before the tap of a drum and a round of fireworks coming from the top of the obelisk gave the signal to disperse.

Within a half hour, the townsfolk had extinguished the numerous lights, and the Common sat in silence once again.

Molineux ascended his home's long flight of stairs. Though invigorated on the inside, his body was beginning to feel the weight of its half century.

If only his father could see him now—in America, the land of opportunity. Far from the disappointments of the past. A place where he and his children could stay for generations.

He took a deep breath of night air then made his way inside.

Life was good.

CHAPTER FIVE

⌀⌒⌒

Over the Line

November 25, 1766—November 5, 1767

A *basket* filled with decorative gourds sat in the middle of the large table in the council chambers.

Molineux slammed the six-month-old newspaper into his hand. His temples throbbed. "Seven days."

Several of the merchants sitting around the table jumped.

"We only had seven days in which to celebrate."

"Please have a seat, Mr. Molineux, and we will begin," one of the merchants said.

Molineux found a chair then scrutinized the group. There were a few things to be thankful for this harvest season—Hancock's election as one of Boston's representatives. Too, Otis had reclaimed his seat despite Tory accusations he suffered from unstable health. The general court had been wise to select them, and Samuel Adams, as the committee to meet with the merchants.

"Several months ago, London merchants developed their own tax scheme," Adams said. "We are here to listen to your concerns and to receive the petition that addresses them."

Molineux put both fists on the table. Adams would refuse to state the obvious, that those merchants had designed their plan to crack down on American smugglers.

"Victory over the Stamp Act should give you a sense of empowerment." Adams surveyed the men with an air of expectancy. "With this in mind, who would like to begin the discussion?"

"As I stated during the writs case," Otis said, "if the customs men are allowed to search your goods at will now, a future tyrant could legally control, imprison, or murder anyone within his realm."

"Those are harsh words," Rowe said. "Is it not a stretch to connect the two?"

Otis leaned back in his chair. "Mr. Rowe, as a leading merchant of this town, you of all people should understand that if a man's property is not his to do with as he pleases, then the entire foundation of his liberty is at stake."

"His life *and* liberty," Adams said.

"But we lost the writs case"—Molineux turned to Otis—"despite your amazing performance, I might add. Do you not believe we would suffer the same fate again?"

"Times are different now," Otis said. "I think there is greater understanding within the House—a greater understanding of our rights."

Molineux pressed on to other concerns. "If England moves forward with her plan, it may not matter if they can search our warehouses and homes. Their telling us what we can do with our goods is as harmful as a search, is it not?"

"Many of our neighbors have begun to refer to themselves as Americans," Rowe said. "I shudder to think of how the Motherland will respond to that."

"Thanks to our own Mr. Otis, we Americans can now keep a watchful eye on our more local officials from the gallery he commissioned to be built."

"We appreciated too your leading the effort to remove Mr. Hutchinson from the multiple offices he once held."

"It was a dangerous situation and needed to be addressed," Otis said.

Rowe tapped his fingers on the table. "Back to the matter at hand, if you please. Will England really require us to purchase from them most of the manufactured items we need?"

"Yes," Molineux said. "The people of our town deserve the opportunity to work for an honest day's wage. The Manufactory House provides that."

"What becomes of the items we manufacture here, insignificant in number as they may be?" another merchant asked. "Without the motivation to produce our own goods, the Motherland would be in complete control."

"They are already," Adams said. "Remember, they have declared America is subordinate both to the Crown and to Parliament in all cases whatsoever."

Expressions of agreement went up from around the table.

Adams stood. "Then I propose we forward the petition to our agent in England who can present it to the House of Commons. We must make our concerns known."

Molineux nodded to Hancock and Rowe. Each would have his pen ready to sign the document. A glance around the table convinced Molineux others would as well.

A sundry of gentlemen's houses and the Liberty Tree sparkled in the glow of lanterns to mark the anniversary of the repeal of the Stamp Act. Faneuil Hall stood statuesque against the late winter sky. Inside, a throng of people drank to the royal family's health. Toes tapped to the tunes emitting from Molineux's fiddle, still warm from St. Patrick's Day.

Joy quickly dissipated a few months later when news of yet another act of Parliament reached America. October provided opportunities for the town to plan its response.

Molineux sat in his store with his boys as rain pelted the roof.

A light knock on the door gave them a momentary start.

Dr. Joseph Warren poked in his head. "Walk up together?"

"C'mon in. Be ready shortly." Molineux turned back to John who was practicing his bookkeeping. "You can finish up later. Gather up your things to take home."

"John is going to catch up with Junior before long," Dr. Warren said.

"He has already outgrown him on the inside." Molineux grabbed his jacket.

With the foursome outside the store, Molineux rattled the doorknob. It was secure. He had learned his lesson in '58 when some villain stole the running rigging off his vessel. He slung water from his hands then shielded his head to miss the blowing rain.

Thunder pealed in the distance.

"Be careful what you touch, Papa," John said. "Remember Mr. Franklin and his kite."

"Ah, our beloved Mr. Franklin," Molineux said with a fake smile. "The one whose less-than-accurate testimony we can thank for our current dilemma. At least Mr. Hutchinson has not been as much of a factor since his stroke."

"True," Dr. Warren said, "but it was mild, so expect him to return."

Molineux turned to John. "Take care going home and see that no one waits up for me."

"I will, Papa." John ran to catch up with Junior.

Molineux and Dr. Warren made their way to Faneuil Hall.

The Townshend Acts placed duties on colonial importations of lead, glass, painters' colors, paper, and tea. Since the British government required the colonies to purchase these items only from them, paying the duties or smuggling were the colonists' only options—or so Britain thought. And to discourage the smuggling of tea from Holland, this law would lower taxes on tea as it passed through England on its way to the colonies and give the struggling British East India Company an advantage over its illicit counterparts.

"Durn Brits." Molineux's thoughts shifted to the issues at hand. "Haven't they learned their lesson? And to think they want to use our money to pay for the new board they plan to set up to make sure we're behaving. It simply adds insult to injury."

"Absolutely."

"And weren't they listening when we told them we wanted juries, not judges, to decide our fate if we do misbehave?"

They climbed the stairs to the building and entered.

Dr. Warren stopped at a portrait of Isaac Barre, which the town had recently hung in his honor. "He is a brave man to have stood up to Parliament."

As if on cue, Molineux straightened his back and placed one arm across his waist. "Mr. Townshend"—Molineux looked at the doctor and began to recite Mr. Barre's speech as best he could remember it—"you say the Americans were planted by our care. Were they? No. Your oppression is what planted them in America. They fled from your tyranny to an uncultivated land where they exposed themselves to a multitude of hardships. And yet, they were actuated by principles of true English liberty. They met all these hardships with pleasure compared with those they had suffered in their own country from the hands of those who should have been their friends."

Molineux walked around the gathering crowd who showed signs of delight with the impromptu demonstration. He continued. "Were they nourished by your indulgence? I think not. Instead, they grew by your neglect. As soon as you began to care, you sent persons to rule over them—people sent to spy out their liberties, misrepresent their actions, and prey upon them."

Dr. Warren responded to Molineux's pleading eyes by placing an imaginary gun on his shoulder. "Were they protected by your arms?"

"No, indeed," Molineux said, reclaiming his rhythm. "Rather these Americans have so nobly taken up arms in your defense. And believe me"—Molineux raised his palm upward for emphasis—"the same spirit of freedom which actuated the people at first, will accompany them still. What I deliver are genuine sentiments of my heart, Mr. Townshend." Molineux placed his hand above his eyes and peered into the distance. "I claim to know more of America than most of you, having seen it with my own eyes. The people are as loyal as any subjects the king has. Yet they are jealous of their liberties, and who will vindicate them if ever they should be violated once again!"

Molineux took a bow amid laughter and applause. He cleared his throat and gestured toward the assembly hall. "Shall we?"

"I wonder if Mr. Otis will be here," Dr. Warren said as they walked into the large meeting room.

"Front and center as usual, no doubt. Even the recent burial of his mother will not keep him from his longstanding role as the meeting moderator."

"Speaking of burials, it was quite odd to see him and Mr. Hutchinson carrying the Grand Master's casket a few weeks ago," Dr. Warren said.

"An awkward pair indeed. With the passing of such a prominent attorney, I believe Mr. Otis may be the one to slip into his shoes."

The two men found seats, and Otis called the meeting to order.

Molineux leaned toward Dr. Warren. "At least Mr. Adams has finally convinced Mr. Otis to apply his writing skills to the newspaper rather than to scholarly essays. If we are to succeed, we must reach the masses."

Otis began. "Some believe this new act is as dangerous as the Stamp Act. Nevertheless, we must make a distinction between the taxes themselves and the five commissioners of customs who will simply come to fulfill their duties."

Adams requested the floor. "England has armed those officers with writs of assistance, so they will be able to search ships and collect duties. With all due respect, sir, I believe this will make them the greatest political curse that could have been sent among us."

Another from the crowd stood. "And what should we make of the fact the act will allow Parliament to use our money to pay wages directly to their colonial appointees?"

Otis rose to full stature behind the podium. "Some fear it would result in our losing power to influence the local authorities. The governor, judges, and other royal officers would move at the direction of those not affected by their decisions." Otis raised a hand. "The Townshend Acts are multifaceted. I assure you we will get to each issue, but one at a time."

Molineux listened to the various views. Some expressed concern the new act would threaten the country with poverty and ruin. Others worried about how Parliament would respond if the colonists pushed back.

The town finally agreed to put the squeeze on Britain in the very area she sought to tax them: imports. Boston would no longer purchase British superfluities such as apparel, hats, shoes, silks, furniture, clocks, nails, and cheese. Instead, they would embrace thriftiness and seek to manufacture some of the items themselves.

Molineux shifted in his seat. Did anyone remember the lack of success in past decades?

He noted smiles on the faces of non-merchants. For them, in the midst of economic depression, it would not be a very hard sell. He knew all too well—they were already not buying. The faces of merchants, on the other hand, showed signs of concern. Those dealing with the post-war competition, such as himself, might not be able to endure the boycott. The issue tugged at Molineux, both as a merchant and as someone who desired to help the poor among them.

Mr. Otis called for a short recess, and Molineux took the opportunity to observe how some of the key players were responding to what had transpired. Hancock seemed pleased, and Adams was already speaking with the less enthusiastic merchants. A glance at Otis revealed his disapproval of Adams's activities of persuasion.

The meeting resumed and turned to the second item on the agenda—what kind of welcome they would give the agents expected to arrive in early November. After some debate, Otis's restrained approach won out over Samuel Adams's more provocative ideas.

The meeting adjourned, and as everyone dispersed, Molineux sat for a moment, reviewing all that had transpired. No matter his response, action or inaction, risk was involved. On his deathbed, what decision would he look back on with satisfaction? Which would cause regret? He took a deep breath, pushed himself away from the chair, and hurried to the front of the room to make his intentions known. He wanted to be among those waiting when the agents sailed into Boston's harbor.

Evening had fallen on Pope's Day, and save a seditious handbill placed under the Liberty Tree, quiet had prevailed. Cold drops of rain dripped from the edges of Molineux's felt hat, yet this year's float made him smile. Its sign held a simple message: "Liberty, Property, & No Commissioners."

The Boston clans gathered around the crackling bonfire, leaving it to the effigies to mock the commissioners as they disembarked with their families amid calm. Even so, Molineux was sure any misconceptions the agents might have had during their arrival would quickly evaporate. This appointment would not be for the faint of heart.

For three-and-a-half years, Britain had provided the firewood—first the Sugar Act, then the Stamp Act, and now the Townshend Acts. As winter approached, colonial newspapers provided kindling by publishing the first in a series, "Letters from a Farmer." The essays reiterated colonists' objections and inspired them in their path forward.

A small body of soldiers—a lieutenant and twenty-seven men—arrived from Halifax and were housed at a fortress in the harbor.

Molineux's patience had run out. He was ready to add his fuel to the fire.

CHAPTER SIX

⁕

Troublesome Times

February 11–March 21, 1768

Molineux growled under his breath as he hurried past Long Wharf. February's climate gripped his bad knee while his flapping cloak went unattended. The evening's gathering was foremost in his mind, yet other thoughts vied for attention.

Had taking a second job been a good idea? Or was this his third? Managing properties seemed to suit him. Doing so for Charles Ward Apthorp, a Tory, gave others reason to pause, but for Molineux, someone's persuasion or lot in life seemed irrelevant—at least for a business deal. Besides, Apthorp's move to New York kept the reins comfortably loose. Controversies closer to home had been enough to keep his mind in a whirl. Six weeks into the year and already so much activity.

Dead-of-winter shadows enveloped Molineux as habit led him to the coffeehouse around the corner from his warehouse. Coffeehouses and taverns dotted Boston's landscape, and men of Boston swarmed around them like bees around a hive. There they feasted on gossip as much as on the food and drink.

Whether political, business, or social, Molineux enjoyed the myriad of clubs that met there and stirred his vivacious spirit. Memberships in the Caucus and the Merchants Society kept him both connected and informed. He admired Samuel Adams's populist approach, and his frugal and backroom ways helped balance Molineux's flamboyant nature.

Mrs. Cordis's British Coffee House hosted the Merchants Society where they spent many an evening mulling over current events, often with non-merchants who would join them. High social rank, rather than occupation or political persuasion, provided the ticket in.

Molineux barely noticed the beefy aroma of his favorite stew permeating from the coffeehouse. He made his way to the front room where the Society had met for the past twenty years. A half dozen had already assembled.

Molineux found a seat around the large table. A few acknowledged his arrival while others stayed focused on their fellow merchant who had the floor.

"I think we all agree Mr. Otis and Mr. Adams make a powerful duo."

"Are you referring to the letter they sent to the other colonies?" Molineux asked.

Several nodded.

Molineux grimaced. "It was much softer in tone than I would have liked."

"But the letter was intended to unify," another of the merchants said, "not divide the colonists in their opposition to the recent acts."

Molineux scowled.

"Mr. Adams and I," Otis said, "were commissioned by the House to make others aware of our concerns."

"Our right to property," Molineux said, "and taxation without representation. What was the third item?"

"That Parliament act in accordance with the British constitution," someone said.

Otis leaned back in his chair. "The letter also addressed issues that might stem from civil officers receiving their salaries from those other than whom they serve."

Molineux pushed aside the mug in front of him. "No doubt Governor Bernard appreciated that."

"Our governor continues to display his ever-present lack of wisdom," Otis said, "by sharing letters with the House he has sent to London. We are obligated to both condemn his less-than-favorable words and provide more accurate reports to our true friends there."

One of the men laid down his spoon and wiped his mouth. "The subsequent petition Mr. Adams wrote to the king should arrive there soon."

"The one in which he sought to reassure them we desire redress rather than independence?" Otis asked.

The man nodded and smiled. "I believe Mr. Adams's prediction may come true. The letter may indeed be spurned by the royal foot rather than touched by his Majesty's hand."

A few laughed. Not Molineux. "At present," he said, "I believe most of us care more about the situation with Mr. Folger."

"Are he and Dr. Franklin still working on the Gulf Stream maps?" Rowe asked. "Dr. Franklin may have his postal ships in mind, but I need the drawings in order to give me a few days' advantage over merchants elsewhere in the world. Faster ships allow for quicker sales."

"You know that is not the topic to which I am referring. As a fellow smuggler, you are well aware of recent events."

Several leaned forward.

Three weeks earlier Captain Timothy Folger, with well-known sympathies toward merchants, had run into difficulties when he reported to the commissioners his seizure of a sloop. *Cornelia* was loaded with eighteen casks of Bohea tea for which duties had not been paid.

The coffeehouse conversation quickly turned to the motivations of key players. According to policy, bounty from seized smuggled goods were to be divided three ways—a third to London, a third to the governor, and a third to the customs officer who seized the vessel. As the evening wore on, Molineux's forbearance dissipated, and John Temple's reputation bore the brunt of his pent-up frustrations.

"Mr. Molineux," Rowe said, "many times I have been in your company, but never have you been guilty of such indiscretion."

Molineux cast a sharp glance in Rowe's direction and continued. "Mr. Folger would never benefit from any seizure, now or in the future."

"Who then would receive his share of the benefit?" someone asked.

"Mr. Temple, of course," Molineux said.

Temple, born in Boston but raised in England, had returned to Boston in time to win friends among the merchants during the writs case. His addition to the new Board of Customs Commissioners, however, put him at risk to receive Boston's fury. His appointment by the Crown gave Molineux enough reason to be suspicious.

Another, knowing firsthand what it was like to have a ship seized, weighed in. "Surely you cannot believe the general guilty of so base a design, and you have behaved very ill in making the company think so."

"I *do* believe it," Molineux said, "based upon his sly agreement with Mr. Folger."

"Indeed, Mr. Molineux, disengage from such rhetoric, and we will forgive this transgression."

Molineux jumped up. "I will not."

Several gentlemen shifted in their seats. A cleared throat gave someone the opportunity to prevent the matter from escalating further.

"Mr. Folger's commission itself is on shaky ground."

Rowe motioned for Molineux to return to his seat, which he did with a pout.

Otis, along with John Adams, provided Folger's legal representation. "The commission was good." He pulled a paper from his pocket. "But one expression gives some people pause." He held the page up in front of him and read. "'I, the surveyor-general of his Majesty's customs, do hereby appoint Timothy Folger to make diligent search for any goods, wares, or merchandise prohibited to be imported or exported, or whereof the customs or other duties have not been duly paid, and the same to seize *in my behalf* to his Majesty's use.'"

"In my behalf." Molineux's fist rattled the dinnerware. "Now, gentlemen, you see, I am right in what I have said. From the beginning, Mr. Temple intended to be the beneficiary of seizures made by Mr. Folger."

Molineux rose from the table, waved his hand in the air. "Gentlemen, I rest my case."

Voices of the men rose and fell in conformity with the sporadic noise coming from the *Gazette*'s printing press in the room below. Molineux had stopped by to check on things. Scattered papers on the table before Samuel Adams and Otis indicated their labor had been intense. With the latest edition now at press, they seemed pleased to see a fresh face.

Adams put his elbows on the table and rubbed his neck. "It is not the first time a newspaper has been censored."

Molineux pulled up a chair. "No?"

"The Franklins ran a paper here forty or fifty years ago," Adams said. "When they were no longer allowed to print what they pleased, they left town."

"The Franklins are from Boston?"

Otis nodded. "Once suppressed, two of the brothers moved to Newport while Benjamin went to Philadelphia."

Adams squinted at Otis. "I doubt it caused quite the stir as recent events."

Molineux quizzed Adams with his expression.

Otis stood and stretched his back. "I believe Mr. Adams is referring to our governor's claim that I recently behaved like a madman in the House."

"Mr. Hutchinson did not appreciate the House's response to newly discovered letters by his Excellency," Adams said. "He says our comments about him were the rudest ever sent to a governor."

Otis returned to his chair. "I would consider that to be kind compared with the council's reaction to Dr. Warren's verbal attack on our governor."

"What did they do, the House?"

"They declared Dr. Warren's printed words a scandalous libel and they censured him," Otis said. "I believe our governor is disappointed they did not do more. Some say he would prefer to appoint his own council."

"No doubt he would," Molineux said. "Keeping the wishes of the people out of the way would free him up to run the province however he desires."

Adams shuffled through the papers then held one out to Molineux. "Here is the edition, if you care to see it again."

Molineux found Dr. Warren's words about the governor. He stood and began to read aloud. "'We have for a long time known your enmity to this province. We have had full proof of your cruelty to a loyal people.'" He looked up and raised a fist into the air. "Hear, hear," he said then looked back at the paper. "'But when a diabolical thirst for mischief is the sole motive of your conduct, you must not wonder if you are treated with open dislike. For it is impossible to feel any esteem for a man like you.'" He laid the paper on the table. "'Tis true."

"Do not leave out the ending." Adams picked up the paper and read. "'We never can treat good and patriotic rulers with too great a reverence. But it is certain that men totally abandoned to wickedness can never merit our regard, be their stations ever so high.'"

"And it was quite clever to conclude with a rhyme," Molineux said. "The town will not soon forget it." He raised one hand and looked toward heaven. "'If such men are by God appointed, the devil may be the Lord's anointed.'" He took a bow prompting his audience of two to applaud and cheer.

"It is words like these," Adams said, "that our governor and his lieutenant desire to silence."

"They are harsh, no doubt, but if a man cannot speak his mind, I for one would rather die than be forced to keep my mouth shut."

Otis laughed. "And, Mr. Molineux, the entire town would be surprised to hear you say otherwise."

Outside the Molineux home, flags fluttered in the late winter breeze to mark the second anniversary of the repeal of the Stamp Act.

Inside, two dozen friends lifted their glasses, and Molineux leapt onto the staircase in their spacious entrance hall and proposed a toast. Some of his drink splattered onto his vest during the ascent. Brushing it off, he smiled at his lovely wife whose ball gown twinkled in the light of the chandelier. The perfectly coiffed wig he had imported for her from England merely accentuated her natural beauty.

He raised his glass. "May the repeal ever remain in the memory of all true Britons—and Americans."

Glasses clinked amid the cheers.

"And another." A grin spread across Otis's broad face. "To the *Boston Gazette* and the worthy members of the House who vindicated freedom of the press. May we ever be this free."

"Hear, hear!"

"Enjoy the remainder of the evening, dear ones," Molineux said, motioning to the harpist to resume the melody, "and please let us know if there is anything we can do to make your time with us more pleasant."

He vaulted from the staircase and rejoined Adams and Otis in the parlor where the fresh scent of greenery filled the room. "Not everyone has arrived."

"I asked several to stay and keep the crowds at the Liberty Tree and in King Street under control—eight hundred of them at last report," Adams said. "It seems they were becoming a bit too mobbish."

Otis chimed in. "I heard their tongues got quite loose as they paraded past the governor's home."

Adams frowned. "I heard the same."

"The commissioners have apparently found a good place to hide." Molineux took a sip from his glass. "No one I spoke with today had been able to find them."

Otis's eyes lit up. "They fear they will be forced to resign like Mr. Oliver."

"The Sons removed the effigies from the tree as soon as they appeared," Adams said.

Molineux set his glass onto a passing tray. "Is it true Parliament may send the commissioners home?"

"No one knows, but the rumor is enough to keep the forces in check."

Otis smiled. "No mobs, no confusion, and no tumults. Right, Mr. Adams?"

"Correct. We know who has abused us but should not let a hair of their scalps be touched."

Molineux crossed his arms. "And why not, Mr. Adams?"

"Mr. Adams has his reasons," Otis said. "He knows this town and her people well."

"Make no mistake," Adams said, "the time is coming when they shall lick the dust and melt away."

His answer would have to do—at least for now.

Two days later a windstorm blew through the town, ripping apart the harbor's ships and wharves. Late the next afternoon, Molineux surveyed the damage and began to clean up. The harbor's low tide lapped against his jackboots as he carried pieces of the wharf to shore. Chunks of ice slowed his progress. Molineux shivered as he threw planks into a small pile. The sound of crunching sand made him look up to see Rowe walking toward him.

"Every day is an adventure with you," Rowe said.

"It must be done, and spring will not come simply because I beckon it." Molineux wiped his hands on his jacket. "Believe me, I have tried."

Rowe smiled. "The proprietors of the wharf will take care of this in due time. But patience is not your strong suit, is it, Mr. Molineux?"

Evening shadows had begun to run long upon the shore.

"If you have a moment, follow me to my store where I can thaw out. And do not fret—the harbor and I have not been playing together very long. I will be fine."

The two men walked the few hundred yards as Rowe told Molineux about his day. The town desired to thank Mr. Dickenson, the farmer whose essays had appeared in the papers.

"I have come from the committee meeting," Rowe said. "We hope to share our letter to Mr. Dickenson with the town tomorrow."

"Do I recall correctly that Mr. Adams and Mr. Hancock are part of the committee?"

Rowe nodded. "Along with Dr. Warren and Dr. Church."

"Care to give me a preview?" Molineux wiped droplets of water and ice from his clothes as they moved along.

"We thanked Mr. Dickenson for giving voice to the friends of liberty who had previously feared all was already lost."

Molineux cast a questioning glance at Rowe. "I assume you reiterated the place of the laws of nature."

"Yes, and also of the British constitution. We also expressed appreciation he was armed with truth. I believe that is how we phrased it."

"Good," Molineux said.

Rowe continued. "The letter also mentions, in the current state of things, it seems those in authority believe for us to reject is to revolt and to reason is to rebel."

"Preposterous. If they will not even hear us out, it is they who are being irrational."

They arrived at the entrance to Molineux's shop where he scraped mud from his boots before they went in.

"Please, have a seat," Molineux offered as he stoked the fire.

Rowe perched on the edge of the chair. "I shan't stay long."

Molineux sat in front of the fire and took off his boots. "Were you able to attend Mr. Folger's trial this morning?"

"I was there. The arguments centered around whether he had the authority to make the seizure. They have adjourned until Saturday when the lawyers will plead before the judge of the admiralty court. I really must be going." Rowe stood then paused. "We plan to vote on the new minister soon. I trust you will give him your support."

"As much as in the past." Molineux began to rise from his chair to see Mr. Rowe to the door.

"Stay by the fire, dear sir. To look at you makes me cold. We would not want you to come to tomorrow's meeting as a snowman."

"I wish that were the worst of our problems. If the past year is any indication, our spring shipments of goods will carry with them boatloads of trouble."

"We shall see, Mr. Molineux." Rowe opened the door. "We shall see."

CHAPTER SEVEN

Hancock's Vessels

April 9–June 13, 1768

Hancock held his lantern over the hatch to *Lydia*'s cargo hold. As winter loosened its grip on Boston, its harbor had come to life with ships carrying merchants' seasonal orders.

"Mr. Richards?" Hancock asked.

Silence.

The merchant intensified his tone. "Mr. Richards, we know you are down there."

The shuffling of crates from below made Hancock wince, then the customs official appeared at the foot of the stairs. "I did not expect you to return at this late hour."

Hancock let out a puff of air. "Both I and the captain of my ship have asked you not to intrude into the belly of my vessel. It is beyond your jurisdiction." The merchant glanced at the eight men standing behind him then turned back to the man in the hold. "I ask you to please remove yourself. Otherwise, I will request my men to assist with my request."

"I am not going anywhere and am merely following orders from my superior customs official."

"Orders?" the ship's owner asked. "Do you even have a commission?"

The man pulled documents from his pocket, and Hancock motioned to one of his sailors to retrieve them.

Hancock turned up the wick in his lantern then handed it to another of his men. He took the papers and held them up to the light. "None of these are dated."

The customs official grunted. "I received them yesterday."

"I have no way of knowing that, do I?" Hancock asked. "What about a writ of assistance?"

"There wasn't time."

Hancock placed a fist on his hip. "You have enough time to snoop beneath the deck of my ship, yet there was none to get permission to do so? Maybe you simply desire to discover cargo for which you can benefit financially."

"If you have something worth finding," the customs official snapped, "then the bounty is mine to share. That is no fault of mine."

Hancock turned to two of his men. "Please assist Mr. Richards to the deck."

The men scurried into the hold, seized the intruder by his arms and thighs, then lugged him up the steps. The man squirmed against the hands which constrained him.

"So, Mr. Richards," Hancock said, "do you still desire to search my vessel?"

The man shook his head, and the merchant gave a cautious nod to the sailors to release their captive. The customs official straightened his hair and clothes.

"You may search my vessel, but not tarry below. The captain tells me you have been down there for hours."

"I have what I need." The official glared at the ship's owner then turned to go. "Take note, Mr. Hancock. This will not be the last you hear from me."

At the annual meeting in May, Hancock noticed that the town picked its own battles. It asked the selectmen to deny the governor and his council use of Faneuil Hall for the annual Election Day dinner if they intended to invite the commissioners. Neither should the governor expect the traditional escort by the cadets. Hancock was certain no one questioned tension existed between the town and the governor, and everyone wondered not if, but when, there would be a more serious confrontation. He feared the opportunity would come soon enough.

Several weeks later, Hancock looked out the window of his counting house situated on Long Wharf. His Majesty's Ship *Romney* and her fifty guns bobbled in the distance, yet within plain view.

The Friday evening sun glimmered off the rising tide as it splashed against the building. The scent of tobacco drifted in from a nearby shop.

The merchant's bookkeepers had left for the day, and Rowe sat at one of the counting tables. "Everyone knows of your taste for the finest wine," Rowe said. "And you made it clear you would pay no duties."

Hancock walked over and sat down. "And my ship sailing in from the Madeira Islands would most certainly be carrying the duty-bearing commodity. Is that what you are implying?"

Rowe shrugged. "Why wouldn't they be suspicious when a sloop comes to port carrying a mere twenty-five casts of wine?"

Hancock half smiled at his fellow merchant.

Rowe continued. "I was at the Custom House the day the inspector reported them. You would have been proud—he did not even flinch."

"But now, with *Romney* here to protect him, the inspector sings a different song."

"I am truly sorry your captain could not be here to support your account of the event."

Hancock took a deep breath. "His heart attack was certainly ill-timed, wasn't it?"

"*Romney* seems to be doing its job as a man-of-war ship very well—terrifying our inhabitants into submission—not only with its guns, but also by forcing our men to serve on her."

The last of the sun's orange rays had disappeared. Rowe stood and walked toward the door. "I must go if I am to miss the horde of laborers as they get off work." He paused. "They seem especially loud even for this time of the day."

Hancock joined him. The two men stepped onto the wharf and were nearly knocked over by those rushing past them. One of the workers pointed north as he ran.

Then the two merchants saw it—a commotion a few hundred yards across the water. At Hancock's Wharf. Hancock pulled Rowe back into the building then hurried to the window.

"The excitement is indeed at my wharf."

Rowe joined him then put his hand on Hancock's shoulder. With his other hand, he pointed toward *Romney*. "Are those longboats leaving His Majesty's Ship and—and heading toward yours?"

"They are, and with plenty of sailors and marines aboard." Hancock scanned back to his ship then grabbed Rowe's arm. "They would not dare." Hancock pointed toward his sloop. "They have marked *Liberty* with the king's arrow."

Rowe's eyes widened. "Then they intend to seize it."

"There must be hundreds of them."

Neither moved while they watched in disbelief, then Hancock spoke. "Is that the commissioner and customs collector in the midst of them?"

"I believe it is—Joseph Harrison and Benjamin Hallowell."

The two men stood in silence as they watched the king's men attach then tow *Liberty* into HMS *Romney*'s protective shadows amid a shower of stones from the men on the wharf.

The roar from Hancock's Wharf grew louder. Rowe's mouth fell open. "The mob is now trying to stone Harrison and Hallowell."

Hancock lit a lantern. "I must find Samuel Adams. He will know what to do."

Molineux stood on the front porch of his home. The grandfather clock in the hall struck midnight. The crowd from the wharf had swelled to more than two thousand and now caroused at the foot of Beacon Hill. Indian war cries, shattering glass, and a crackling bonfire on the Common filled the night air.

Junior had returned with the details. The casualties—windows in the commissioners' homes and Harrison's pleasure boat. Hancock, Adams, and Dr. Warren were attempting to disperse the mob.

Molineux motioned to his son for silence as he heard a voice from below rise above the rest. "We will defend our liberties and property by the strength of our arm and the help of our God. To your tents, O Israel." And then, the throng faded into the night.

Molineux said good night to Junior then went to his desk and pulled out pen and paper. He and the other Sons of Liberty must distance themselves from such extreme revelry.

He expressed regret to Harrison for the frenzy of the night then sat back in his chair for a moment before he continued. The whole must not be condemned for the actions of a few. After all, every major city in the world contains this sort of people, and this lucky incident may have kept them from greater evils. He finished and addressed the letter then made his way up the stairs to his bedroom with light from the lantern. More episodes were sure to come, and he must be ready.

At midday on Monday, Molineux sat on the edge of his bed while Dr. Warren examined his elbow. After Friday's riot, someone had placed notes in the Liberty Tree encouraging the town to rid the country of the commissioners and their officers. Patriots worked to squelch the violence associated with such notions.

"You took quite a tumble, Mr. Molineux," Dr. Warren said.

"Someone put the papers higher up in the tree than usual."

"I want to see the commissioners gone as much as anyone," Dr. Warren said, "but Mr. Adams says it should be done without tarnishing the town's image."

Molineux used his free arm to adjust his sitting position. "Do you happen to know who the officers were milling around town a few weeks ago?"

"They were from New York. I know nothing more." Dr. Warren pushed the curtain of the four-poster bed further out of the way then lifted Molineux's arm.

"Ouch. I brought you here to help me, not hurt me."

"My apologies. Unfortunately, sometimes pain is a matter of course. You should have sent for me sooner."

The patient smirked. "Mrs. Molineux said the same."

"Hold still while I bandage you up." The doctor placed a splint of wood against Molineux's arm then secured it with linen bandages.

"Will this slow me down?"

Dr. Warren bowed his head and stared at him. "That is the hope. You need to be careful if you want to get better."

"Where do things stand with my neighbor?"

"Mr. Harrison and Mr. Hallowell agreed to return the ship to Mr. Hancock if he would post bond while awaiting trial. Hallowell has a few bruises, so I met with him at his home. We settled the negotiations this morning."

"They are snakes in the grass."

Dr. Warren smiled. "Some say Mr. Hallowell obtained his position due to his opposition to the cause of liberty."

"It would not surprise me."

Dr. Warren began to pack up his supplies. "We have a meeting at Mr. Hancock's this evening. Mr. Otis and Mr. Adams will be there. They will likely agree with you."

The doctor pointed at Molineux. "Take care of this arm of yours. You only have two."

Molineux laughed, and they walked down the stairs together.

Maryann met them at the front door. "You have tied him down, I see."

"Not possible, but I have done what I could."

"Thank you for coming, Dr. Warren," Maryann said.

The two men stepped onto the porch.

Molineux nodded toward Hancock's home. "Maybe I will see you there in a few hours."

"Good day, Mr. Molineux."

Molineux paced around Hancock's parlor where the candles had been burning for hours. Adams had asked him, as the uninvited guest, to remain silent. Otis and Adams leaned forward in their chairs. Dr. Warren sat rubbing his chin.

Hancock's fingers tapped the armrest of his wingback chair. "Having one of my ships sit idle for untold months would be very costly."

"We have been over that." Adams extended both hands. "Which is worth more to you—financial security or freedom from tyranny?"

Hancock remained quiet yet thoughtful.

Otis stood, walked toward the mantel, and stared at the empty fireplace. "The seizure was simply not legal. Not protesting would send London the wrong message."

Adams lifted a hand toward Molineux who tightened his lips to prevent words from spilling out.

"And *Liberty* sitting in the harbor under the king's guns," Adams said, "would remind our fellow Bostonians of what is at stake. A peaceful demonstration if you will."

"It seems the commissioners do not anticipate peace," Dr. Warren said. "Four of them and their families sought refuge aboard the *Romney* this very day."

Hancock interlaced his fingers and rested them on his lap. "I will submit to your wishes and withdraw from my previous agreement."

The room fell silent then Adams spoke. "Dr. Warren, will you be so kind as to relay this change to Mr. Hallowell? Even though the hour is late, I believe it would be wise to do so tonight."

"Let him know we believe our case is strong," Otis said, "and we will simply let it play out in the court of law."

"Mr. Hancock," Dr. Warren said, "your decision is final?"

"It is." Hancock rose from his chair and saw Dr. Warren to the door. "Please give Mr. Hallowell my regret for any trouble I may have caused by the reversal, but I must do as my conscience demands, regardless of the cost."

CHAPTER EIGHT

Stalemate

June 13–30, 1768

*H*utchinson stared out the window of the governor's office. "Messrs. Harrison and Hallowell have joined the commissioners at Castle William. Without the island fortress, I do not know where they would have found refuge. They will be safe there."

"Yet it is a temporary fix." Bernard sat behind his desk. "They have not only requested additional war ships but soldiers as well."

Hutchinson turned to the governor. "You fear an insurrection against the Crown's officials, do you not?"

Bernard laid a hand upon his desk. "My not applying for troops does not mean they are not wanted. I have relayed this sentiment to the commander of Britain's North American forces, General Thomas Gage."

"I pray it will not take long for your letter to reach New York," Hutchinson said.

"I begged the general to keep the letter to himself as much as possible since knowledge of such things tends to awaken the trained mobs."

"I am afraid the danger to officials will not blow over quickly." Hutchinson rose to leave. "And aid from beyond our fair town may, in fact, be required to keep the peace."

The lines in the governor's face furrowed. "Until the atmosphere is more stable, I will take refuge at my home in the country."

The two men exchanged their goodbyes, and the ride home provided Hutchinson with the opportunity to consider what might transpire without troops to protect them. Tomorrow's town meeting would likely provide an answer.

The next evening, rain beat against the roof of Hutchinson's carriage as he traveled to Bernard's country home. His Excellency had requested the lieutenant governor's immediate counsel.

Hutchinson tilted his head. Thunder? Then the source of the noise came into view—a line of eleven carriages on the road moving toward him. Although curious to know who was among the town's delegates to the governor, he chose to keep his face hidden from view. He would get Bernard's account of the meeting soon enough.

Upon Hutchinson's arrival, he and the governor exchanged few pleasantries before comparing notes from the eventful day.

"It was perhaps the largest town meeting ever assembled," Hutchinson said. "They met first at the Liberty Tree—or Liberty Hall as they now refer to it."

"The rain did not deter them?"

Hutchinson shook his head. "They paraded past the Town House to Faneuil Hall before finally moving to Old South in the middle of the afternoon. Fifteen hundred by my estimation."

"That church is cavernous. It will hold four times as many," Bernard said.

"And more."

Bernard picked up a piece of paper and handed it to his lieutenant governor. "This is what the twenty-one delegates, with Mr. Otis as their leader, presented to me."

Hutchinson blinked at the mention of his nemesis. "My source tells me Mr. Otis closed the meeting by declaring they would resist unto blood."

"Do you believe they will?"

"No. He added his hope that it may never happen and encouraged the people toward peace and good order. I believe the people wish for the latter much more than the former. An insurrection would not be in anyone's interest."

Hutchinson looked down at the petition and read the first line.

The inhabitants of the town of Boston have gathered in a legally assembled meeting.

He looked up at Bernard. "They did not gain permission to meet until late in the day. And ignorant as they may be, the heads of a Boston town meeting influence all public measures."

The governor motioned to the document. Hutchinson continued to read silently.

The British constitution has established no man shall be taxed but by himself or representative. We have not given our consent, and petitions have been cruelly and insidiously prevented from reaching the Royal Presence.

Hutchinson kept his eyes focused on the document. "No one can deny they have sent many a complaint to London."

We find ourselves invaded with an armed force—seizing and impressing our fellow subjects contrary to express acts of Parliament. All navigation is obstructed, upon which alone our whole support depends. And the town is at this crisis in a situation nearly such, as if war were formally declared against it.

Hutchinson's eyes widened.

Bernard shifted in his chair. "Have you reached their demands?"

Hutchinson continued to scan the page. "Ah, here they are." He read aloud. "As the Board of Customs have relinquished their commission here, we flatter ourselves your Excellency will in tenderness to this people use the best means in your power to remove the other grievance.

Namely, your immediate order to the commander of His Majesty's Ship *Romney* to remove it from this harbor."

Hutchinson looked up. "Have the commissioners notified you of their resignation?"

"I am afraid the people have misinterpreted the board taking refuge at the castle."

"I see. And what of the town's request for you to remove the *Romney*?"

Bernard stood. "I have not given an official reply. It is a delicate matter and what you and I will spend the remainder of our evening debating."

"We carry a heavy burden," Hutchinson said, "for the fate of this province—and, indeed, of all of America—may depend upon the measures the town takes at tomorrow's meeting."

Molineux stood at his parlor window, his leg bouncing in anticipation. Evening shadows ran long across the floor.

Maryann sat in her rocker knitting. "Will, you have looked out the window fifty times since you arrived home."

"I've got to know what happened," Molineux said. "The committee will almost certainly return to Hancock's home, since that is where they assembled before going to meet with the governor."

"You know what they say about a watched pot." Maryann grinned.

"Once they arrive at Hancock's, they will want to rendezvous. Then it could be hours. Besides, I am not watching—" Molineux spotted the lights of the eleven chaises. He shot out the door and ran toward them.

"Confound it!" He grabbed his elbow then found a more comfortable trot to accommodate the pain. Reaching the caravan, he hopped on board the first carriage in line, careful not to reinjure his arm.

"If you please, Mr. Molineux," Mr. Otis said. "There is an old man sitting in my chair who has no need of a surprise. And I am not referring to Mr. Hancock."

"Begging your pardon, my dear man, but I would do no less than to speak to the leader of this posse."

Otis's round frame shook with laughter.

Molineux acknowledged Hancock with a nod.

"What can I do for you, Willy?" Otis asked.

"Tell me of the success—or failure—of your mission."

Otis drew in a long breath then exhaled slowly. "The governor received us quite politely."

"And then what?"

"He had wine handed around to us all."

Molineux gave Otis the evil eye. "You know that is not what I am asking."

"The governor will provide us with a written answer tomorrow."

Molineux's face dropped. He had hoped for an answer today.

"What do you tell your children the night before a big celebration?" Otis asked. "Sleep, for tomorrow will surely come."

The chaise jerked to a halt in front of Hancock's mansion.

"Ah, my dear friend," Otis said, "today's journey has come to an end. You will have an answer tomorrow afternoon along with every other anxious soul in this fine town."

Molineux arrived at Old South in plenty of time for the four o'clock meeting. Samuel Adams's place of worship was impressive. What the Puritans had left out of the structure in ornamentation due to their religious beliefs, they had more than made up for in architectural design. Box pews running across the width of the building, coupled with a large gallery above, gave everyone a sense of closeness to the speaker who would stand at the high pulpit against the long wall. Large, arched windows all around gave a sense of openness no matter the size of the crowd. White everything, minus the floors and wood accents, reflected the virtues sought after by the segment of society who had built it nearly four decades before.

Many of the committee—Rowe, Hancock, Samuel Adams, and Drs. Church, Warren, and Young—had already found seats at the front. Molineux joined Drs. Warren and Young. Molineux's leg bounced until Otis stepped to the platform and called the meeting to order. The piece of paper Otis carried caught Molineux's eye.

After Otis conveyed information about the pleasant reception the committee had received, he read aloud the governor's response to the town's petition:

> *Gentlemen,*
> *My office and station make me a very incompetent judge of the rights you claim against acts of Parliament, and therefore, it would be to no purpose for me to express my opinion thereupon. All I can say is I shall not knowingly infringe any of your rights and privileges but shall religiously maintain all those which are committed to me as a servant of the king.*

Molineux gritted his teeth. He glanced around the room. To his dismay, people seemed pleased.

Otis continued to read.

> *In regard to impressing men for the service of the king in his ships of war, I shall use my utmost endeavors to get it regulated so as to avoid all the inconveniences to this town. I have no doubt of my succeeding therein.*

Molineux let out a slight cough. That would be welcome relief.

> *I am obliged by all kinds of duty by his Majesty's special orders to protect, aid, and assist the commissioners of the customs. And whether they shall or shall not relinquish the exercise of their commission, I must not fail to give them all the protection, aid, and assistance in my power. If in so doing I shall give offence, I shall be sorry for it, but I shall never regret doing my duty.*

> *I have no command over His Majesty's Ships, and therefore, cannot issue such orders as you desire regarding the Romney.*

Otis looked up. "Signed by his Excellency, Francis Bernard."

Molineux leaned over and whispered to Dr. Warren. "Duty, duty, duty. Mr. Hutchinson's fingerprints are all over that last paragraph."

Dr. Warren smiled but continued to look straight ahead.

Otis cleared his throat and looked at Molineux. "Now that we have heard the governor's reply, I believe there is another item to address before we can bring this meeting to a close. I have been informed that after much debate, those selected to handle the situation regarding Mr. Hancock's vessel have reached a decision. They believe it best to deal with the matter through written instructions to the town's representatives to the House. As you know, Mr. Hancock, Samuel Adams, one other, and myself are those representatives."

The town selected a committee to prepare the instructions, then the meeting closed.

Molineux stood. "Congratulations, Dr. Warren, on convincing John Adams to join our meetings and for whatever manners of persuasion you used to convince him to play an active role."

"My pleasure," Dr. Warren said. "The fate of America may depend upon Boston's ability to stand firm behind whatever resolves we propose."

"I will look forward to hearing what you and the rest of the committee draw up." Molineux scanned the crowd. "Now, if you will excuse me, I must find Mr. Adams and speak with him myself."

Molineux pushed his way through the crowd to John Adams who was nearing the door. "Mr. Adams. A moment of your time, if you please."

Adams scanned the room until his eyes landed on Molineux.

Molineux bowed his head to acknowledge Adams's attention. "It has been a pleasant surprise to see you here these last few days. Have I heard correctly—you have settled in the white house near the concert hall?"

"For now—until I am able to find a more permanent place to live." Adams's eyes darted to the door then back to Molineux.

"Then you are perhaps a half mile from where I reside. You and your lovely wife are welcome to drop by anytime. I enjoy being surrounded by you young folk."

Molineux and Adams stepped aside as people exited the building, then Molineux continued. "Dr. Warren indicated you preferred to stay away from these meetings because it is here that madness lies. Is Mr. Otis why you believe this?"

"The actual phrase is 'O that way madness lies.'" Adams said. "And, no, any issues Mr. Otis may have are another matter entirely."

"I am not sure what it means, but it sounds clever."

"It is from Shakespeare and refers to total obsession with a problem to the extent all else is neglected and the mind becomes riddled with madness."

"Then it is a great honor to welcome you to our town, to my neighborhood, and to the asylum," Molineux said with a bow.

Adams smiled.

"And may I thank you, in advance, for your service to your new hometown," Molineux said.

"Boston may have celebrated too soon with regards to Parliament's desire to tax us," Adams said.

"Indeed. Too much cash has gone out from America through trade, never to return. Or worse, to the support of royal officers who live in idleness and luxury."

"We must reemphasize our loyalty, reverence, and submission to those ruling in the Motherland," Adams said. "Yet, at the same time, we must assert and vindicate our rights and liberties—even at the utmost hazard of our lives and fortunes."

"You will be a great asset to the committee, Mr. Adams." Molineux dodged those moving toward the exit. "What do you think of the seizure of my neighbor's vessel?"

"Such an illegal action is alarming. Even more so are the rumors the homeland desires to use additional ships of war and military force to intimidate us into passive obedience."

"Well said. And what of our local leaders?"

"Many are good, but anyone who solicits the importation of troops during times of peace, as we have now, should be considered an enemy."

Molineux beamed. "I believe you will make your cousin proud. May he and the others in the House remain committed to the people they serve—and not to those who seek to suppress us."

"Thank you, Mr. Molineux," Adams said. "Now if you will please excuse me, I have matters to which I must attend."

Molineux turned his gaze to the platform and his thoughts to the governor's refusal to give an adequate response to their request. What will it take to convince him and his dutiful assistant they are defending the wrong side? As for the people of the town, can they not see the harm in mindlessly accepting whatever comes from the governor's hand? He took in a sharp breath then exhaled. Will it take the likes of a nor'easter for the ship to return to its rightful course? If so, may it come upon us quickly.

Hutchinson sat in his place overlooking the activities of the Massachusetts Bay House of Representatives. The lieutenant governor sighed. The new British secretary might as well have included matches in the packet the governor had received from him the day after the town meeting.

Much could change in the months it took to communicate with London. Responding to the circular letter the province had sent to other colonies in February, Lord Hillsborough's latest correspondence demanded that Governor Bernard instruct the Massachusetts Bay House to rescind the letter. Bernard had enjoyed newfound popularity after his positive reply to the town a few days before. The governor did not expect it to last a week—he had been right. A few days later, Bernard obeyed the order. And now, the consequences of the governor's actions played out before Hutchinson through a rant by Otis.

"The king has appointed none but boys for his ministers," Otis said as he paced about, "with no education but traveling through

France." Otis wiped sweat from his flushed face. "It is from thence they return full of the slavish principles of that country."

How quickly Otis had dismissed the kind words he had lavished upon the governor less than a week before. Bernard had even noted how uncommon and extraordinary Otis's comment had been.

Hutchinson caught a glimpse of Molineux among the crowd in the public gallery, which poured out both doors and energized Otis. Odd—Molineux had his fiddle.

Otis raised his arms, took a deep breath, then continued. "They knew nothing of business when they came into office and did not stay long enough to acquire knowledge which is gained from experience."

The people sat in awe. Those in the front row leaned forward to hear the scathing words being bestowed upon those in authority on both sides of the water.

"And who are these ministers? The very frippery and foppery of France, the mere outsides of monkeys."

Otis bowed his head then slowly lifted his eyes to his audience. "And the people of England themselves do not know what the rights of Englishmen are," he said, then shook one fist toward the heavens. "But we do—and we will guard them with our lives."

After two hours of venomous attacks, Otis finally relinquished control of the floor.

Other members of the House spoke their minds, but none as violently as Otis. They argued they had already received official support from other colonies for the correspondence they had sent out in February.

Hutchinson held his breath when it came time for the vote on whether to rescind the letter.

The results were tallied, and the announcement came.

Ninety-two nays and seventeen yeas.

The crowd cheered and ran out of the Town House onto King Street.

As soon as the building was clear, Hutchinson moved down the hall to the council chambers. He cracked opened the door to the balcony and stood in the shadows as he observed the celebration. He recognized the tune coming from Molineux's fiddle—one that had gained popularity in recent days. In the street just beyond the balcony, the townsfolk lifted their voices in song.

> *Come join hand in hand, brave Americans, all,*
> *And rouse your bold hearts at fair liberty's call.*
> *No tyrannous acts shall suppress your just claim*
> *Or stain with dishonor America's name.*

> *In freedom we're born, and in freedom we'll live.*
> *Our purses are ready,*
> *Steady, friends, steady,*
> *Not as slaves, but as freemen, our money we'll give.*

Some began to dance a jig as the throng moved down the street toward the harbor. Hutchinson moved out of the shadows and pushed the door further open.

> *Our worthy forefathers, let's give 'em a cheer,*
> *To climates unknown did courageously steer.*
> *Thro' oceans to deserts for freedom they came,*
> *And dying bequeathed us their freedom and fame.*

> *In freedom we're born, and in freedom we'll live.*
> *Our purses are ready,*
> *Steady, friends, steady,*
> *Not as slaves, but as freemen, our money we'll give.*

Molineux danced, cheered, and played his fiddle with as much energy as Hutchinson had ever seen. Tears welled up in the lieutenant governor's eyes. Such spirit, yet terribly misdirected.

> *For our children shall gather the fruits of our pain . . .*

Hutchinson looked beyond the jubilation to the harbor where *Liberty* continued to bobble, representing a cause the people believed was worthy of a fight.

By uniting, we stand, by dividing we fall . . .

As they continued toward the harbor, the voices grew faint, yet Hutchinson could still make out the words.

All ages shall speak with amaze and applause,
Of the courage we'll shew in support of our laws;
To die we can bear, but to serve we disdain,
For shame is to freedom more dreadful than pain.

Molineux lifted his fiddle. "Here's to the ninety-two men who voted to stand against tyranny!"

"Huzzah for ninety-two!" the crowd shouted back.

Hutchinson collected himself then went in search of the governor who, as Hutchinson had suspected, confirmed he would do as London had requested and end the legislative session. It was the only way to silence the voice of the people.

"I fear England has a difficult task," Hutchinson confided in Bernard, "to keep the colonies in due subordination while finding a way to continue to benefit from their commerce."

"A revolt itself, I believe, will concern them at least as much," Bernard said. "I suspect Lord Hillsborough will instruct me to collect evidence against those who have actively resisted British law. He will need the information if he decides to summon them to England to stand trial for treason."

Hutchinson nodded. "May I suggest that your informants begin by investigating a certain fiddler who resides on Beacon Hill."

CHAPTER NINE

The Unthinkable

August 15–September 29, 1768

In mid-August, Molineux and his fiddle entertained the large group of Sons of Liberty gathered around their tree on the south side of town to celebrate their founding. The fiddler spotted Rowe in the distance, played a few more bars, then wrapped up the tune.

"Do not go far, gentlemen, for more is yet to come," Molineux said. He tucked his instrument under one arm then trotted toward his fellow merchant. "Mr. Rowe, you are coming to us late."

"I had to make merry in Roxbury before I could join you here. They are quite jovial there, too. About a hundred of them, I would say."

Molineux waved his bow in the air. "I am sure there were ninety-two."

"Ah, yes," Mr. Rowe said, "a joyful ninety-two."

"And I have no doubt a mere seventeen dined around our governor's table today."

A voice rose from among the group. "May I have your attention?"

The crowd grew quiet.

"I would like to make a toast to the prosperity of the fine land in which we live."

"Hear, hear!"

A minister stood up. "May fifty thousand troops with fifty men-of-war never be able to compel us to import, buy, or consume English goods."

"Huzzah!"

"What but a standing army can be worse to a people who have tasted the sweets of liberty? Long live our liberty!"

"Huzzah! Huzzah! Huzzah!"

Molineux played a brief tune then proclaimed, "Now to our chariots for a parade." He ran and jumped onto the first of the sixty carriages then searched the crowd for his next-door neighbors. "And shan't our leading merchants, Mr. Hancock and Mr. Bowdoin, be given a place of honor in the pilgrimage to join our brothers in Roxbury?"

"Huzzah!"

Molineux helped the men aboard then hopped down to lead the procession on foot for a few hundred yards. He poured his heart and soul into his playing. The people of Massachusetts Bay had defeated those who sought to suppress them, and life was good once again.

Molineux stood at the counter of a local merchant with his son John. The weight of the gun in Molineux's hands felt right. "You say it is the last of this size you have?"

The merchant nodded. "People have been streaming in all day."

Molineux handed the weapon to John. "You are a young man now. A gun is not a toy. Use this to your advantage but always with great care."

"I will, Pa. I promise."

Molineux pulled out his purse then spoke to the merchant. "Fortunate for us, Mr. Rowe let the cat out of the bag."

"They tell me Governor Bernard leaked the news to him this morning," the merchant said. "From there word spread quicker than the 1760 fire."

"It seems our governor had been planning this for some time but did not want to let on until the last possible minute. No one knows exactly when the troops will arrive, but when they do—like the paper said—our lives will be in our own hands."

The merchant retrieved his copy of the newspaper and set it on the counter. "The shop has been bustling so I have not had an opportunity to read it."

"If you'd like, John will be happy to read it to you," Molineux said. John beamed. "Sure, Pa."

Molineux searched for the correct page and read one line. "The Motherland has broken its portion of the compact, leaving the colonies unattached." He handed the paper to John and pointed to the section. John adjusted the pages then read aloud.

If an army should be sent to reduce us to slavery, we will tell them we are willing and desirous to be their fellow subjects. We are Englishmen and claim the privileges of Englishmen, but we are never willing to be slaves to our fellow subjects. If this will not satisfy them, we will put our lives in our hands and cry to the Judge of all the earth, who will do right.

John set the paper back onto the counter.

"We hope the troops will understand we are ready and that will be enough to scare them away." Molineux picked up the gun and walked with John to the door. He turned back to the shopkeeper. "If not, well, only the Lord above knows what will happen."

Molineux rubbed his forehead as he left his warehouse and set out for the town meeting. Faneuil Hall came into view. His uncle had told him stories about watching it go up in 1742. Michael Molineux, a ticket porter at the time, believed the town's new market and meeting hall provided one more reason to make it their North American base of operations. Michael's willingness to cover the Nova Scotia portion of the business gave them an additional edge. Molineux noted the grasshopper weathervane atop the cupola. Even his headache could not prevent a grin from spreading across his face. Since his warehouse sat at the east end of Faneuil Hall, the creature had amused him many times. It also gave him a sense of camaraderie with merchants in London, whose Royal Exchange bore a similar image.

Dr. Thomas Young's greeting interrupted his thoughts. His move to Boston had given Molineux a friend like no other, even though his age eclipsed the doctor's by nearly fifteen years. Each had roots in Ireland and a nonconformist spirit. Regular contact through their ties to the Sons of Liberty and North End Caucus had strengthened their bond. Dr. Warren thought less highly of him and had claimed "Youngisms" equated to "inaccuracy, malevolence, bad grammar, and nonsense."

Smells from the market below added to Molineux's fogginess as he and Young climbed the steps to the meeting space.

They settled into their seats, and a local clergyman opened the meeting with prayer. With his head bowed, Molineux's mind reviewed what he should expect. He, Otis, Adams, and a few others had met at Dr. Warren's house over the weekend to map out the plan.

Otis, in his familiar role as moderator, called the meeting to order. After some initial business, the town proceeded with the real purpose of the meeting—to consider the critical state of public affairs, both civil and religious, and how the town should react upon the troops' arrival. It pleased Molineux when the town appointed him to one of the two committees that would report back to the town meeting tomorrow.

The next day, Hutchinson sat at the long table in the council chambers. "It cannot be. It simply cannot be," he said to Governor Bernard in response to news from the informant who stood before them. "The town has ripped the authority right out of your hands, Governor."

"It certainly appears that way," Bernard said.

"Do they not understand a lack of representation was their own doing?" Hutchinson asked. "They are the ones who chose not to rescind the letter. And you were simply following orders from your superior when you disbanded the assembly. No one can place blame at your feet for that."

"Blame or no blame, they have chosen to move forward by their own devices."

"Perhaps other parts of the province will refuse to go along with the plan. Maybe they will be wise enough not to send delegates to the unauthorized convention."

"Perhaps." The governor faced the informant. "What else transpired at today's town meeting?"

"They did not take kindly to your refusal to supply information regarding the possible arrival of troops and where you plan to quarter them. They are fearful if the king's men do come, they will seek to disarm the town."

"Not a bad idea," Hutchinson said.

The young man shuffled his feet. "Four hundred of our militia's Brown Bess muskets lay scattered about the floor of the meeting hall."

Hutchinson gasped.

Bernard stretched his arms onto the table. "They were placed there temporarily while the storage room underwent a few changes."

Hutchinson found it difficult to breathe. "What did the people do with the muskets?"

"Nothing for now, but Mr. Otis indicated they would be delivered to the people, if and when an attempt is made against their liberties. The town record may be a bit confusing, as they couched the entire discussion in terms of protecting themselves against an attack by the French."

"The French?" Bernard said.

"Yes, your Excellency. I believe it was an attempt to disguise the true nature of their argument. Mr. Otis spoke of the legality of arming oneself against an enemy, and Samuel Adams mentioned nature and reason also declare these rights."

"They play the role of pied piper well, do they not?" Hutchinson said.

"The larger committee—including Samuel Adams, Otis, Hancock, and Molineux—presented a rather lengthy report, which reiterated past concerns over laws enacted without their consent. They specifically referenced taxation and having a standing army during times of peace."

"A city of peace is not what enters my mind when I evaluate the last few years." Hutchinson swallowed the rage that crept up his throat. "My own home—"

Bernard held up a hand toward Hutchinson then looked at the informant. "What did the town decide?"

"In the end, they agreed to greet the troops with a dignified cooperation, even though Mr. Adams was not as pleased with the decision as much as Mr. Otis was."

"Dare I ask," Bernard said, "for any additional news?"

The informant looked at his feet. "There are two more items that may be of interest."

"Then let us hear them."

"At one point during the meeting, Dr. Thomas Young took to the floor."

"Ah, yes," Bernard said, "a firebrand and eternal fisher in troubled waters."

"And the only one as riotous as Mr. Molineux," Hutchinson said.

Bernard kept his eyes on the informant. "Go on."

"Dr. Young invoked the spirit of the seventeenth century English philosopher John Locke, who suggested death as just punishment for those who sought absolute power."

"What was the response?"

"Most, save Samuel Adams and a few others, waved for him to sit down, and he obliged."

"The second item?" the governor asked.

"The town voted to observe next Tuesday as a day of fasting and prayer—a day to call upon the Ruler of the world for wisdom at such a time as this."

"Rest assured," Hutchinson said, "the Almighty will not answer the prayers of an immoral people."

"Any mention of the tar barrel atop the pole on Beacon Hill?" Bernard asked.

"They did much like the selectmen—acknowledged the situation then ignored it. Privately, some question whether it even contains the spirits needed to signal an alarm." The informant smiled. "Several of the Sons of Liberty have complained of headaches, however, since the barrel went up. I can neither confirm nor deny a connection."

"Very well. Thank you for your very helpful report. I will see you are compensated."

The informant left, and the governor stood and walked to the window. "They are still streaming out of Faneuil Hall."

"What are your plans concerning the barrel?" Hutchinson asked.

"The sheriff will oversee its removal—without fanfare, if he is wise." Barnard walked back to the table. "But that is the least of my worries."

"Oh?"

"I have heard rumors Mr. Molineux plans to lead five hundred men in an attack on the castle. He believes the troops will be garrisoned there."

"With the *Romney* now watching over the fortress, only a lunatic would attempt such a feat," Hutchinson said.

"I not only hold Mr. Molineux in such regard," Bernard said, "but believe he may also attempt to take possession of the treasury."

Hutchinson refused to let the fear within him manifest itself outwardly.

"And I have no reason to believe he will stop there," Bernard said. "May I suggest, Mr. Hutchinson, you be on guard as I believe he will eventually come after the two of us."

Two weeks later, Hutchinson sat at his desk in the Town House. Early rays of the autumn sun filtered through the open window and flickered across the newspaper spread out before him. He closed his eyes. Shots from the local militia fired in the distance. Drills had begun soon after the governor acknowledged two regiments were on the way to Boston. Bernard had discussed with his council where they would house those already in route, but he had not disclosed his mentioning to Lord Hillsborough additional troops might be needed.

Hutchinson opened his eyes, stood, and walked to the window. The week before, Faneuil Hall had welcomed seventy delegates who had streamed into Boston from sixty towns for the unauthorized convention. Others continued to trickle in. The victory of Otis's refusal to appear at the convention had been short lived. Over the weekend, he had yielded to pressure from Samuel Adams and other Sons of Liberty to attend.

The lieutenant governor returned to his desk and picked up the paper. What had become of the town's ability to reason? Tories had threatened the so-called patriots with the whipping post and other physical harm once the troops arrived. Those threatened had declared the liberty of the press and freedom of speech were under attack, and a platform, not punishment, should have been the appropriate response.

Delegates to the convention and the governor were in a squabble of royal proportions. Bernard had refused to receive the petitions from the unsanctioned assembly. Signed invitations to the meeting, as evidence against the offenders, had been hard for royal officials to come by.

Hutchinson closed his eyes again. Toasts from the previous week to the king's health were a distant memory. The province was in disarray, and Bernard had been right to encourage London to relinquish the Massachusetts Bay charter and reorganize the local government. The people must be reminded wherein lay the true authority—and it was not with the commoners.

A few days later, word came of the troops' imminent arrival, and the *Boston Chronicle* reported the nearly one hundred convention delegates "rushed out of town like a herd of scalded hogs."

An informer brought Hutchinson news of a meeting at Molineux's home. Samuel and John Adams, Paul Revere, Dr. Warren, and Josiah Quincy Jr. had gathered there to finalize plans for receiving the troops. The outcome was unknown.

Hutchinson sailed to the castle in a small vessel to ensure the barracks were ready. As he approached, the fortress discharged skyrockets, and the customs commissioners erupted into song.

> *Yankee Doodle came to town,*
> *a-riding on a pony.*
> *He stuck a feather in his hat*
> *and called him macaroni.*

The commissioners had apparently received word additional safeguards were on the way.

> *Yankee Doodle, keep it up!*
> *Yankee Doodle, dandy!*
> *Mind the music and the step,*
> *and with the girls be handy!*

Then Hutchinson saw their cause for jubilation. About a dozen ships neared the castle. No doubt they were the troops expected from Halifax, Nova Scotia—the Fourteenth and Twenty-ninth British Regiments. The ships cruised past the fortress as breakers rocked Hutchinson's boat.

He grabbed the rim of his vessel and watched from a distance. The war ships lined up in siege formation in Boston's harbor, aiming more than a hundred guns at the shore. Hutchinson's entire body relaxed. Order had at last returned to his beloved town.

CHAPTER TEN

○○○

Troops
October–November 1768

At high noon on Saturday, October 1, 1768, Hancock watched one thousand well-armed troops disembark at Long Wharf and march in formation up King Street. Officers led the way with swords drawn, daring anyone to hinder them from taking possession of the town.

The noise of drums and fifes saturated the scene. Yellow jackets stood in stark contrast to the drummers' black skin. Crimson sashes draped the officers' shoulders while silver breastplates protected their chests.

Wide-eyed townsfolk lined the street, complying with the patriots' request for calm, yet Hancock heard muted grumblings all around. A few teenage boys mumbled something about "lobsters" as soldiers dressed in bright red coats paraded in front of them. Older men denounced a minister's comment that the town's grievances had finally been "red-dressed." And whispers ran rampant that local officials had sent word to General Gage to send more troops.

Hancock scanned the crowd for Sons of Liberty, but they were few and far between. Those present remained as quiet as a moonbeam.

The commanding officer strode to the head of King Street and into the Town House. The hands of the clock seemed to stand still as the people waited for him to emerge. How would he respond to instructions to re-embark the king's troops and take them to the barracks at Castle William? The fortress technically falling within the town limits would be of little consolation to the officer.

Time continued to crawl. Then, a red-faced Lieutenant Colonel William Dalrymple appeared in the doorway. He stormed down the stairs to his officers to whom he gave orders. Orders too quiet to make out, yet the subsequent movement of troops made it clear—the soldiers would not be returning to the ships. A small detachment turned south, and one full regiment marched north toward Faneuil Hall. Hancock waited. Where would the remaining regiment go? Then, as he feared, they marched forward—toward Beacon Hill. The troops would set up camp on the Common.

Hancock helped Aunt Lydia into his carriage then extended his hand to the lovely Dorothy Quincy. All in their Sunday best.

Aunt Lydia found her spot then straightened her skirt with several flicks of her hand. "The sound of drums and the ear-piercing fifes still ring inside my head. Not to mention the shouts of officers conducting their drills. Who could possibly focus on what the minister had to say under such conditions?"

"Yes, my dear aunt," Hancock said. He steadied Miss Quincy as she stepped up into the carriage. "It is unfortunate."

The skin on Aunt Lydia's face tightened, and she dropped her hands into her lap with a groan. "Many of us fear the army's disrespect for the Sabbath will have an ill effect upon the younger part of our community."

Hancock climbed in and settled into the empty seat, then he signaled for the coachman to take them home. "Since the troops' behavior is contrary to the law, the selectmen have heard our share of complaints from the older inhabitants."

Miss Quincy smiled ever so slightly. "The noise cannot be mistaken for rumors."

"Speaking of rumors," Hancock said, "someone told me at church this morning you were among those the officers of the Crown invited to attend their dance."

Miss Quincy blushed. "'Tis true." She glanced down then up again. "Of course, I declined, citing the inappropriateness of gaiety during our country's time of mourning."

Hancock grimaced. "It is not simply for their own pleasure they hold these gleeful assemblies, but also to silence Boston's claims of misery." Hancock grabbed a strap in anticipation of the next bump in the road. "Even some of Boston's men find it difficult to shun these opportunities."

"Some of the fair maidens among us choose to support the plain and manly defenders of this country," Aunt Lydia said, "rather than embrace the feathered and embroidered aggressors who come from afar. Is that not so, Miss Quincy?"

"It is." Miss Quincy cast a grin at Hancock. "Yet it is not the feathers and embroidery that give the offense."

Aunt Lydia beamed, then her face fell. "Yet not all women are able to resist the offenders, no matter how they are dressed. Some say Mr. Rowe's adopted daughter has fallen for one of the Crown's men—drawing Mr. Rowe even closer into forbidden circles, I fear."

"My path crossed with his the day after the troops arrived. You would have thought he had seen a ghost," Hancock said, looking out the window.

"What happened?"

"He had come from an encounter with the captain of one of the armed schooners. Let's just say the captain had no inhibitions with regards to his language."

Aunt Lydia inhaled. "Did the captain threaten Mr. Rowe?"

"In so many words," Hancock said. "The captain indicated he wanted to see Mr. Rowe hung in his shoes."

"With all the drunkenness and profanity the regiments have brought to this town, it does not surprise me," Aunt Lydia said.

Miss Quincy looked at Hancock. "Do you believe the accounts in the newspapers we have received from New York? It paints a dark picture of what is happening here."

"I do not believe all of them," Hancock said. "Our governor is correct to say Samuel Adams fabricates some of the reports which find their way to the other colonies."

"Mr. Adams holds Governor Bernard and the commissioners responsible for our current situation due to the letters they sent to London. He claims it is their exaggerations which brought the soldiers here in the first place."

Hancock nodded. "A gentleman I spoke with last week believes the government desires to see mob-like behavior for it provides the need for soldiers."

"Then the disorders surrounding the seizure of your vessel made them happy?" Aunt Lydia asked.

"It did," Hancock said. "Mr. Bowdoin is preparing the address to the governor to counter claims that the people, rather than the Crown's officials, incited the riot."

"Mr. Bowdoin?" Miss Quincy asked.

"He lives on the other side of Mr. Molineux and is part of the governor's council. With Mr. Hutchinson no longer sitting in on their meetings, Mr. Bowdoin is a key player for the group. The council will request General Gage move the troops to the castle."

"Thank heavens our trip home does not take us by the Town House," Miss Quincy said. "It reeks. Do the soldiers housed there ever bathe?"

Aunt Lydia scrunched up her nose. "Did Mr. Otis's concerns go unheeded? He believes the stench could be hazardous to the health of those who need to conduct business there."

Hancock smiled. "Guards stationed at those legislative doors and a cannon placed across the street have been of greater concern."

"They leave no question as to who now holds the authority in this town," Aunt Lydia said. "Do they?"

The carriage began its climb up Beacon Hill. The Common, with row after row of soldiers' tents, came into view.

"Some say the town is a perfect garrison," Miss Quincy said.

"Mr. Otis is correct. It is utterly derogatory to administer justice under such conditions," Hancock said. "Mr. Adams believes this treatment impresses our minds with ideas of a military government and will eventually induce us to give up our rights and privileges."

"It seems," Miss Quincy said, "the patriots are attempting to keep demonstrations under control to prevent that argument from carrying any weight."

Aunt Lydia gestured toward the encampment. "At least the soldiers of the Twenty-ninth receive one good sermon a week from their chaplain. John, have you heard Samuel Adams speak of the need for Bibles among the troops?"

The carriage came to a halt in front of the Hancock home.

Hancock helped Miss Quincy from the carriage. "I have," Hancock said. "He has mentioned a few of his ideas to me."

Aunt Lydia extended her hand. "If they are going to practically live on our front lawn, I would at least like for them to have a dash or two of religion."

"No guarantees, but I will see what I can do."

Molineux and Rowe searched the coffeehouse for a seat. As during the rest of October, it was abuzz.

"Ah, Mr. Molineux, what a delight," Nicholas Boylston said. "And Mr. Rowe. Will you join me?"

As they claimed their seats, Molineux caught Rowe's silent message—don't cause any trouble.

All three men, charter members of the Boston Society for Encouraging Trade and Commerce, had joined in petitioning for various causes throughout the years. Life had been good to Boylston, which he evidenced through his estate, gardens, and wardrobe selections. Though Boylston claimed moderation in his political beliefs, he acted as an informant on smugglers and refused to support the nonimportation agreement earlier in the year, which his brother Thomas had signed. Their sister was married to Hallowell.

"Have I heard correctly," Boylston asked, "that both of you have honored General Gage's request to help the troops with their winter housing dilemma?"

"I can spend the Crown's pound as easily as one of my own." Molineux said. "Besides, Mr. Apthorp welcomed the opportunity."

"Nonetheless, Whigs may want to avoid Wheelwright's Wharf for the foreseeable future," Boylston said. "It may contain more red-coated lobsters than they would be able to properly digest."

"I know Mrs. Molineux will stay away," Molineux said. "During the past month, she has grown weary of seeing them within view of our front door."

"Certainly," Boylston said, making room for the additional food and drinks coming to the table. "Mr. Molineux, did I hear your trial is quickly approaching?"

Molineux's tongue had been a bit loose when he referred to Robert Cotton, former clerk of the court but known more recently for insane behavior. Cotton sued Molineux for libel, demanding two thousand pounds.

"Yes, it is," Molineux said. "Even John Adams whispers Mr. Cotton is indeed insane. I just happen to speak my mind louder than most. The boys around town have made up songs about the lunatic."

"I am not so sure John's cousin replacing Mr. Cotton as clerk has resulted in any more sanity in the House," Boylston said.

"Ah, we think differently along those lines," Molineux said. "And I trust the courts will take my view of things." Molineux searched for a way to pivot the conversation. "Your concern should not be for me but for Mr. Rowe. He and General Gage are getting along a bit too well."

Boylston questioned Rowe with his expression.

"General Gage has treated me kindly," Rowe said, "and desired to engage in conversation. Entertaining him in my home was quite appropriate."

"And Colonel Dalrymple?" Molineux asked.

"Appropriate for him to attend as well, considering the nature of the general's visit."

"Were they successful in removing the squatters from the Manufactory House in order to make room for the troops expected from Ireland?" Boylston asked.

Molineux grinned. "No. It seems the tenants preferred to share their place with the sheriff rather than with the troops. They locked him in the cellar when he tried to displace them."

"With the encouragement of you Sons, no doubt."

Molineux chuckled. "Oddly enough, it was the soldiers who eventually rescued him. The sheriff finally gave up on removing them. I am certain the troops will find the Wheelwright's Wharf to be much more welcoming. For Mrs. Molineux, they cannot move there fast enough."

Molineux lay in bed listening. Never had migrating birds been so loud.

A faint light upon his eyelids indicated it was barely dawn.

He reached to Maryann's side of the bed. No one.

He threw off the covers, sat up, and rubbed his eyes.

Drums? At this hour?

He shuffled to the window.

The soldiers' tent city had vanished from the Common. In its place, a thousand troops marched to the beat of a rolling drum.

The sound of death.

Then he saw a lone soldier dressed in white, standing before a firing squad.

Desertion among the troops had plagued Lieutenant Colonel Dalrymple throughout October. Falling night temperatures and pamphlets circulated by Molineux and Junior had encouraged soldiers to escape in search of a better life. Now, it appeared Dalrymple wanted to stop the bleeding.

A chaplain stood beside the soldier. An officer motioned for the minister to step away from the one condemned. Then shots rang out. The soldier's life snuffed out as a vivid reminder to others who might contemplate betrayal and to the town that their grip on it was firm.

Drums still rolling, the regiments slowly filed past their former comrade. Several of them lifted the limp body into a simple coffin then carried it to a nearby grave where they lowered it into the ground and the chaplain read a few parting words.

On the tenth of November, Molineux led soldiers of the two new regiments to the quarters he would provide. The Sixty-fourth and Sixty-fifth Regiments had arrived from Ireland with smallpox on board. The remainder of the troops took up housing around town and at Castle William. With new safeguards in place, the commissioners moved from the castle back into town. A few days later, they appeared in public. General Gage left before Thanksgiving Day, stating Boston was firmly under military control.

Molineux returned home to read another of Adams's editorials. One section stood out.

> It is a very improbable supposition any people can long remain free with a strong military power in the very heart of their country. A wise and prudent people will always have a watchful and jealous eye over it.

Molineux sat deep in thought for a while. With the grand total of unwelcomed troops in Boston at four thousand—one soldier for every four residents—he wondered who was really doing the watching.

CHAPTER ELEVEN

Financial Woes

March–June 1769

*M*olineux shivered as he entered Revere's shop. "Brrr." The half-mile walk from his own store had chilled him to the bone. His red cape would surely come in handy about now. Too bad it was on reserve for special occasions.

Revere set down his work and stood. "The winds of March followed you, I see."

"It is more the Ides of March that are haunting me."

Revere laughed. "Debts are coming due, eh?" He walked over to a table laden with wares and began to search. "You will be able to pay me, I trust."

"I can pay you as soon as the general pays me. Otherwise, I will need to break into my piggy pot."

"The troops continue to lodge at no charge, I take it."

"Oh, we are charging. They just aren't paying. The colonel says to expect payment any day. When it arrives, I may begin spending it as if I am one of the drunken sailors sitting in our harbor." Molineux rubbed his forehead. "I had to sell my Harvard Street property to help make ends meet."

Revere lifted an eyebrow.

"I held onto it for twenty years. The time had come for me to turn it back into cash."

Revere pulled a silver coffee pot from among the wares and placed it on an empty table near his customer. "Will this suit Mrs. Molineux? Business has been brisk so I will cut you a deal. Only five pounds—ten shillings off the usual price."

"You are a good man, Mr. Revere. It is a pleasure doing business with you."

Revere patted the coffee pot. "These are in demand right now."

"Unfortunately, it is where some of the ladies hide their tea."

"True."

Molineux picked up the merchandise and secured it under his arm. "The ladies are not my only concern. Mr. Rowe's desire not to continue as a selectman also bothers me."

"Do you believe he is still importing the baneful weed, as some refer to it?"

"Maybe. There has been talk of him taking on more responsibilities at our church. That may explain things. Still, I will keep a watchful eye."

Molineux sauntered to the door. "I must be on my way." He pulled his cloak tight then placed his hand on the doorknob before turning back to Revere. "Someday I will repay your kindness to this poor soul."

At the annual meeting in March, Molineux was delighted when the town voted him as chairman of the committee to consider suitable methods for employing the poor. A few weeks later, Boston reconvened in Faneuil Hall to hear various chairmen present their reports.

Molineux shifted in his seat as he listened to the report on what could be done to vindicate the character of the town. He smiled. The presentation, which emphasized employment of those less fortunate would keep them out of trouble, set the stage for the statement burning a hole in his own pocket.

With little discussion, the town accepted the report and passed it in the affirmative.

Otis returned to the podium as the moderator. "Mr. Molineux, your report, please."

Molineux bolted from his chair to the stage and scanned those seated before him. The drooping eyelids of the afternoon crowd breathed additional life into him. He raised both arms and began with a burst of energy.

"My fellow Bostonians, it is with great pleasure I address you today on behalf of my committee." He grinned. With their attention intact, he continued. "We have conversed with the overseers of the poor and find there are almost two hundred and thirty persons in the almshouse and about forty in the workhouse who are proper subjects of the former."

He reported the town had spent more than six hundred pounds for their care in the previous two years, and costs would only increase due to the great decay of trade.

"The only way to lessen this expense or prevent its increase," he said, "is to employ those who occasion it. There are above two hundred poor of this town who are now ready and desirous to be employed in the carding and spinning of wool, and I am happy to inform you, the enthusiasm is daily increasing."

The committee proposed the town set up schools in various parts of town and employ mistresses to teach children to spin. They could sell the resulting yarn to those recently arrived in Boston who were masters at manufacturing fabrics and could produce men's summer wear.

Molineux walked to the right of the stage to keep their attention. Samuel Adams quickly shooed him back and pointed to the sounding board above the podium. The merchant nonchalantly meandered back while, on the inside, cursed the restraint.

He continued. "Your committee believes this plan would be of unspeakable advantage to the town as it would, in a few years, save considerable expense."

He examined faces in the audience—open yet nervous in anticipation.

Molineux turned his right palm upward and lifted it slightly. "It would annually lessen the number of those who are esteemed proper subjects of the almshouse. And it would keep great numbers out of idleness which, as the parent of vice, would promote intemperance and all the diseases naturally produced by this course of life. Moreover, it will transform those who are currently a burden to society into more useful members of the same."

Molineux paused before making his final plea. "The committee is not fooled into believing such an enterprise would be carried into execution without expense. Nor do they believe it can accomplish what those of decades past, despite their best efforts, have been unable to."

Several in the audience perked up. Molineux proceeded with caution.

"Rather than attempt to raise the needed funds from gentlemen who reside among us, we believe it to be in the interest of the town to choose a different course."

Molineux knew all too well the past failures of similar ventures—for he had been part of them. Curious looks from the crowd encouraged him to continue.

"Allow the treasurer to borrow and furnish the overseers with the small amount of five hundred pounds. These funds can be used to empower the poor through their gainful employment and through the efforts of a responsible gentleman."

He hesitated. Surely, they remembered the three thousand pounds others had requested the previous year. Five hundred was a mere fraction. Yet eyes widened. The town's financial state was not much better than the merchants', and apparently many understood Molineux referred to himself. He had opened the door and must now walk through it.

"Grant that gentleman two hundred pounds, then lend him the remaining three hundred to be payable in two years. Funds would be used to hire a suitable number of rooms and schoolmistresses to teach as many persons to spin as are desirous to learn. This gentleman," Molineux said, once again referring to himself, "would at his own cost furnish them with spinning wheels and with a sufficient quantity of wool to keep them employed until they were thoroughly acquainted with the business."

Molineux scanned the room to ensure the gentlemen understood his willingness to cast his lot in with the town.

"He would further commence to keep the spinners employed at said business for the space of two years, provided they will work upon reasonable terms. By which time it is highly probable the business will be so well established as to find them full employment. For all this, and not to the gentleman's own advantage, the town will receive a much greater benefit than the two hundred pounds they shall have granted."

Molineux picked up the report and took two steps back from the lectern.

"All of this is humbly submitted," he said with a bow, then returned to his seat.

Otis resumed his place at the lectern and led the discussion. The town accepted the report and directed the town treasurer to borrow five hundred pounds and place into the hands of the overseers of the poor. They would give two hundred pounds to Molineux for expenses and lend him three hundred pounds to purchase wool.

After addressing a few other items, the meeting dissolved.

Molineux left amid a wide range of stares. His heart was set on the project, and he wanted to revive the efforts and prove it could succeed. Failure would have no place in this latest endeavor.

Molineux fingered the tumbler on the coffeehouse table. His rising popularity had afforded him the opportunity to sit on the committee that would draft instructions for the town's representatives for the coming session. The town had provided a near unanimous vote to keep Otis, Hancock, Cushing, and Samuel Adams as its delegates.

"And where shall we begin?" the chairman asked the half dozen men sitting around the table.

"There are so many offenses, it is hard to know," Molineux said.

"Then let us begin by simply listing them. Afterwards we will seek to explore each one more fully."

Dr. Warren looked hard at his mug. "The cannon and guards must go."

"They are meant to awe and intimidate," John Adams said, "and no legislative body should be expected to carry on its business under those conditions. Such men cannot be considered free."

"What else?" the chairman asked.

"As much as my wife enjoyed having the troops on our front lawn"—Molineux provided a sarcastic grin—"they need to return to the place from whence they came."

"Should the province pay for expenses incurred thus far with regards to the troops?" Dr. Benjamin Church asked.

"No indeed," another chimed in. "No one who has housed these men, including Mr. Molineux, should expect to receive a single shilling from us. Let those who sent them here bear the full burden of their actions."

"The province has but little money to give even if it were demanded," Molineux said.

"True," the chairman said. "And, Mr. Adams, I would imagine you have something to say of the recent expansion of the admiralty's jurisdiction."

John Adams's jaw tightened. Boston's desire to maintain trials by jury was under attack. Adams, as Hancock's representative in the *Liberty* case, claimed not allowing such trials effectively repealed the Magna Carta. Again, in May 1769, Adams's plea for a jury trial went unheeded in the case of a sailor standing trial for murder on the high seas while resisting impressment.

"Next to Parliament's demand for revenue, I would say it is our greatest grievance," Adams said. "It seeks to overturn our constitution and repeal a portion of the Magna Carta."

"A fearful thing indeed. Your trials certainly put the town in a fuss."

"And we have all heard about the letters our governor sent to London last year."

"Not too flattering of us."

"His words must be dealt with for they poison our reputation," Dr. Warren said. "An effectual antidote must be found, or it will surely lead to our demise."

"Quite a few items to address," the chairman said. "We will take them one by one, and when we are through, may our representatives have no question as to our desires."

A few days later, Molineux sat in the front row at the town meeting. The committee had presented its proposed instructions for the representatives, which the town accepted. Several newspapers would publish them. Then someone took to the lectern to read the gathering's official view on the nonimportation agreement.

Molineux reviewed what had brought the town to this point. For more than a year, Boston's merchants had enjoyed varying degrees of success in implementing a nonimportation agreement. Merchants, retailers, and other tradesmen had agreed with those in New York and Philadelphia not to import—or purchase from any who should import—tea, glass, paper, or other goods commonly imported from Great Britain. They would abide by the 1769 agreement for all, until Parliament repealed the acts that imposed duties on these articles.

For months, Molineux had heard rumors not all merchants had been faithful to their word. A merchant-appointed committee had investigated and reported only a half dozen of the two hundred eleven signers had imported. Rowe was among them, yet his imports and those of others were too small to be of significance. Newspapers had reported importations of the two dozen nonsubscribers were small and consisted of articles allowed by the agreement. Only six or seven had imported as usual. Some submitted their cargo to storage under the watchful eye of the Committee of Inspection.

The clerk cleared his throat, and Molineux leaned forward in his seat to absorb every word.

"It gives high satisfaction to the town to be informed that our merchants have strictly adhered to their agreement relative to nonimportation of European merchandise."

Molineux beamed. The town recognized his sacrifice and that of his fellow merchants.

The reader continued. "It be hereby recommended to the inhabitants not to purchase any goods of those few persons who have imported any articles in the vessels lately arrived from Great Britain, not allowed by said agreement."

Molineux looked around for the offenders.

"On the contrary, they should promote the trade of those gentlemen who have nobly preferred the future welfare of their country and all North America to any present advantage of their own."

Molineux nodded then his lips tightened. One British politician had claimed Parliament would not think of repealing the hated act until America lay prostrate at its feet. Molineux growled under his breath. If the townsfolk would put into practice what they said they believed, they would show London otherwise.

The meeting adjourned. Molineux would watch to see which merchants remained true to the cause. Meanwhile, he would busy himself preparing suitable methods for employing the town's poor.

Molineux surveyed the work going on inside the Manufactory House. Noise from the hammers and saws invigorated him. Sixteen years in Boston's harsh winters coupled with unruly occupants had taken their toll on the factory, but revitalization efforts would eventually pay off. He was sure of it.

Samuel Adams's voice broke through the clamor. "Anyone home?"

Molineux followed the voice and found the visitor near the entrance. "Mr. Adams, how wonderful for you to drop by."

"I see you have replaced the disorderly tenants with more useful tradesmen," Adams said above the commotion.

"And they are doing a fine job—" A loud thud caused Adams to flinch. "A fine job of getting this place back into working order."

Molineux extended a hand toward the door. "Maybe we should take our conversation outside."

The two men exited into the late spring sunshine.

"Dear me," Adams said. "It is loud in there."

"The sound of men hard at work—music to my ears," Molineux said. "I must admit, however, this fresh air might do me some good. Now to what do I owe the pleasure of your visit?"

"Ah, yes." Adams held up a newspaper. "I am afraid the war of words continues."

"The other side did not believe the importations to be as trifling as we claimed?"

"Correct. The *Chronicle* desires to make the number of importers appear as large as possible and, therefore, has no qualm lumping our local clergy in with the true merchants."

"What do you propose we do?" Molineux asked.

"We published the names of the handful of real offenders."

Molineux laughed. "Yes. And that is what started all of this."

"Now we will dare Mr. Mein to do the same. Publish an entire list of those he wishes to embarrass publicly."

Molineux's face lit up. "I see. A game of chess."

"I do not expect Mr. Mein will want to upset so many of his subscribers. Instead, he will back down, and we will gain the upper hand."

"A good plan indeed. Let me know if there is any way I may assist."

"Now if you will excuse me, I must continue to Mr. Hancock's place. I trust he and the committee will be receptive to the idea." Adams took a few steps toward Beacon Hill then pivoted back to Molineux. "I know you were not the town's first choice to manage this project," he said with a gesture toward the factory, "but I must say you are doing a fine job."

Molineux acknowledged the compliment with a nod. "It is my honor to serve our town's poor in this way. They suffer the most from the nonimportation agreement, and I want to help them by any means I can."

"They do benefit, but the products they manufacture will provide all of us with the goods we need to survive until Parliament gives us reason to once again trade with London."

"I have ordered four hundred spinning wheels," Molineux said. "After they arrive, you should expect to see our townsfolk dressed in homespun glory."

"A patriotic sight to behold," Adams said. "The dock workers tell me their wives and children are ready to do as you bid them. When I pass by, I already hear joyous shouts of 'Paoli Molineux.'"

Molineux laughed. "I may never be able to provide as much inspiration as the Corsican revolutionary, but may I live up to the Paoli name. I will do my best."

"You command a different type of army," Adams said. "One made up of common people with no official ties to the government. As with your namesake, however, you may someday need to lead them into battle against those who seek to deprive us of what is rightfully ours. But we trust it will never come to that." Adams lifted his chin toward his destination. "Well, I must be on my way. Good day, Paoli Molineux."

Molineux watched Mr. Adams begin his ascent up Beacon Hill. He scanned the Common, devoid of troops. His mind drifted to the petition, which sought to remove them from the town for good. That would be a glad day. Then sounds from the factory house pulled him back to the tasks at hand. He walked toward the building, unable to shake the troops from his mind.

CHAPTER TWELVE

Uproot the Enemy
July–August 1, 1769

Several weeks later, Hancock sat in John Adams's parlor discussing the legal wrangling over his ship *Liberty*. The piercing sound of a military fife, a stone's throw from the front door, accompanied their conversation.

Hancock raised a hand to his ear. "How do you live with this every day?"

"It is certainly enough to drive a man and his wife mad." Adams rose and poured each of them a drink. "We are not surprised, however, since the officers refused the selectmen's request to remove the troops from town during the annual election. How much less would they be mindful of complaints from a handful of irritated citizens?"

"Even Mr. Hutchinson refers to the Twenty-ninth as bad fellows," Hancock said. "If the troops remain as disrespectful as they were last Sunday, every parishioner in town will oversee their lynching before sundown."

Adams handed a tumbler to Hancock and returned to his chair. "And every clergyman with them, if the solders continue to drown out sermons with their contemptuous rendition of 'Yankee Doodle.'

I believe my cousin may be correct. His Majesty's men have brought more disruption to this town than we had before they came."

The fife ceased, and the two men sat quietly for a moment, then Adams spoke. "I am uncertain which is worse, the troops or the small-pox you and the other selectmen must fight against."

"Some wish the latter would spread to every soldier among us," Hancock said.

"Their being here certainly sets a bad precedence with regards to the law."

"Does anyone else see irony in the governor's actions?" Hancock asked. "To have the representatives meet outside the city."

"There is no need for troops where there is no mob."

"And where there are no watchful eyes of patriots," Hancock said. "Yet he is among those who beckoned them here." His shoulders drooped. "The travel back and forth to Cambridge has wearied me."

"Did I hear correctly, you and your colleagues in the House stumbled a bit?"

Hancock gave a sheepish grin. "All of Boston would have come after us had we not moved quickly to modify our mistake."

Adams smiled. "You had no way to know the general would respond the way he did."

"Thankfully, our clarification as to which laws concern us was enough to pacify him. The Sixty-fifth Regiment should leave for Halifax soon. It will be a relief to have them and the Sixty-fourth far, far away."

"It is unfortunate the others remain."

A rap on the door beckoned Adams to answer it. A few moments later, he returned with one of Hancock's manservants.

"For me?" Hancock stood.

The servant held out a piece of paper. "I have a message from Samuel Adams for you, sir."

Hancock took the note, read it, then looked at his host. "Additional news has arrived from London to which I must attend."

He turned to his servant. "Please tell Samuel Adams I am on my way to him now."

The servant bowed his head then departed.

Hancock picked up his hat. "Thank you, Mr. Adams, for all of your efforts on my behalf. If I can ever repay you in kind—"

"Continue to do your part to remove the troops, and I will be more than pleased," Adams said.

Hancock stared at the floor for a moment in search of the proper words then lifted his head. "Though I am not yet at liberty to say how, you may get your wish above and beyond your wildest dreams."

Hancock settled into his usual chair in the small meeting room of Faneuil Hall. It, rather than the Town House, provided a safe location to discuss the matter for which Samuel Adams had called him. Otis sat on the other side of the table. The deep lines around his red face left little doubt the new information would be worth his time.

Adams stood at the head. "We have received word that more of Governor Bernard's letters are on their way here."

Hancock glanced at Otis then back to Adams. "Letters he wrote about Boston?"

Adams nodded. "If those we have already received are any indication, the new ones should be enough to petition the king for our governor's removal."

Otis planted his fist onto the table before him. "And put the final nail into his coffin."

Hancock grimaced. Was Otis intoxicated?

Adams appeared not to notice. "This should please our fellow citizens. At least ninety-nine in every one hundred in this province hate him, including most of those in the House."

Otis grinned.

Adams took a deep breath. "We do not yet know the specifics of the accusations, but that will be revealed soon enough. I will look forward to seeing them firsthand."

Molineux paced the floor of the room above Edes and Gill's printshop. Samuel Adams, Otis, and a handful of others sat around the table. Copies of a half dozen letters their governor had written to London last year lay scattered before them. Through the efforts of the patriots' friends, Bernard's accusations had finally come to light, as had those of General Gage.

The governor had announced London had called him home for consultation. He would soon be out of the way, but the damage he had done would remain.

"High treason?" Molineux shook both fists in the air. "He is accusing us of high treason?"

"According to Governor Bernard," Otis said, "we are mad people."

Adams looked at Otis. The attorney's mental state was slipping, and some believed he had taken to the bottle.

"We are not *all* mad," someone said. "And even the mad among us may be more sane than those who desire to see our heads on a silver platter."

"Dr. Church characterized our governor quite well." Molineux spit on the floor then put his attention on those seated around the table. "Fob, witling, favorite stamp man, tyrant tool. Or all those mighty names in one, thou fool!" His fist came down on the table.

Adams raised his trembling, palsied hand and asked for calm. "The letters clearly contain gross and material mistakes."

"And your proposal for dealing with them?"

"First, the town must know of these letters. We will let the governor's own words hang him."

Edes and Gill glanced at each other then nodded. "The press is ready."

"Gather round," Adams said, picking up one of the letters, "for we must decide which items to include in tomorrow's paper."

Molineux stood inside his Merchants Row shop by the rain-drenched window. Steam rose from the harbor in the late July storm, and thunder rolled in the distance.

"Are you glad you signed?" Molineux said to the thirty-something young man sitting in a nearby chair. William Dennie had joined Molineux and others in various petitions during the previous fourteen years but had shied away from the patriots' more radical ways. Since his brother had gone bankrupt the previous year, Dennie was spending more and more time with the Sons of Liberty.

"The troops have been here long enough," Dennie said. "We had to do something."

"And now we will be rid of our dictator," Molineux said, walking over and taking a seat beside Dennie. "That is how the *Gazette* has referred to him in today's paper."

"A bit harsh, wouldn't you say?"

Molineux leaned back and let out a deep breath. "He constantly misrepresented us. He sent for the troops and prorogued the court so we could have no means of redress. *That* is harsh."

"I suppose you are right."

"I am fearful, though, that Parliament's decision to remove most of the duties will produce additional defectors among our fellow merchants." Molineux smirked. "And with the threat of smallpox coming in on ships from Philadelphia . . . the good news shows no signs of stopping."

"Was the removal of duties not good news?"

"You heard the discussion at the meeting a few days ago. The remaining duty on tea is intended to keep us under their control. Like a rudder—small yet powerful."

Dennie remained silent for a moment before he spoke. "The committee hopes to bring the strayers back into the fold."

"That is the hope." Molineux glanced out the window then patted Dennie on the back. "Well, my lad, the rain has stopped. You are welcome to stay, but if you do, I shall put a broom in your hand. My place is a mess."

"I would love to help, but my stepfather is expecting me. He can always use a hand at the town warehouse." Dennie moved toward the door.

"Please give him my best."

"Thank you, again, for sheltering me."

"Always a pleasure to see you."

The next day all the bells in town rang for joy, cannons fired, and flags flew from the Liberty Tree. News had come that Governor Bernard had boarded a ship bound for England the previous evening. During his tenure, the governor had tried to squelch bonfires for, according to him, they were used to call a mob to action. To celebrate his departure, the town built one on King Street and another on Fort Hill. Molineux threw another log onto the fire. Hancock had donated lumber from two of his vessels sunk in the storm the day before.

The mantle now passed to Hutchinson who took the reins of Massachusetts Bay. Would Hutchinson as acting governor be better or worse than what they had just sent away? No one dared ask the question aloud. For now, they would simply celebrate.

CHAPTER THIRTEEN

❧

Fractured

August 4–October 5, 1769

*M*olineux took two steps at a time heading into Faneuil Hall then went directly to the small meeting room where he planted himself in front of Mr. Rowe. Molineux wiped the dewy sweat forming on his brow. Other merchants seated around the table slid their chairs back a few inches so as not to get caught up in the fray.

"Mr. Rowe, I need to have a word with you," Molineux said. "What is this I hear of Porter beer being on board one of your ships?"

"'Tis true," Rowe said. His forehead furrowed. "And how I regret it, for it has caused me great uneasiness."

"And so it should."

Interrupted by the chairman's call to order, Molineux's inquisition came to an end. He dropped into a chair, crossed his arms, and muttered. "And you say you are one of us."

"I beg your pardon, Mr. Molineux?" the chairman said.

"Nothing."

The chairman addressed the group. "As you know, there are conflicting opinions among us as to what constitutes a breach of the nonimportation agreement. Unfortunately, a handful of the first merchants of our town—including Nicholas Boylston, Richard Clarke & Sons, and Thomas Hutchinson's sons—have not subscribed to the agreement at all. And every Scottish merchant in town is an importer. If we refuse to stand united against the acts of Parliament, they will cripple us all."

Molineux unfolded his arms and leaned into the table.

"Even those in the same family have found themselves on opposite sides of this argument," the chairman continued. "The gentleman presenting our first report today is an example. Thomas Boylston, brother and business partner of Nicholas, will bring us up to date on the activities of his committee since our last meeting." The chairman extended his hand toward Boylston then sat down.

Boylston arranged the papers in front of him then stood. "As you will recall, my cohorts and I were commissioned to deal with those merchants who had refused to comply with the nonimportation agreement. Although it took a bit of coercion, we ultimately met with success."

Another committee member interrupted. "At least one expressed appreciation for the civility of our visit." He glanced at Molineux. "And indicated not all had been so kind to those with differing opinions."

Boylston cleared his throat and continued. "Theophilus Lillie, William Jackson, and a few others have recently signed an abbreviated version of the original agreement."

Molineux sat up. "Abbreviated?"

The chairman frowned in Molineux's direction. "Would you do us the favor, Mr. Boylston, of reading the agreement to which you refer?"

"Certainly." Boylston picked up one of the pages before him. "Whereas we the subscribers have not heretofore entered into the agreement of the merchants for nonimportation, we do now promise, we will not send for any goods to any part of Great Britain until January next, directly or indirectly."

"No doubt many of them," someone said, "have already placed their orders."

Boylston held up the paper. "The final sentence states any such goods which arrive will be delivered up to the committee of merchants."

The chairman stood. "Let me see a show of hands of those in favor of accepting these new documents."

Most around the table raised their hands. Molineux did not.

"You expect us to simply forget the trouble these new signers have caused?" he asked.

"Is not a signature now as good as an earlier one?" Boylston said.

"No indeed."

"But why then would we have requested them?"

Molineux grimaced while others shared their views. As the discussion proceeded, the tables turned more to his liking.

"Mr. Molineux," the chairman said, "I trust you are satisfied. We will reject the new documents and send for Mr. Lillie to come meet with us at once."

They waited. And waited.

But Lillie never came.

Molineux stood in the doorway of his shop blinking against the summer sun. The committee had met and once again requested Mr. Lillie's attendance. He refused, and the committee voted him and others as enemies of their country.

Molineux decided to stretch his legs with a walk to Edes and Gill's print shop.

"Mr. Dennie," Molineux said to the young man atop a horse outside the shop. "What brings you here?"

"Have you not heard?" Dennie patted the leather pouch strapped around him. "Our disapproval is now in black and white, and the committee has given me the honor of distributing the handbills throughout the countryside."

"I had not. I have been held up in my warehouse all morning attempting to get blood out of a turnip."

"Then you may not know, but the sign on Mr. Lillie's store was defaced," Dennie said. "And those committed to our cause took great pains to discourage customers from providing him with their business."

"Ah, but Samuel Adams says we must be careful not to go overboard with our displays of enmity."

"I suppose," Dennie said. His horse snorted. "I must be on my way."

"God speed to you," Molineux said with a wave. "And may no one attempt to stone you during your mission."

Dennie smiled and urged his horse into a gallop.

The Sons of Liberty dined in the field outside Robinson's Liberty Tree Tavern in Dorchester on August 14. Four years had passed since their fight for freedom had begun.

Molineux played his fiddle as more than three hundred joined him in song. He smiled at Otis who had penned the words.

> *Come join hand in hand, brave Americans, all,*
> *And rouse your bold hearts at fair liberty's call.*
> *No tyrannous acts shall suppress your just claim*
> *Or stain with dishonor America's name.*
>
> *In freedom we're born, and in freedom we'll live.*
> *Our purses are ready,*
> *Steady, friends, steady,*
> *Not as slaves, but as freemen, our money we'll give.*
>
> *Our worthy forefathers, let's give 'em a cheer,*
> *To climates unknown did courageously steer.*
> *Thro' oceans to deserts for freedom they came,*
> *And dying bequeath'd us their freedom and fame.*

Molineux roamed the crowd as they sang the chorus. Hancock, Otis, Dr. Warren, and Dennie were all there. The net had widened to include Revere and his artisan friends. Samuel Adams raised his mug and reveled in the sentiments of the forty-five toasts while his cousin John expressed surprise no one had become intoxicated.

The melody rolled on . . .

> *Their tree their own hands had to liberty rear'd,*
> *They liv'd to behold growing strong and rever'd;*
> *With transport they cried, "Now our wishes we gain,*
> *For our children shall gather the fruits of our pain . . ."*

> *In freedom we're born, and in freedom we'll live.*
> *Our purses are ready,*
> *Steady, friends, steady,*
> *Not as slaves, but as freemen, our money we'll give.*

> *How sweet are the labors that freemen endure,*
> *That they shall enjoy all the profits secure.*
> *No more such sweet labors Americans know,*
> *If Britons shall reap what Americans sow.*

> *In freedom we're born, and in freedom we'll live.*
> *Our purses are ready,*
> *Steady, friends, steady,*
> *Not as slaves, but as freemen, our money we'll give.*

Cheers went up as they launched into the final stanza.

> *All ages shall speak with amaze and applause,*
> *Of the courage we'll show in support of our laws;*
> *To die we can bear, but to serve we disdain,*
> *For shame is to freedom more dreadful than pain.*

> *In freedom we're born, and in freedom we'll live.*
> *Our purses are ready,*
> *Steady, friends, steady,*
> *Not as slaves, but as freemen, our money we'll give.*

A few more toasts, then the Sons loaded onto the more than a hundred awaiting carriages. Hancock led while Otis brought up the rear.

"It has been a most agreeable day," Samuel Adams said to Molineux as he carefully pulled himself up into one of the carriages.

"Indeed it has."

Hutchinson sat alone at the desk in his Town House office with the door closed and the *Boston Chronicle* spread before him. A late August breeze from the open window warmed his face. Mein had finally responded to the challenge the agitators had presented earlier in the year. "Why?" Hutchinson said aloud. He knew the answer. At least two things had provoked Mr. Mein.

A lawsuit, which had dragged on for a year and a half, had recently wrapped up. If Mein had not demanded that the *Gazette* reveal the name of its anonymous writer who was critical of the *Chronicle*, the matter would have simply died a natural death. Instead, Mein had flown into a rage and attacked Gill with a club. "Very unwise, Mr. Mein."

The acting governor looked at the stack of newspapers on his bookcase. "The rebels have once again pushed you to your limit, haven't they?" He walked over and shuffled through the papers until he found the one. "The town should boycott the eight offenders, including Theophilus Lillie, two of Hutchinson's sons, Richard Clarke & Sons, and John Mein." He sighed. "Why could you not have left well enough—?"

A light rap on the door interrupted him.

"Father?"

Hutchinson opened the door to find his two grown sons.

"We heard voices. Are you with someone?"

"No." He swung the door wide and motioned for them to enter. "I was merely discussing a matter with myself." He held up the newspaper and returned to his chair.

Thomas Junior nodded. "The battle rages on."

Hutchinson examined the faces of his sons. "Mr. Mein came to America as a businessman and has always attempted to publish both sides of an issue."

"Until now, some would say," Elisha said.

"In these times, even neutrality is considered criminal," Hutchinson said.

Thomas walked to the window. "Being a Scot does not help Mr. Mein's case."

"Nonetheless," Elisha said, "it is unfortunate the agitators chose to cast him as a merchant when he is not one of us."

Hutchinson picked up the *Chronicle*. "His list of names does not discriminate. He claims one hundred and nine people imported from Great Britain during the first five months of this year."

"May I see?" Elisha reached for the paper. "He is quite detailed: one hundred sixty-two trunks, two hundred seventy bales, one hundred eighty-two cases, two hundred thirty-three boxes, one thousand one hundred sixteen casks, one hundred thirty-nine chests, and seventy-two hampers." He set the paper back on his father's desk. "Where does he get his information?"

"Do you not know?" Hutchinson asked.

Thomas leaned forward in his chair and looked at his brother. "Mr. Mein is the lone supplier of stationery to the commissioners. They are quite cozy."

"One more burr in the rebels' saddles," Hutchinson said.

Thomas motioned to the paper. "The list also includes Mr. Rowe and Mr. Hancock. It seems Mr. Mein would like the town to assume these men encouraged others to sign the nonimportation agreement as a means of crippling their competition."

Elisha shrugged. "But aren't certain imports of little consequence?"

"Technically," Hutchinson said. "Yet resentment burns against Mr. Mein in the breasts of most people in town."

"Some speak of revolution," Thomas said.

Hutchinson shook his head. "They will eventually see the absurdity of such talk."

"Back to Mr. Hancock," Thomas said. "Did you know two London firms have hired him to collect a considerable debt from Mr. Mein?"

Elisha perked up. "Mr. Mein claims Mr. Hancock is the milk cow of the so-called patriots."

"And has bandages tied over his eyes"—Thomas placed one hand over his eyes and pulled invisible money from his cloak with the other—"which allows people to dip into his well-disposed pockets."

Hutchinson stood, and the three men moved toward the door. "There is little doubt Samuel Adams does so. How else could he eat?"

"Father," Elisha said, "we dropped by to share our concern about your new role. You are approaching sixty. Are you up to the demands?"

Hutchinson raised a hand. "With a birthday right around the corner, I know this all too well." He opened the door and extended his hand. "Yet our province is in need of my help. I was born here and plan to die here. Until then, I aim to serve her to the best of my abilities."

The young men walked out the door.

Thomas pivoted. "Father, we almost forgot. Have you heard of the change to the merchants' committee?"

Hutchinson tilted his head.

"Someone stepped down. Mr. Rowe and Mr. Hancock remain," Thomas said.

"Another has stepped into the vacant spot," Elisha said.

Hutchinson squinted his eyes. "Who?"

The brothers looked at each other, then Thomas responded. "William Molineux."

Hutchinson stood quietly for a moment. "I see." He put a hand on Elisha's shoulder. "Thank you both for a most illuminating time. I wish it could be extended, but I have work to do."

The boys left, and Hutchinson returned to his desk. He pulled out his stationery and quill. Authorities in London must be informed of the role the committee had assumed. Much like his revolutionary namesake of the Mediterranean, Paoli Molineux was especially troublesome. The traditional leader of the South End clan might have named his son Paoli in the spring, but no one questioned it was Paoli

Molineux who now oversaw dirty matters in Boston. The people referred to Hancock as brig Paoli. Although his direct influence on Boston's streets might be less than Molineux's, as the reference to the small ship indicated, his ability to fund the cause helped keep it afloat. The two men had become toasts of the town—at least, among the more radical—and London must be encouraged to keep a watchful eye on them.

Two weeks later, Molineux fought his way to the front of the two-thousand-strong crowd gathered at Faneuil Hall. Way too many bodies filled the space, but townsfolk wanted to get a firsthand account of what had happened at the brawl the previous evening. An accomplice stood before the judges for a preliminary hearing.

Molineux elbowed a few more people until he found Dennie.

"What do we know?" Molineux asked as he vied for enough space around him to be comfortable.

"Were you not in the streets last evening preparing to see the comet with everyone else?"

Molineux shook his head. "We thought our hill would provide a better view."

"One of the commissioners, Mr. Robinson, hit Mr. Otis over the head with a cane—or maybe a sword—at the British Coffee House. According to Dr. Young, it is a pretty bad gash. One of the seventeen was involved." Dennie nodded toward the man standing in front of the justices.

Copies of letters the commissioners had written to London had found their way back to Boston two weeks before. Otis had taken no pleasure in being called out as a traitor. He had placed an advertisement in the *Gazette* to declare his allegiance to the Crown and put the commissioners in the same camp with Bernard.

"They are getting back at him," Molineux said.

"Calling Mr. Harrison a liar when he tried to apologize probably had an adverse effect."

"He referred to him as a liar *and* senile. And he said Mr. Robinson was a superlative blockhead."

"John Adams may be correct," Dennie said. "Mr. Otis has become the most talkative man alive."

"We saw it firsthand at Monday's merchant meeting."

"I am fearful his own words will send him to the grave."

"Mr. Otis threatening to break Mr. Robinson's head was the final straw," Molineux said. "The tables were turned."

The judges completed their proceedings and began to disperse. Molineux and Dennie moved toward the door amid the mass of people.

An angry voice arose from a few feet away. "Not so fast."

Molineux and Dennie whirled around to see a small group grab the wig of the patriots' least favorite judge. Another placed it atop a pole and slung it around. "A cold head to go with a cold heart."

Those sympathetic to the justice surrounded him and moved him away from the offenders.

"No matter," one from the crowd said. "Was not Mr. Mein at the coffeehouse the night of the attack?"

The mob hissed.

"And is not his bookstore in need of some paint?"

"Hillsborough's paint," the crowd shouted in unison.

Dennie gave Molineux a look of disgust. "Mr. Adams would have our hides."

"Rest assured," Molineux said, "we will find some other way to express our frustration—a way that keeps our pants up."

Dennie smiled.

"The winds are at our backs and the people are with us," Molineux said. "All we need is the right catalyst. When it comes, we will make our move."

Maybe it was his imagination, Hutchinson thought, but the Town House balcony felt less sturdy than usual. That and the hurricane-damaged ships and wharves sprinkled about the harbor were the least of his worries. Mr. Mein's practice of printing ship manifests in the *Chronicle* had continued for weeks, causing tensions to rise. Yet a new calm had fallen over the town.

Fragments of letters Hutchinson had written to London scrolled through in his mind.

"If the troops had not been here, there would have been more than a cudgeling match between a demagogue and a commissioner of the customs," he had written. "I am not sure we are yet out of danger, for many people are enraged to a degree of frenzy."

In another letter he had written, "If we could keep the influence of Boston at bay for twelve months, I think we could bring the rest of the province to their senses."

The influence of Boston. A sad smile spread across Hutchinson's face. People, not an impersonal Boston, had done the influencing. Thus, his most recent letter to England. "Molineux's influence," Hutchinson had written to Bernard in early October, "is as great as it ever was."

Despite the current state of the town, Hutchinson felt an uneasiness. Boston could not remain calm for long. He was sure that Molineux would see to it.

CHAPTER FOURTEEN

War of Words
October 4–November 6, 1769

Yellow and red leaves, still mixed with a fair amount of green, waved at Molineux as he made his way to the town meeting. He had not been inside Faneuil Hall long before he heard Samuel Adams call his name. The merchant spun around with a smile.

Adams's face exuded curiosity. "How did you make out with Saint Nick?"

Molineux grinned. "Nicholas Boylston is no saint, I can assure you, but he did provide me with a gift." He pulled a key from his pocket and placed it in his open hand. "The cargo from the big bad *Wolfe* has been stored away."

"Well done," Adams said. "For a moment, I feared the arrival of fall goods by the infamous few would do us in." Adams dodged those entering the meeting hall. "And what of Mr. Lillie?"

Molineux took a deep breath and put the key back in his pocket. "He was a tougher nut to crack. And not willing to be thoroughly broken."

Adams's expression egged him on.

"He met with us—Mr. Dennie and the rest of the committee—but only at the urging of his friends who feared for his safety if he did not come."

Adams rubbed his chin and smiled. "He has wise friends."

"It took some persuasion." Molineux pounded a fist into his other hand. "But he now considers the previous paper he signed to be in force. He would not, however, be intimidated into agreeing to the document signed by the nonimporters."

"I see," Adams said, looking toward the stage. The two men continued their conversation as they made their way to the front. Adams handed a piece of paper to a man on the stage, then Adams and Molineux took seats in the front row.

"An important document?" Molineux asked.

Adams nodded. "Some merchants will be pleased. Others will not."

Molineux scanned the crowd. "No sign of Mr. Otis."

Tears welled up in Adams's eyes. He put his trembling hand on Molineux's arm. "Mr. Otis continues to slip away from us, both in mind and spirit. One moment he wishes for a grand revolution, and the next he says he has done more mischief to our country than can be repaired."

"'Tis unfortunate," Molineux said. "For a decade he has been a mighty warrior for our cause."

"Indeed he has," Adams said.

The meeting began, and those assembled listened to a clerk read the latest letters and memorials received from London. The town appointed a committee to determine what measures it should take to vindicate their character in response to the gross misrepresentations to the king.

Then the meeting turned its attention to the uncooperative merchants.

The clerk read:

The merchants not only of this metropolis but throughout the continent have nobly preferred the public good to their own individual profit, with a view to obtain a redress of the grievances so loudly and justly complained of, having almost unanimously engaged to suspend their importations from Great Britain.

Molineux glanced around. Other merchants also seemed pleased.

Such a measure will be regarded by posterity with veneration. The town cannot but express their astonishment and indignation that any of its citizens should be so lost to the feelings of patriotism and the common interest and be so infamously selfish as to obstruct this very measure by continuing their importation.

Molineux felt Adams's hand on his arm. Their eyes met briefly, and Adams gave a slight nod toward the speaker.

Be it therefore solemnly voted, that the names of those persons— namely, John Bernard, Nathaniel Rogers, Theophilus Lillie, James McMasters and Company, John Mein, Thomas Hutchinson Junior, and Elisha Hutchinson—be entered in the records of this town, that posterity may know who those persons were that preferred their little private advantage to the common interest of all the colonies. Those who not only deserted but opposed their country in a struggle for the rights of the constitution. And who, with a design to enrich themselves, basely took advantage of the generous self-denial of their fellow citizens for the common good.

A quiet reverence filled the room, then a voice from the back broke in. "Some of those in that list are now ready to sign."

The place stirred as everyone turned to see.

The sound of the gavel brought the gaze of the assembly back to the front.

Then Adams stood and faced the crowd. "It is too late in the day to consider this suggestion. The previous conduct of those mentioned in the document could not be made right on this side of the grave.

God, perhaps, might forgive them, but I and the rest of the people never could."

The people unanimously voted to accept and have printed in several public newspapers what had been presented. Then the meeting adjourned.

"Mr. Molineux," Adams said, "I trust your schedule is flexible in the coming days."

"How do you mean?" Molineux asked.

"The men mentioned in the document may be more anxious than before to speak with your committee. You need to be available."

Molineux provided a sinister grin. "It will be my pleasure."

The nervous optimism that infused the conversation around the table at the British Coffee House sent a tingle up Molineux's spine. He, Dennie, and three other committee members awaited the arrival of the subjects of the meeting. Molineux studied the floor. Blood left from the previous month's brawl between Otis and the commissioner had vanished.

Nicholas Boylston had informed the merchants that the Hutchinson brothers were nervous about their unsanctioned eighteen chests of tea, which had arrived aboard the *Wolfe*. The Hutchinsons were now inclined to concede to the nonimportation agreement.

Thomas and Elisha arrived and, after brief niceties, Molineux dove in.

"We expect your goods to be stored on the same conditions as the others." Molineux delivered his most piercing stare. "That is, until those who have not imported might be allowed to do so—assuming Parliament changes its ways."

"But that is too uncertain for us," said Elisha Hutchinson. "Should we be expected to keep our wares in storage for two or three years, if the winds of decision dictate?"

"We need to remain united, regardless of time or cost," another of the committee members said. "Others have agreed to these terms, albeit after some debate, and you must as well."

"We are ready to conform to the present agreement in every respect and no further."

Deep breaths and looks of determination went around the table, then a committee member placed the agreement and a quill in front of the brothers.

"Our intentions shall remain verbal," Thomas said.

Molineux gritted his teeth. This would be the best they could do.

Thomas pulled a key from his pocket. "This is for our storage located on the north side of town. You will find the tea there that we have lately imported."

A couple committee members provided halfhearted acknowledgments of the offer, and wide-eyed Thomas and Elisha rose.

Molineux took the key. "We expect you to honor your word, signatures or no signatures."

The brothers nodded then left.

Molineux looked at the committee. "A key with no signature is better than no key at all. Until Parliament has met our demands, we will keep our eyes on the Hutchinson boys."

Hutchinson reviewed the letters on his desk he had written to London.

> *The seller of Dutch tea made the greatest clamor . . . . My sons were the butt of it for they have imported from England nearly two hundred chests of tea since the agreement, which they have been able to sell so low as to discourage illicit trade. This has enraged the smugglers who expected a great harvest from the agreement not to import goods.*

He sat back in his chair to reflect on all the committee had achieved.

They had threatened to break Lillie's neck and bones if he did not submit to inspection of goods in his shop. He succumbed.

They had driven Bernard's son to a nervous breakdown.

They, or those they had directed, had twice desecrated the home of his nephew Nathaniel with the vilest filth imaginable.

And the merchants had managed to extend the nonimportation agreement until Parliament repealed their hated acts.

The acting governor picked up the letter to prepare it for delivery. Something in the doorway caught his eye. There stood a disheveled Mr. Mein.

Hutchinson hurried to him, took his arm, and led him to a chair. "Are you all right, Mr. Mein?"

Mein first nodded, then shook his head. "Once again the merchants' committee has threatened me. I beg for your assistance."

"As we have already discussed, without the names of potential assailants, I have no authority to provide protection." Hutchinson sat down. The most recent *Chronicle* sat on his desk and cried out for his attention. He hesitated then looked at Mr. Mein. "You did not heed my warning," he said. "You stirred the pot."

Mein bristled. "But Samuel Adams *does* have a hypocritical appearance, and Mr. Hancock *does* wear a fool's cap on his head."

"But saying this in your paper"—Hutchinson glanced at it again—"and that Mr. Otis is the counselor muddlehead and Mr. Molineux is the knave, leave the radicals less than amused." Hutchinson sat back. "You have given the people of Boston a great uneasiness."

"I know."

Hutchinson rose from his chair. "It is regretful, Mr. Mein, but I cannot unmake the bed you yourself have made."

Mein stood and walked to the door. "I understand." He patted a pistol at his hip, which Hutchinson had not noticed before.

"Be careful, Mr. Mein," Hutchinson said.

"It is those who threaten me who should take care."

The next day saltwater lapped beneath Molineux's feet as he stood near the town end of Long Wharf. The late afternoon sun cast long shadows over Boston. Movement from the front of Mein's bookstore a few hundred yards away prompted Molineux to signal to the men waiting on Merchants Row. At least three other Sons of Liberty were among the small group.

Molineux grabbed his club and joined his comrades who strode toward the two men who had emerged from the store. Mein and his business partner made their way up King Street toward their print shop, apparently unaware of the swarm behind them.

The posse inched closer, then one of them spoke. "We want to have a word with you."

The two businessmen whirled around. Mere feet separated them from the clan. The speaker jabbed Mein's ribs with his cane.

A captain whom Mein had dubbed an unclean beast took two steps forward. Within minutes, the commotion had pulled in a dozen gentlemen who surrounded and pushed the two men up the street toward the Town House using sticks, canes, and brickbats.

"William the Knave, eh?" Molineux said. "'Tis you, not I, the town believes to be a scoundrel."

Mein pulled and cocked a gun as he and his colleague backed farther up King Street. "Leave me be or I'll shoot."

People poured out of shops into the street. Molineux caught a glimpse of Samuel Adams. Cautious yet infuriated, the crowd kept moving toward the Town House.

"How'd you like us to use that whipping post?" one of the harassers asked, as they continued pushing the two men up the street.

"Kill him!" someone said.

One of the attackers grabbed a shovel from a nearby store window. When Mein attempted to find refuge in a nearby office, the man drove the sharp edge of the shovel full force onto Mein's shoulder.

The pistol went off.

Molineux caught Adams's eye. They nodded in agreement then darted off to find a justice of the peace who could issue a warrant for Mein's arrest for firing into the crowd.

While on their mission, a church bell rang to alert the town to the emergency.

Once back on the scene, Molineux clung to the warrant as he elbowed a path through the crowd. He glanced back to ensure Adams was in his wake.

"There must be a couple thousand here now," Molineux said.

Several of the townsfolk pointed toward the guardhouse. Careful not to collide with the lanterns emerging amid the darkness, Adams and Molineux arrived at the military post, but their efforts to find Mein proved to be futile.

Molineux growled. "Mein has not seen the last of us."

"No doubt, my friend," Adams said, panting from the hunt. "No doubt."

Light from the lantern flickered against the walls in Hutchinson's office. The acting governor stared at the crumpled piece of paper on his desk. Mein claimed he could now identify by name those who had threatened him, and he sought protection. Hutchinson had sent word to Lieutenant Colonel Dalrymple to order his troops to arm themselves, but to stay out of sight.

Hutchinson moved the lantern to the small table in the hallway. He returned to his office and closed the door, leaving only a trickle of light to pass through. Then he walked over to the window.

Huzzahs from the street below echoed through the glass, and activities unfolded beneath his gaze. With Mein's whereabouts unknown, the mob's vengeance had turned to a customs informant. The tarred and feathered seaman sat in a cart holding a large lantern as the mob, more than a thousand strong, hauled him through the streets.

"Mr. Hutchinson?"

The voice from inside the Town House startled Hutchinson. He collected himself, walked to his office door, and opened it. He stepped into the flickering light of the lantern. "I am up here."

The courier had returned.

"Were you able to relay my instructions?"

Yes, sir." The messenger walked up the stairs. "And I have news from the lieutenant colonel."

Hutchinson extended his hand to receive the document.

The messenger shuffled his feet. "Due to the urgency of the hour, he did not take time to write it down."

"What is it?" Hutchinson let his arm fall to his side. "What word do you bring?"

"It is regarding Mr. Mein. He was able to escape from the garret disguised as a British soldier."

Hutchinson smiled. "He did, did he?"

"Yes, sir. And he found refuge at Colonel Dalrymple's dwelling."

Hutchinson's muscles relaxed. "Any more news?"

"The people have tarred and feathered a man they believe is an informant."

"I saw."

"When I passed by them a few moments ago, they spoke of taking him to the Liberty Tree."

Hutchinson peered at the lantern for a moment. "The nine o'clock curfew will be here soon. The people are wise enough to disperse by then." Hutchinson picked up the lantern and led the courier to the stairs. "I apologize your ascent was in darkness."

"It was a small thing compared to the evening Mr. Mein has endured."

"Indeed it was. Thank you for the news."

"Will Mr. Mein be all right?"

"We shall have to see, won't we?"

Nine days later, Hutchinson employed the courier once again. Pope's Day celebrations provided enough of a distraction for the townsfolk that arrangements could be made for Mein to board a British schooner set to sail for London a few days later.

The messenger reported that an effigy of Mein had made an appearance at the annual festivities. "There is a slogan printed on one of the broadsides," the agent said. "Mean is the Man and Mein is his name."

"Thank you," Hutchinson said. "That will be all for today."

He returned to his desk to ponder the previous twelve months. British troops had been in Boston one year without a serious riot, but the truce was now broken. A minister had bemoaned someone's person and property would be at risk if he spoke respectfully of the king. And the note from the British colonel articulated everyone's greatest fear: "The crisis I have long expected comes on very fast."

In two months, a new decade would begin. Surely it would be better than the one they had just endured.

CHAPTER FIFTEEN

Dissension Spreads
January 12–17, 1770

Molineux's whole body shook as he spoke to fellow merchants gathered in the large meeting room. Candlelight from wall sconces cast deep shadows on faces of both friend and foe.

"Were it not for the law," Molineux said, "I would with my own hands put to death any person who should presume to open their goods."

No one moved.

Those durn Hutchinson boys. The new year gave them no right to remove their contraband from storage—at least not until the more faithful merchants had time to order and receive their wares from Britain. News of the impending repeal of the Townshend duties, except for tea, hadn't helped matters.

After an awkward few moments, a meek voice came from the group. "It is primarily the young shopkeepers who have given offense."

"Inexperience is no excuse." Molineux walked back and forth in front of the crowd. "And breaking into storage for which the boys had submitted their key three months ago should make it obvious they were doing something against our wishes."

Five additional merchants had followed their lead. When the Committee of Inspection voiced its concerns, the guilty had turned a deaf ear.

"Perhaps you and the rest of the committee can convince them of their blunder."

"That we shall." Molineux beat his fist into his hand. "I have heard Mr. Lillie has once again made his contraband tea available for sale. It must be removed from all store shelves."

"Word has arrived from England the nonimportation agreement had an impact." The words came from a friendly face.

Molineux raised his arm. "And *now* we turn our backs on it?" He resumed pacing. "Rest assured our devoted Mr. Hutchinson will eventually squelch such encouraging reports."

"You speak ill of a man who seeks to do us good." Rowe's voice was unmistakable.

Molineux stopped and faced him. "I suppose you would like to give us a full report of what he and your other dinner guests shared with you the other evening. Colonel Dalrymple, Nicholas Boylston, and others who seek to suppress us dined at your home, did they not?"

Rowe blushed.

Hancock rose from his chair. "Regardless of the impact of our previous agreement, we did vote to rescind its strictest portion."

Molineux squinted at Hancock. "I am beginning to think your trip to New York and Philadelphia may be at the root of our troubles."

The man in the seat beside Hancock jumped up. "That is an unfair accusation, and you know it. Mr. Mein is the one who planted seeds of distrust and dissension, not Mr. Hancock."

Another merchant chimed in. "Mr. Mein sent publications all over America, thousands of them best I can tell—from Nova Scotia to Florida."

"And without charge," another gentleman said. "A parting gift to us all."

Several chuckled.

Molineux returned to his seat in the front row but sat on its edge so he could face the group.

"Regardless of who is to blame," another merchant said, "our image is tarnished. Many in the port cities to our south no longer trust us, and without their support, the more stringent agreement was unable to hold."

"When you are finished debating water already under the bridge"—the voice came from the back of the room—"I would like to discuss the recent proposition made available to us by the two fellows from Glasgow."

A few men groaned. Others countered with words of encouragement.

"Hear him out."

"Those men are our salvation."

"A blessing."

The man in the back continued. "The Scottish captains seek only to provide our shipbuilders with employment."

"If we sell our souls," someone said.

The lips of the man in the back tightened. "They would require that we allow shopkeepers to purchase English goods. This would help fund their endeavor."

Molineux grimaced. "More specifically, they asked us to refrain from rebuking them for their importation."

"I spoke with enough of you prior to this meeting to know many have no reservations regarding my proposal." The man in the back reached toward his chair. "So I have brought with me a petition we can sign in order to move the process forward."

Molineux jumped up. "At your own peril."

"I say we sign," one of the merchants said.

Several others verbalized their support, and within minutes, dozens surrounded the petition and began signing their names.

The meeting officially adjourned, and Molineux grumbled as he tramped past them. "You will regret this. Mark my words."

Molineux's family had settled into the parlor for the January evening. The fire crackled in response to his stokes. He smiled once again at the thought of the petition scattered about the Town House floor in tiny pieces. Its seventy signatures were for naught once a justice of the peace had his say. And the Scotsmen had scurried out of town quicker than—

"Pa?"

His twenty-one-year-old daughter's voice brought Molineux back. "Yes, Anne?"

She pointed to the newspaper in her lap. "Do you agree with Mr. Lillie?"

Molineux jabbed the fire a few more times before he responded. "Mr. Lillie said quite a few things. To which do you refer?"

Anne picked up the paper and studied it. "Do you believe it is proper for those who contend for civil and religious liberty to deprive others of their own rights?"

Molineux leaned the stoker against the stone face, took a deep breath, and glanced at his wife. "That is how Mr. Lillie views things. Not everyone sees it the same way, however."

"He goes on to say if one group of private citizens seeks to punish another group, it is the very thing government should seek to prevent."

Molineux walked over to his chair, pushed aside his red cape, and sat down. "When the government itself is corrupt, we have to take matters into our own hands. At times, it involves sacrifice."

Elizabeth stood behind her father. "Like our relatives in Wolverhampton?"

Molineux raised an eyebrow. "Some of the manufacturing towns in England are suffering due to our refusal to import from them. We seek to help Parliament change its mind by causing pain to those they supposedly serve. Of course, we do not want to hurt those we love, so we encourage them to come here. They could help America produce her own wares."

"Then is our sacrifice like that of the pilgrims?"

"Both we and they suffered great loss to be sure." Molineux leaned forward and drew his intertwined fingers to his mouth. He dropped them and stood. "Sometimes we must sacrifice for the common good."

John glanced up from the game board. "A few weeks ago, I overheard one merchant say he was no longer willing to make those kinds of sacrifices. Several agreed with him."

"Each person must decide for himself whether the cause is greater than the sacrifice he has been called to make."

"Like the *Gazette*," John said, "calling for your committee to do its duty against the importers?"

Molineux walked back to the fireplace. "It is my way of fighting against those who seek to enslave us." He looked at Maryann. "For those of us with posterity, to sacrifice is often an easy decision."

"But, Pa," Anne said, "Mr. Lillie says he would rather be a slave to one master than to many."

Molineux stoked the fire. "Unless Mr. Lillie changes his ways, he may live to see the results of his wish." He turned back to the family. "I hope to spare him the regret his desire would eventually cause."

Molineux shook the knob of his shop door to ensure it was secure. Puffs of his breath wafted by and assured him it would be a cold walk home.

"Ah, Mr. Molineux." Samuel Adams's voice resounded behind him.

Molineux pivoted. "As usual, Mr. Adams, you are not a minute too late."

"May I accompany you to your destination?"

Molineux placed a hand on Adams's shoulder. "If you have no fear of smallpox, then you certainly may."

"In that case, I will talk fast," Adams said.

Molineux smiled. "Mr. Apthorp has asked me to check on the barracks. Mr. Hancock and the other selectmen say it is under control, but I want to see firsthand."

The men strolled toward the wharves. Aromas coming from the market and coffeehouses made the grey sky almost bearable.

"Mr. Hancock would himself be a topic of conversation," Adams said.

"He has lost favor with you as well?"

"Losing, not yet lost." Adams lifted his shoulder in half a shrug. "But if he continues to wane . . . well, we shall see."

"What brings you to my doorstep today?"

"Another of our adversaries—Mr. Hutchinson," Adams said. "He has delayed the general court until late March. He claims he received orders from the Majesty himself."

"Oh?" Molineux drew his coat tighter against the wind from the harbor.

"Needless to say, our carefully laid plans are no longer valid," Adams said. "The Sons will need to meet and form a new strategy. I will provide more details as they become available. Can I count on you to attend?"

Molineux bowed. "At your service, my lord. And if I run into any Tories along the way, shall I take them out as one of our clergy proposed?"

Adams raised a hand. "He made no such suggestion. He merely indicated the sixth commandment may not apply to our treatment of Tories."

"Hence they are fair game?"

Adams peered at Molineux. "You know better. We can go to the edge, but never across the line."

"You are a strict master, but I shall obey." Molineux grinned. "At least while you are watching."

Thankful the merchants had accepted the committee's suggestion to swing wide the doors for a more diverse group to attend their meetings, Molineux surveyed the hundreds gathered at Faneuil Hall. Anyone concerned with or connected to trade clearly included shopkeepers and artisans, but the *Gazette* had cast an even wider net by claiming this would embrace every inhabitant and be known as The Body. No surprise to see Samuel Adam and Otis, but also among the catch were several informants for the Crown.

Molineux found a seat, the meeting was called to order, and those gathered quickly selected a moderator—a member of the Committee of Inspection who was one of Molineux's neighbors. The committee reported most of the violators of the nonimportation agreement had submitted their goods to storage and released the locks' keys to the committee, only to retrieve their goods by force or otherwise break their promise in recent days. The moderator presented the question at hand—what should they do about those who had broken the agreement? Lieutenant Governor Hutchinson's sons, Elisha and Thomas Junior, and William Jackson seemed foremost in everyone's mind.

The committee suggested legal, yet spirited, measures.

"I motion," someone said, "that we select a committee to beckon the offenders to this meeting."

Molineux spun around in his chair. "Do you not think a more enthusiastic measure is needed?"

"Such an action," someone from the committee said, "might have the opposite effect of what we are trying to achieve."

"And we must ensure any measure taken is legal."

It had been so long since Molineux had heard Otis's voice, it almost sounded foreign.

"Then our first activity," the moderator said, "must be to send a small committee to the offenders to request their attendance. Then we can hear of their intentions firsthand."

The assembly selected a committee to deliver the invitation, but they returned empty-handed. Not all of the offenders could be found, and those who were refused to come. Jackson, however, would allow his store to be inspected.

Molineux stood and gazed out over the group. "The entire body must pay a visit not only to Mr. Jackson, but to the brothers as well."

"Agreed," the moderator said. Then the meeting appointed him, Molineux, and a few others to lead the way.

A cleared throat from one side of the room caused everyone to turn. There, two men stood. "No visit is needed to the Hutchinson brothers," one of them said. "We assure you, if required, they will submit to the demands regarding the tea in question. A visit by the Committee of Inspection could be arranged to work out the details."

"So be it," the moderator said. "We shall proceed with visits to the others. But those of this body who desire to accompany the committee must remain outside, orderly and peaceable, while the delegation speaks with Mr. Jackson."

The Body voted to go first, *en masse*, to confer with Jackson, and appointed Molineux as the spokesman.

While everyone bundled up, Molineux walked to the door where he held up his hands to restrain the crowd. A few minutes later, he motioned for everyone to follow.

Molineux hardly noticed the cold bite of the mid-January air as he escorted the five-man delegation, along with a thousand concerned citizens, the short distance through Dock Square and to Jackson's shop. As they made their way, several murmured Mr. Jackson might well wish he had left town ten years before, after causing the great fire which nearly burned down the entire town. He had gained no additional friends with his latest faux pas.

"Look," Molineux said, pointing to Jackson's place. "He is expecting us."

The object of their attention had pushed open an upper window as the throng approached.

Molineux wasted no time declaring the purpose of their visit. "Mr. Jackson, we demand entrance into your shop and release of the goods."

"I am no longer willing to provide either," Jackson said.

Molineux took a deep breath. His jaw tightened. Someone touched his back and reminded him to remain calm. He shook loose and stayed focused on the man in the window.

"Sir, do you know I am at the head of two thousand men?" Molineux exaggerated. "It is beneath the dignity of this committee to be parleyed within the street." He gritted his teeth. If one fell away, how would the others respond? Fuming inside yet determined to follow orders, he spun around as if a well-trained soldier. With the wave of his arm, he ushered the group back to Faneuil Hall.

Molineux, Adams, Dr. Young, and others shared a few abusive remarks with those gathered then dismissed them before heading to the coffeehouse themselves. With news the Hutchinson brothers were ready to submit to the committee's demands once again, the Sons of Liberty had reason to celebrate. Surely others would follow suit.

CHAPTER SIXTEEN

Hutchinson's Stand
January 18–23, 1770

The next morning Molineux scanned those seated behind him at Faneuil Hall—another full house. He shook his head at Dr. Young, who sat next to him. "Maybe others believe the Hutchinsons' claim of misunderstanding, but not I."

"Mr. Jackson's firm stand," Dr. Young said, "must have provided encouragement for the brothers to turn away the wagons sent to receive their tea."

"Quite the opposite of what we had hoped," Molineux said.

The moderator called the meeting back to order. "The Hutchinson brothers will allow inspection, but not confiscation."

Molineux rose and turned toward the group. "Then we shall visit them *en masse* as we did with Mr. Jackson yesterday."

"Such an action would be considered treason." Quincy, a young attorney and new son-in-law of the moderator, sat on the edge of his seat. "For it would mean going to the home of their father, where they also reside—and the elder represents the Crown."

"It is not the father with whom we wish to speak," Molineux said. "His sons are the sheep who have broken out of the fold and need to be brought back, lest others follow."

Dr. Young stood up beside Molineux. "I wholeheartedly agree, and those who do not should be deprived of their existence." He scowled. "People to whom the government rightfully belongs should take it into their own hands."

"Hear, hear," Molineux said, grateful Samuel Adams had not yet taken all the rashness out of his comrade. "Only the *people* can save the liberties of their country."

The two men remained standing.

"What if it is a trap?" Quincy asked.

Heat crept up Molineux's neck. "Then we will die together. There is no other means by which we can sustain the agreement. And without it, there is no means of redress."

Quincy turned to Otis and one of the justices. Otis, whose head bore a scar from his September attack, stood and lapsed into one of his less lucid moments. His attempt to address the matter produced expressions of confusion and embarrassment, and his legal colleague remained silent.

"A small committee then?" Molineux said, grasping at straws.

Former allies, including Hancock, shook their heads and continued to resist Molineux's suggestion to wait upon the Hutchinsons at their home.

Molineux scanned the room for inspiration as to how he might sway the crowd. A bench caught his eye and he leapt upon it. Several gasped. With everyone's attention, he placed his hand across his throat, and declared, "Without your support, I am ready to die this very minute!" He jumped down and rushed toward the door. "I will leave the movement unless you join me."

Dr. Young cried out. "No, Mr. Molineux! For God's sake—stay!" Then taking to the bench himself, he turned to the crowd and said, "Can you not see it? If Mr. Molineux leaves, our plan will be overthrown by the powers seeking to enslave us."

Molineux squinted and examined the faces of the crowd. Beneath their shock was a glimmer of willingness to consider his proposal. He strode back to the front of the room with his head held high. Every muscle in his being still tense from the demonstration, he stood facing the group as they discussed the options.

An underlying fear of possible consequences for visiting the Hutchinsons infused the debate. No one wanted to be part of the committee that would oversee the visitation. After additional persuasion, Otis and two others offered to join Molineux and Adams in the endeavor. They would lead the crowd to the home of the acting governor.

As Molineux prepared to leave, he felt Samuel Adams's trembling hand on his arm.

"Remain calm," Adams said. "Violence might erupt again, but not today. See to it."

At two p.m., the five men led The Body, more than a thousand strong, to the lieutenant governor's home to confront his sons. An upper window squeaked open, then the father appeared in its frame as if a living portrait.

Molineux stepped forward and addressed the man in the window. "We are here to speak with your sons."

The elder Hutchinson turned away from the window and made a motion. One of the young men joined his father.

Molineux pulled a document from his pocket. The assembly had provided him with the exact words to say, leaving no room for rogue behavior. Assured he had the Hutchinsons' undivided attention, Molineux began.

> *Sir,*
>
> *Merchants and traders of this town, at their present meeting, have had before them a report from their committee, wherein it appears you have violated your solemn and voluntary agreement. It is, therefore, the determination of this body to demand of you the immediate delivery of all such goods as you have heretofore agreed should be stored. They should be*

deposited to the Committee of Inspection and by them kept
with equal safety as their own until a general importation
may take place.

Your decisive answer is immediately expected.

Molineux folded the paper and put it in his pocket.

Hutchinson's son refused to comment, but his father requested a copy of the vote.

"We have only the original." Molineux patted his pocket. "I have no copy to give."

The elder Hutchinson surveyed the crowd. "I see six or seven among you who destroyed my house several years ago," he said. "At the time, I was a private citizen. Now I represent his Majesty, the king. What you do to me will be considered done to him."

"This assembly comes in peace," Molineux said.

Hutchinson gestured toward Otis. "I see you have a great legal mind in your midst. He should know better than to be part of this illegal assembly." The one accused stood in silence.

"We merely seek an audience with your sons to discuss the matter at hand," Molineux said. "If they refuse, we shall be on our way."

Hutchinson and his son exchanged a few private words then the elder faced Molineux. "My sons have already communicated their intentions and have nothing further to add."

Stonewalled, the committee led the crowd to the other half dozen importers. Receiving similar responses, The Body adjourned until the next morning.

Molineux's shoulders drooped as he made his way home. Resistance seemed as cold and hard as the frozen harbor, with no spring thaw in sight. If the importers did not join their fellow merchants in refusing to purchase goods from Britain, the agreement would produce no pain for the Motherland, and she would have no reason to listen to her colonists' complaints.

Molineux stood on the Faneuil Hall stage and smiled. Despite the bitter cold and Hutchinson's call for his council to help put a halt to the meetings, an even larger crowd had turned out for Friday morning's meeting. Molineux related to them what had transpired at the Hutchinson home then reported on visits to the others.

Mr. Lillie had declared, "I have nothing left but my life, which I will deliver up, if you please."

Mr. Taylor claimed to have almost no items to submit for he had already sold them.

Mr. Jackson refused to open his shop to them.

Two others were not at home, and one previously out of town would turn over his goods to the care of the committee.

Molineux motioned to the back of the room. "And now I present to you our very capable moderator who, I believe, has additional information to share." Molineux took his seat, and the moderator came forward to the stage's lectern.

"I have just met with the lieutenant governor and am pleased to report he has directed his sons to deliver up their tea along with any money they have received for the sale of the same."

An audible sigh rippled through the hall, and the assembly wasted no time voting to accept Hutchinson's proposal. After several scurrilous and abusive speeches from Molineux, Adams, and others, The Body adjourned until Tuesday morning.

Relieved, Molineux took in a deep breath then let the air slowly pass between his lips. The tide had turned in their favor once again.

Hutchinson sat at the large table in the council chambers. All other chairs were empty. While awaiting word as to what was transpiring at the meeting of The Body, he reflected on the past week. His own council had refused his request to condemn the recent meetings. In the asset column, he had managed to remove his sons from the dispute and, thus, any perceived conflict of interest. Yet he had maintained his honor by refusing to submit directly to the mass visitation. Perhaps it would provide him more sway with those who had previously opposed him.

He drummed his fingers on the table.

Heeding the advice of his Tory friends had not prevented the violence they wished to avoid. Had he not pacified the radicals, however, the situation could have been much worse than a few broken windows and a failed attempt to burn down Mr. Jackson's store and home.

Hutchinson pushed away from the table, stood, and walked over to the portrait of the king. "The meetings border on high treason, your Majesty, yet I can get no one to stand with me to condemn them. Even some of your justices have turned a blind eye and claim there are exceptions to the laws of the land." The acting governor wilted. The justices had claimed, with other channels shut down, meeting together was the only way for the people to preserve their rights and liberties.

Hutchinson raised one hand, palm up, to the king. "I have warned the moderator if any of the meetings should result in violence, those responsible will pay with both their lives and their estates. No level of society would be immune—not even the so-called gentleman with a store on Merchants Row."

"Mr. Hutchinson?" The voice of the sheriff resounded in the empty room.

Hutchinson pivoted to the door. "Enter, please."

"I have come from the meeting."

Hutchinson extended his frame to full stature. "And what do you have to report?"

"Once again, it is a mixed group," the sheriff said. "In addition to the merchants, shopkeepers, and artisans, there are several attorneys, justices of the peace, and three of Boston's four representatives in attendance."

Hutchinson nodded.

"The discussion has turned to the people's frustration over quartering of the troops within the town. I thought you would want to know."

"Thank you," Hutchinson said in a voice so quiet he wondered if it could be heard. "I will, of course, prepare a statement for you to take to them. Please wait elsewhere in the building while I collect my thoughts."

The sheriff did not move. "I also have news regarding the other importers."

Hutchinson motioned for him to continue.

"They have informed the committee they too will respect its request regarding their goods." The sheriff took a breath. "Yet they have rejected your advice to sue those causing them grief. They believe no fair trial can be had amid Molineux's promise that radicals would always have eleven of the twelve jurymen."

"I see," Hutchinson said. "Thank you for the news." He walked the sheriff to the chamber door. "I will call for you when I have completed the message I wish for you to convey."

The sheriff walked out the door then turned back to Hutchinson. "Several of the violators of the agreement now sleep with a gun by their beds."

Hutchinson did not flinch. "Thank you. I will take all you have conveyed into consideration as I draft my reply. Nevertheless, the people must be taught to submit to those who have ruled them for generations. No action on their part should deter us from helping them return to a proper way of life. I will see to it."

Hutchinson walked to his office and pulled out a piece of paper, his inkwell, and a quill. He faced the icy window. This would provide an opportunity to do what the council and justices refused to do.

"To the People Assembled at Faneuil Hall," he wrote. "Your assembling together for the purpose you profess cannot be justified by any authority or law."

The unwelcomed event at his home the week before flashed through his mind. He continued to write. "Your going from house to house and making demands of property must strike the people with terror from your great numbers."

He touched the feather to his mouth then raised it slightly. "Lest there be any misunderstanding," he said aloud. He returned the quill to the paper. "Even if it be admitted it is not done in a tumultuous manner, it is of very dangerous tendency."

Now to address those the radicals had sought to ensnare. "You who are persons of character, reputation, and property have exposed yourselves to the consequences of irregular actions by those who assemble with you, although you may not approve of them nor have the power to restrain them."

He sat back in his chair for a moment before he presented his plea. "Therefore, as the representative of his Majesty, who is the father of his people," he wrote, "I must, from a tender regard to your interest, require you to separate and disperse and to forbear all such unlawful assemblies in the future."

He laid down his pen and went in search of the sheriff.

Hutchinson returned to the warmth of the council chambers to await the reply. The minutes dragged by until the sheriff returned.

"There must have been a considerable debate," Hutchinson said.

"There was," the sheriff said, "followed by additional proceedings I wanted to be able to report to you." He held up a piece of paper. "Mr. Hancock prepared the reply, which states they believe their meeting is warranted by law."

Hutchinson took the paper and scanned it. "Hence their meeting continued."

"They voted the importers, including Messrs. Jackson and Lillie, were enemies of their country and should be driven back into the hole from whence they were dug."

Hutchinson frowned.

"They believe it is their duty to themselves and to posterity," the sheriff said, "since the importers are subverters of their country's rights and liberties." The sheriff walked closer to the fire and rubbed his hands together. "They did, however, agree to obliterate names from the record for those who deliver their goods to the committee tomorrow."

Hutchinson nodded. "Any more activity?"

"They reacted to yesterday's piece in the *Chronicle* with a vote to recommend total abstinence from tea."

"If only Mr. Mein's business partner had sailed to England with him."

The sheriff gazed into the hearth. "It would certainly have meant less kindling for the fire."

"If the *Chronicle* is correct and the radicals get their way," Hutchinson said, "there are a hundred thousand pounds of tea around town available to those faithful to the Crown. A silver lining in the cloud, wouldn't you say?"

CHAPTER SEVENTEEN

Market Day

February 1770

*H*utchinson sat in the mahogany-paneled drawing room of his country home in Milton. A cup of tea warmed his fingers amid the early February chill. The two weeks of quiet had soothed his soul. His stand had halted the rebels' momentum. Even a member of the Committee of Inspection had grown cool to the cause.

Then there was Molineux, along with a few other Sons, who remained restless. The acting governor sighed. But even they had backed down, and the committee had suspended its efforts.

Yet less bold demonstrations remained. Teatime had all but disappeared in an attempt to force Parliament to remove the tax on the controversial herb. With patriotism as their rallying cry, the ladies of the North and South Ends had convinced upwards of a hundred to pledge not to drink the forbidden brew. If common people could reform the law, what would become of law and order?

The fire crackled as he took another sip.

Would the prophesy of some come true? Would tea, now a forbidden fruit, only produce a greater longing for it? He smiled.

Weeks of tension had taken their toll, and both sides had welcomed the much-needed respite. He would enjoy it.

A knock at the door interrupted his thoughts. Hutchinson set his empty cup on the table and walked to the door. A messenger brought word of a scuffle in the streets of New York between British troops and Sons of Liberty. Rumors were running wild in Boston, and bells were ringing for joy. Hutchinson thanked the courier and provided him with a brief message for those who would want to know of his plans. Unsettledness had crept back into Boston's streets so he must return.

He surveyed the peaceful setting he had enjoyed amid the weeks of calm. "All good things must come to an end," he said. "Only God knows what lies ahead."

Molineux stood across the street from Jackson's shop, beating a stick into his free hand. Despite two weeks of relative calm, he could count on Thursdays being abuzz with activity. Country folk came to town for market day, and schools let out midmorning. Molineux kicked a patch of melting snow and grinned. If he had figured it correctly, today should be especially clamorous.

The stage had been set. Wandering schoolboys, not yet ready to go home to practice their penmanship, would not need to look far for a diversion.

Molineux glanced to the corner. A small group of them had gathered.

"Hey, look," one said pointing to the town pump.

He had spotted the wooden sign with a hand painted on it. "IMPORTER" was etched in large letters, and the ominous finger pointed to Jackson's place of business.

Another of the boys found a nearby handbill. "It says Sons and Daughters of Liberty should not buy anything from him."

The boys glanced at each other, dropped their books under the sign, and raced toward Jackson's shop.

Molineux threw down the stick, stepped into the street, and spread wide his arms. "Gather 'round, my friends," he said to those going about their business, "for the show is about to begin."

Molineux moved toward the main attraction but stayed far enough back to give the schoolboys room to maneuver. Several merchants and marketgoers joined him. Others sought refuge in nearby shops. Some halted in their tracks and waited to see what would happen.

"Don't let them go in there," someone said, pointing to the store.

The schoolboys grabbed clumps of ice, rocks, and mud and began to pelt the would-be customers. They hissed at those attempting to dodge their missiles.

Jackson bolted from his store, with arms raised to protect his face, and moved toward the sign. As he reached out to remove it, a rock hit his hand. "Argh. Ye durn boys." He backed away then tried again with similar results.

Molineux stepped forward. "Does the hand disturb you, Belshazzar?" Molineux said, referring to the Babylonian king of old who saw a vision of a bodiless finger writing on the wall of his royal palace.

Jackson shook his own finger at Molineux. "Mark my words, Mr. Molineux. Your day will come." Fending off clubs and sticks, he retreated into the safety of his store to ride out the assault.

By one o'clock, the sign had disappeared, but Jackson's mud-covered shop remained as proof. The truce had been broken.

The following Thursday played out in much the same way, and by month's end, everyone knew what to expect on market day. Shops of the importers drew spectators like a magnet. Molineux arrived in front of Lillie's store shortly after ten a.m. Already it was adorned with one of the "Importer" signs, and the familiar accusing finger sat nearby. A mannequin, complete with a large, wooden head atop a post, brought images to mind of criminals executed in days gone by. Molineux smiled at the four caricatures at Lillie's front door, which did a good job of representing the leading importers.

Molineux spotted Revere, whose new home backed up to Lillie's shop, and quickly made his way to him to get his account of what had happened.

"The boys did a lot of this," Revere said, pointing to the display. "Mr. Lillie's home was tarred and feathered overnight."

Molineux tried to look surprised. "Really?"

"A sign at one of the stores says, 'Don't buy from the traitor.'"

The schoolboys paraded back and forth in front of Lillie's store, preventing entry by potential customers. The boys bombarded patrons with dirt and stones. "Huzzah!"

Molineux began to mingle among the crowd to ensure the level of excitement remained high. Scores had gathered by the time he spotted Ebenezer Richardson. Molineux growled. A wretch if ever there was one. Known as an informer for the customs officials and suspected of incest with his sister-in-law, Richardson had his share of enemies. He had threatened to feed the radicals to the devil for supper and claimed his guns were loaded. "Mere rhetoric," Molineux said under his breath.

Mrs. Lillie emerged from her husband's store. She and Richardson conversed for a moment, then Richardson marched back toward the street. He signaled for a man atop a wagon to ram his cart into the offensive image. "Away with the sign." The countryman shirked back, refusing to have anything to do with the situation.

"You there." Richardson darted to a nearby charcoal vendor. "Strike the sign with your wagon."

Getting a similar reaction, Richardson grabbed the reins of the closest horse and wagon and attempted to destroy the sign himself.

Molineux mumbled. "Such a fool." The commotion grabbed the attention of the schoolboys, who began to throw their makeshift missiles toward Richardson.

Four other Sons of Liberty had joined Molineux. Richardson caught sight of them as he hurried to the shelter of his home, only fifty paces away. The men bore the brunt of his words. "Perjury! Perjury!" He pointed to the sign as he ducked into his home.

"Make your intentions clear," one of the patriots said as they followed him to his door.

Richardson came out waving his fists. "I will make it hot for you by nightfall."

One of the men spat curses at Richardson then added, "And I will have your heart and liver out before you can make good on it."

Richardson fumed. His face turned red, and he went back inside.

"Come out, you fool," Molineux said.

The boys ran over to resume their attacks, and the men stepped back. A woman came out of the house.

"Huzzah!" One of the boys hurled an egg in her direction, and she quickly retreated.

The men laughed. "Blast her again," one of them said.

Emerging with what appeared to be a pistol, Richardson fired off venomous words as he shook his weapon at the crowd. He waved it at the boys as if shooing off a swarm of gnats. "Go off, you juveniles. My gun is loaded and as sure as there is a God in heaven, I will blow a hole through you—a hole big enough to drive a cart and oxen through."

Molineux smirked. The fool had fanned the flames.

"We are as free as you to stand in the king's highway," one of the youngsters said.

Stones, oyster shells, and eggs still flying, Richardson returned to his shelter and, moments later, appeared at an upper window with one of his sailor friends. Richardson knelt.

"Is he loading a gun?" one of the Sons asked.

"Where are they?" Richardson fought to steady his musket on the window's edge and point it toward the crowd.

"You would not dare," someone from the crowd shouted.

Richardson fired.

Then clacking while he reloaded.

Boom . . . clack.

Again and again.

Molineux's nose itched from the smell.

Boom.

"Argh." An older boy grabbed his right hand while the younger boy clenched his chest and fell to the ground.

Seconds later, a nearby church bell called more townspeople into the streets while spectators carried the bleeding child to a nearby house.

"It's Christopher Seider," someone said. "Send for his parents—and a minister."

Molineux stood in a daze. He knew the boy.

Those not attending to the lad stormed Richardson's home. Some ripped apart window frames, made their way inside, and dragged the two men into the street. Richardson's friend gave up without a fight, but Richardson wielded a cutlass at the mob.

"You've killed the boy," someone claimed.

"I do not care what I have done," Richardson said.

The crowd pressed in and subdued him. Molineux, back from his stupor, joined them.

Someone produced rope and began to form a noose. Another brought a sign post suitable for hanging. "A life for a life," someone said.

Molineux fought his way to the center of the turmoil and pushed away the noose. "Justice must be served, but not this way. We must let the law determine their fate."

Some looked disappointed, some relieved.

"We must find a justice of the peace," Molineux said.

The crowd dragged the two men through town until they found an authority who directed them to Faneuil Hall. Amid a thousand onlookers, testimonies provided enough evidence for the judges to commit the men to the gaol where they would await a March trial for "firing off and discharging a gun . . . at one Christopher Seider thereby giving him a very dangerous wound."

At nine p.m., Seider died. The new charge against Richardson: murder.

Molineux paced back and forth in his home's parlor. Four days had passed since the lad's death. Molineux glanced at the clock then walked to the window. The evening sun cast an eerie glow across the snow that had fallen on the Common two days before. Had the hail, thunder, and lightning that accompanied the snow been a sign from heaven?

Five after five. The funeral procession would be gathered at the Liberty Tree by now. Patriots had no need of Molineux's fiery nature today. Instead, those with less volatile tendencies would attend—John Rowe and John Adams came to mind. Samuel Adams had orchestrated a day for reflection and pageantry that would stir the heart.

Church bells tolled in the distance.

As the sun touched the horizon, Molineux caught a glimpse of the schoolboys making their way up the street one block beyond the Common. Four to five hundred lads, walking in pairs, preceded the six who carried their classmate's coffin. The plan would take them as far as the Town House then by the gaol, where Richardson and his accomplice sat awaiting trial. Eventually they would make their way back toward the Common.

"'Tis sad." His wife had entered the room undetected. Molineux felt her hand slip around his waist. His hand met hers, though still in his own world.

They both watched as the parade continued for more than a half mile—two thousand mourners then thirty carriages and chaises. Perhaps the largest event ever held in America.

"The Sons posted a board to the Liberty Tree. You would have liked it." He turned to his wife. "It quoted a passage from the Bible about the fate of a murderer."

"Every death is sad, deserved or not," Maryann said.

Two of their children came into the room and joined their parents at the window.

A copy of the *Gazette* was tucked under John's arm. "The paper referred to him as a little hero." He pulled out the paper and lifted it to catch the light from the lamp. "'The innocent lad was the first whose life has been lost to the cruelty and rage of oppressors.' It says he was the first martyr to the noble cause."

"Papa, tell us again." Elizabeth wiped a tear from her face. "When did you last see him?"

"A week ago. I paid a visit to Mrs. Apthorp to inquire about her son—the one for whom I manage properties," Molineux said. "Christopher worked for her and was there doing chores." He paused to reflect on the difference a week had made then looked at his daughter. "He was only a year younger than you."

"We lived near Christopher's home when Junior was born," Maryann said. "A stone's throw from the Liberty Tree."

Molineux remained motionless. Were his actions to blame for the lad's death? Could he have saved the child from the bullet that claimed his life?

"Come along, children," Maryann said. The trio left Molineux to watch the last of the procession. The burying ground lay just out of Molineux's sight, yet the glow of lanterns grew stronger as friends and family gathered there and twilight turned to darkness.

Bloodshed. Was it too high a price to pay?

Maybe the *Gazette* was right. Young as he was, Seider had died for the country's cause. And his death cried out for vengeance.

CHAPTER EIGHTEEN

$$\mathcal{C}\!\!\sim\!\!\mathcal{O}$$

Blood in the Snow
March 3–8, 1770

Hutchinson glanced at his sister, also seated in the parlor of his Boston home. Her maidservant stood before them. A quiet market day had given way to an unruly Friday. By Saturday, rumors were running wild.

"Thank you again for being willing to share your firsthand account," the acting governor said to the girl. "Please continue."

"Well, the soldier didn't take kindly to being asked to clean the man's toilet, especially since he thought he was going to be offered a real job."

Hutchinson's sister leaned forward in her chair and looked at him. "As you can imagine, with the meager pay the troops receive, they are anxious to pick up any odd job they can find."

"But not cleaning a toilet," the maidservant said.

Hutchinson nodded. "And then what happened?"

"One of the other workers at the ropewalk took the soldier's reply as a threat and jumped on him." The girl leapt forward to demonstrate, startling her audience.

Hutchinson held up a hand to calm her.

"I'm sorry, Mr. Hutchinson. I meant no harm."

Hutchinson motioned for her to continue.

"Well, out from the soldier's jacket fell a cutlass." She pretended to wave one in the air while making the swooshing sound of the blade. She put one hand on her hip and changed her accent. "'Ye came prepared to fight, did ye?' the worker said to the soldier."

Hutchinson was unsure what to think of the maidservant's entertaining style but was grateful for the eyewitness account.

"The private jumped to his feet," she said, "and swearing to get vengeance, ran off to get reinforcements."

Hutchinson's sister motioned for their attention. "Gray's ropewalk is only a few hundred yards from one of the barracks for the Twenty-ninth."

The girl nodded. "Laughter from the men at the ropewalk hounded the soldier all the way back to his hut." She took a moment, swung her head back, and put hands on both hips. "They weren't laughing when the private returned with eight or nine of his comrades, but it didn't take much for the workers to beat them off."

Hutchinson tried to envision it. "Had more joined the two involved in the initial exchange?"

"Oh, yes, sir. Men from the ropewalk shed next door came with their two-foot-long hickory sticks to help fight off the soldiers."

"I see," Hutchinson said.

"The ropewalk workers celebrated for a time. That is, until the soldiers returned in full force. Thirty or forty of them, I'd say. And they came armed with clubs. It was a bloody mess."

"I heard a justice of the peace attempted to break up the disturbance," Hutchinson said.

"Yes, sir—and no offense to the elderly, mind you—but he was too old to have much success. It didn't matter since it didn't take long for the workers to beat the soldiers back up the lane and into their barracks."

"And they stayed there?"

"A corporal made sure of it," the maidservant said. "The soldiers were mad, though—steaming as much as one of those cauldrons of hot tar at the ropewalk."

"Thank you for your report."

"But that wasn't the end of it. There was another brawl between them this morning." The girl glanced at her mistress. "Of course, the townsfolk blame the soldiers."

Hutchinson provided a faint smile. Of course they did.

"Some of the soldiers' wives are madder than a hornets' nest," she said. "I heard one of them say by Tuesday or Wednesday night the troops will wet their bayonets in New England people's blood."

Hutchinson straightened. "The soldiers are not allowed to fire without permission from a civil authority. And I have no plans to grant it."

"But, my dear brother, no musket is needed to do great harm. One of the men from yesterday's scuffle suffered a cracked skull."

"And threats coming from the barracks," the maidservant said, "claim many who eat their dinners on Monday will not be around to eat them on Tuesday."

Hutchinson checked the clock then stood. "I am grateful for the report," he said as he walked them to the door. "I am afraid I have kept you too long. You must hasten or you will not arrive home before the nine o'clock curfew. I will tend to the matters you have brought to me."

Alone once again, Hutchinson prepared for bed. He drifted off to sleep, thankful the Sabbath would give him a bit of a reprieve from all that clamored for his attention.

Hutchinson sat at his desk in the Town House. A Monday if ever there was one. The meeting with his council had not gone well, and a variety of papers had collected on his desk during the previous few days.

A copy of the agreement between Mr. Gray and Colonel Dalrymple claimed Gray would dismiss the offending worker from his employment while Dalrymple would prevent the soldiers from seeking vengeance.

A letter from the Twenty-ninth's commanding officer expressed concerns over abuses his men had received from the town's citizens. They, and the provocative language, must stop—something his council claimed would not happen until the troops were ordered to the castle.

"Mr. Hutchinson?" a voice said from the other side of the door.

The acting governor sighed. "Come in."

One of his messengers entered and held out a piece of paper. "I thought you would want to see the most recent handbill. It has been posted all around town."

Hutchinson took it and leaned back in his chair.

Boston, March 5, 1770

This is to inform ye rebellious people in Boston that ye soldiers in ye Fourteenth and Twenty-ninth Regiments are determined to join together and defend themselves against all who shall oppose them.

Signed, ye Soldiers of ye Fourteenth and Twenty-ninth Regiments

"Thank you," Hutchinson said.

"Two other items may also interest you," the young man said.

"They are?"

"Two days ago, one of the soldiers left a message for a local carpenter who had befriended him. He warned him to keep in his house, for before Tuesday night next at twelve o'clock—that would be tomorrow—there would be a great deal of bloodshed and a great many lives lost."

"And the second item?"

"Yesterday, one of the ministers claimed many townspeople look forward to fighting it out with the soldiers on Monday," the boy said. "He also reminded his congregation that ringing bells would signal an alarm."

The messenger left, and Hutchinson added the handbill to the pile on his desk. He shuffled the papers and retrieved the day's *Gazette*. Not a word about the recent confrontations between the soldiers and the people. He sat back in his chair. Yet plenty about the young lad's funeral. Enough to reignite the flame which, until Friday, had once again subsided. And somehow they had received word Richardson's trial would be delayed.

One would expect tinder from the radicals, but—Hutchinson shuffled through more papers. Ah, there it was—a statement from the commissioners whom he had labored to protect. Their memories were short. He reread the portion where they sought to distance themselves from the defendant. Hutchinson rubbed his forehead. "You, my dear friends," he said aloud, "have only increased the anger against those of us who seek to represent the Crown. Let's pray we do not live to regret your provocation."

The white wig warmed Molineux's head. He tugged at his cape with a free hand to ensure the mask stayed concealed. Monday evening's slim moon helped illuminate the snow-covered town, yet Molineux chose to stay in the shadows and crept through the back corridors toward the center of town. The light snow had ceased, and a thin covering of ice crunched beneath his jackboots.

King Street—at last. Molineux peered out from the alley to ensure his passage across would go undetected. He pulled back. An unusual number of men and boys roamed about for such a cold night.

He peeked, careful to remain hidden. Many carried a cane or club. Sailors, slaves, and laborers from the wharves also moved about the main thoroughfare, flashing their swords for all to see.

It was nearing eight o'clock. Time was running out to make his mark on the night. He stepped back to plan his move. His red cape was not exactly inconspicuous.

"Argh!" The scream came from up the road.

Molineux peered around the corner. A young lad was running away from the Town House—no, running away from the lone soldier who stood watch outside the main guard.

Now or never. Molineux clenched the mask beneath his cape then darted across the way. Surely the shouts from the main guard would be enough to deflect attention away from him and his flapping cloak. He slid on the ice but caught himself. The cold air gripped at his chest. A few more yards, and once again, shadows from a footpath enveloped him.

He bent over and put both hands on his knees. His breath formed white billows of air. "Not . . ." he panted, "the di . . . version . . . I had expected." He stood up. "But I'll take it." Moments later, he made his way down the dark passageway. At the end, he paused.

A few folks milled around Dock Square—but not enough.

Shouts of "Liberty, liberty, fire, fire" cut through the night a few hundred yards to his left—from Murray's barracks. His cape and mask were no match for the well-armed soldiers.

Did the original Joyce Junior have this much trouble when he attempted to behead the king more than a century before?

He took a step into the square then quickly retreated. Several dozen were coming his way. No soldiers. Only townsfolk and rabble.

Molineux pulled the mask from under his cape and placed it securely on his face, then he ran into Dock Square. "Gather 'round, my friends." His voice reverberated behind the disguise.

Many turned toward the masked stranger and gasped.

"Joyce Junior has arrived!"

Molineux smiled. He had captured their attention with his charade.

"Our deliverance!" the townsfolk said.

"He will know what to do."

Molineux scanned the crowd—maybe a couple hundred. Sticks ready. His eyes widened at the sight of a large mulatto who had come with others from the area around the barracks. The giant carried two large sticks as he clomped through the crowd.

Molineux whipped the cape around and motioned for the crowd to draw near. As they did, a hush fell over them.

"Do we like having lobsters among us?" Molineux asked.

"Nay!"

A few hissed.

"Is it time for them to leave?"

"Yea!"

"Too long we have allowed fear to be our master. Too long we have laid our freedoms at their feet." Molineux smiled behind the mask as the mulatto raised his makeshift clubs and shook them skyward.

Molineux grabbed the edge of his cape and flung it open. "Are we ready to be done of them?" He spun around to see each part of the crowd that now encircled him. "Huzzah! Huzzah! And thrice, I say, Huzzah!"

The crowd went wild. "Huzzah!"

"We know where they nest, do we not? And the time has come to do away with them."

"To the main guard!" the crowd said. Many lifted their hats upward and began to run in that direction.

"Huzzah! Huzzah! Huzzah!"

"Lobsters for supper tonight!"

The crowd rushed down one of the byways toward King Street. Molineux lingered. He would need to hide his disguise before joining them. He had played his role well, and his spirit was at peace. The results were out of his hands, but surely it would include ridding Boston of the troops once and for all.

As the crowd ran toward the main guard, Molineux strode toward the barracks. He would circle around to King Street once he had modified his appearance. He removed the mask and pulled it back under his cape.

Bells from the nearby church began to ring, calling more towns-folk from their homes. Several hurried past him.

"I am afraid you will not find a fire," Molineux mumbled.

Above the confusion, a cry came from King Street. "Turn out, main guard!"

Molineux ducked into an alley to avoid a potential stampede from the barracks. Several minutes passed. He took a single step toward the road then back again.

A handful of soldiers stood outside the barracks. Molineux adjusted his position until he was sure the shadows kept him undetected. Then he surveyed the scene. A townsman armed with a stout cudgel had apparently heard the commotion and was on his way to investigate.

As the man neared the barracks, one of the soldiers stepped forward. "And what makes you think you can be out at this late hour?" Without waiting for an answer, the soldier grabbed the man's neck. "You Bostonians think you arc in command. Not so." The private seized the man's coat and ripped his shirt.

"I . . . I heard the bells—"

Molineux watched from his hideout.

A second soldier struck the man on the shoulder while yet another wrestled the club from him. The townsman snatched at his cudgel but drew his hand back empty.

The door to the barracks squeaked open and out stepped an officer. He surveyed the scene then spoke directly to the townsman. "How can Boston's inhabitants wrangle with the soldiers on such a trifling occasion?"

The Bostonian tugged at the tear in his shirt and cast a timid glance at the one who had addressed him. "Can a man be inactive when his countrymen lay butchered in the streets?"

"Mr. Molineux was the author of all this," the lieutenant said.

Molineux smiled at the mention of his name. So they did know who he was.

The lieutenant glared at the townsman and pressed the cudgel into its owner's hand.

Molineux turned to the blackness behind him. He took a moment to gather himself then ran toward the other end of the path. Ice crunched beneath his feet.

"Who goes there?" The voice came from behind.

Molineux did not look back. He needed to get to King Street.

As he approached, the uproar grew louder until one voice rose above the others.

"Fire! Fire!"

The cry hardly seemed like a call for additional buckets.

Molineux slipped then regained his footing. It sounded more like—

Boom! A gunshot. Then several more. Seven? Eight? A dozen?

Molineux quickened his pace. His feet took him as fast as the darkness would allow.

He stepped into the snowy, moonlit byway, and his mind raced to make sense of the confusion. The guard stood at the corner of the Custom House several yards to his right. Seven soldiers, not here when he had dashed by earlier, formed a semicircle.

The nostrils of the captain flared as he thrust up their muskets one by one. "Hold your fire."

Molineux inhaled . . . gunpowder.

Bells were ringing all over town.

Several dozen townsfolk stood in the street—others watched from doorways with leather buckets in hand. Some clenched sticks and others nothing at all. Young lads held oyster shells ready to use as ammunition. A few shook melting snowballs from their hands. Many faces registered shock and disbelief. A number were solemn while others moved about in a panic. Dr. Young knelt in front of the soldiers, pleading with the townsfolk to go home. Knelt?

Then Molineux saw it. A lifeless body lying in the snow.

He moved closer. His mouth fell open. The mulatto who had been among the crowd in Dock Square had taken two bullets to his chest. Molineux dared to look around. Another body lay close by. Yet another, a kinsman of the South End clan leader, lay in the middle of the road.

Three colonists lay dead. Two others groaned, as if mortally wounded. Several clutched their less serious wounds. All at the hands of British soldiers.

"Pa." The call came from behind and above him.

Molineux pivoted to see Junior and two of his friends standing on the balcony of the Bunch of Grapes Tavern. They had apparently watched the event unfold. Junior pointed toward the Town House.

Amid the chaos Molineux had not noticed the beat of the regiment's drum. Three divisions of soldiers had filed into King Street. The front line knelt at one corner of the Town House. All pointed their guns down the street—the one through which they had entered the town a year and a half before.

The crowd continued to swell. Several removed the wounded and dying to shelters more conducive to their needs. The civilians, nearing two thousand, refused to back down from the soldiers who now filled the street. Molineux forced his way up King Street. He kept his eyes on the Town House. He must reach it so he could make their voices heard.

Hutchinson hastened to King Street as soon as he was beckoned. Why had the officer fired upon the inhabitants without permission from a civil authority? He found Captain Preston but strained to make out his response. The noise from the people was simply too great.

"To the Town House! To the Town House!" the crowd chanted at their lieutenant governor. A push to his back thrust him toward the building.

How rude. Could they not see he was already speaking with the object of their frustration?

"To the Town House!"

He cast an apologetic glance toward the captain then gave in to the momentum of the crowd. The path to the Town House through the throng left him a bit disheveled. Upon entering, he took a moment to tidy himself. The shuffling of feet above him indicated many had already gathered. He made his way up the stairs and toward the council chambers. As he approached, he caught glimpses of council members and civil magistrates. Then, with one foot inside the chamber's door, Molineux rushed toward him.

"You will demand the troops return to their barracks," Molineux said. "Immediately."

Hutchinson walked past. Molineux ran around him and planted himself in front of the balcony door.

One of Molineux's merchant friends came to his side. "What say ye?"

"What I have to say," Hutchinson said, "I will say to the people. Now if you will please allow me to perform my duty." He motioned for the two men to let him pass then made his way onto the platform overlooking King Street.

He stood quietly as awareness of his presence rippled through the crowd, then he spoke. "I am concerned over this unhappy event and assure you the law will have its course. I beseech you to return to your homes. A full and impartial inquiry shall be made upon the morrow. Rest assured, I will live and die by the law."

"We want arrests," someone said from the King Street crowd.

"Tonight."

Another pointed to the soldiers in their military stance beneath the balcony. "And get rid of these."

"Return home peacefully, and we will deal with the events of the night in due course."

Several walked away with mutters of "home, home" on their lips.

Progress. He waited a moment, but most refused to budge.

A bit defeated, Hutchinson returned to the chamber. His lips tightened at the sight of Molineux, who met him at the door.

"Ordering the troops back to their quarters," Molineux said in a huff, "would achieve your desired goal."

Hutchinson refrained from comment and scanned the crowded room. He found the Twenty-ninth's commander, approached him, and conveyed his orders. The lieutenant colonel immediately departed to carry them out.

The acting governor glanced back at Molineux, who darted onto the balcony. Hutchinson walked over and began to close the door. He left it ajar and stood close enough to monitor what would transpire. The commander's voice from below confirmed the troops were on their way back to the barracks.

He watched Molineux walk to the edge of the platform and look out over the crowd. "Your presence has been most welcomed this evening," Molineux said, "but your beds now beckon for you to retire. Good day to each of you."

"And what of the murderers?" someone from the street below asked.

Hutchinson opened the door and moved onto the veranda. Molineux stepped aside.

"I have sent word for the justices to come," Hutchinson announced to the people below. "We will begin interrogation this very night. You would be wise to return to your homes. You will receive a full report in the morning."

Hutchinson watched as the crowd began to disperse then turned to face Molineux.

Molineux extended his hand toward the door. "After you." The two men returned to the chamber.

Hutchinson found his chair at the head of the table and called the meeting to order. Some of the men took a seat while others stood. The debate continued for hours until the lieutenant governor issued a warrant. At three a.m., he ordered Captain Thomas Preston to jail.

The men were satisfied, and the leader of the province could return home. It had been a long day, but at last, he and the town could rest—albeit for a few short hours.

Hutchinson's morning had begun with news that the eight soldiers had surrendered to the authorities' custody and that death had claimed a fourth victim. The town had called a meeting at Faneuil Hall for eleven o'clock. The clock had just struck twelve.

The acting governor sat at the head of the council chamber table, reviewing the setting. The council, men wigged and robed in scarlet laced with gold and silver, sat around the long table. Uniformed officers—commanders of the two regiments and a captain of one of the eight war vessels standing guard over Boston—had joined them. Large portraits of royalty observed from the chamber walls.

"We are ready," the lieutenant governor said to the attendant. "Send them in."

A committee from the town meeting filed in—Samuel Adams, Hancock, Molineux, and twelve others. Hutchinson motioned for several of the men at the other end of the table to part so he could see the visitors.

Adams, as plainly dressed as ever, walked to the table, took a piece of paper from his pocket, and unfolded it. "It is the unanimous opinion of this meeting," Adams's palsy-stricken voice read, "the inhabitants and soldiery can no longer live together in safety, and nothing can rationally be expected to restore the peace of the town and prevent further blood and carnage but the immediate removal of the troops."

Adams gazed at Hutchinson a moment, then he continued. "And the town, therefore, fervently prays His Honor would exert his power and influence for their instant removal." He folded the paper and returned it to his pocket.

Hutchinson remained calm. "You, Mr. Adams, and your committee may retire to the next room while we discuss the matter."

The committee filed out of the room, and Hutchinson led the discussion with those who remained. Then he instructed an assistant to retrieve the committee.

The acting governor sat motionless as they entered and did not allow his expression to provide clues for what was to come. With everyone returned to the room, he began. "As you know, it is beyond my authority to grant your request. However, Colonel Dalrymple has most graciously offered to remove the Twenty-ninth Regiment to the castle since it was their original destination." Hutchinson nodded to the attendant holding a piece of paper, who took it to Adams. "This written reply," Hutchinson said, "will provide you with additional details and should settle the matter. Good day, gentlemen."

Molineux rode Adams's heels to the chamber door. On the other side, he held out his hand.

Adams waved him off. "Not until we are outside the building."

Molineux sneered.

The committee walked down the stairs. Once outside, Adams handed the paper to Hancock.

The men navigated the icy streets back to the assembly while Hancock conveyed what was in the document.

"Gentlemen," Hancock read, "I am extremely sorry for—"

"No need to read the niceties," Molineux said.

Hancock cast a disparaging glance at Molineux then continued. "He says they have their orders from General Gage in New York which he cannot counter."

"No surprise they would use that tactic," Adams said.

"This is interesting," Hancock said. "Apparently the council desired *both* regiments be removed."

The men walked along in silence as they listened to the remainder of the message.

"Since the Twenty-ninth has been the problem," Hancock read, "they will be removed immediately while the Fourteenth remains in order to prevent future differences. He says they will stay until orders from New York have been received."

"Always awaiting orders from above," one of the committee members said.

"It keeps him out of trouble."

"So he believes," Molineux said.

The men rounded the corner at Dock Square.

One of the men in front held out his arms. "Whoa." Everyone halted and stared. The hundreds who now overflowed into the streets had joined the crowd the men had left in Faneuil Hall.

"A couple thousand?" one asked. "Plus those inside."

"Old South, here we come."

Adams nodded. "It will provide plenty of space. We do not want to turn anyone away. Their number will provide the clout we need when we return to Mr. Hutchinson with our reply."

Molineux was delighted to be one of the seven The Body chose to help push through their request. He stood behind Adams and Hancock at the end of the council chamber table and squinted at the glare from the afternoon sun filtering through the windows.

With everyone once again in place, the lieutenant governor began. "Am I to presume you have more to convey?"

Molineux sensed a slight edge to his voice. Maybe the lifelong battle with Adams had taken its toll. Molineux glanced at Adams who, although his hands shook from disease, remained stoic.

"The meeting from whence we have come," Adams said, "is now more than three thousand strong and rejects your answer. If you have the authority to remove one regiment, you have the power to remove both. They will be satisfied with nothing less, and nothing less will preserve the peace. Fail at your own peril to comply with this demand."

The Crown's representative did not move. "If violence is the consequence of the illegal assembly of people," Hutchinson said, "and an attempt should be made to drive out the king's troops, everyone abetting and advising in it will be guilty of high treason."

Adams placed his hand on the table and leaned forward. "Treasonous acts have indeed been committed," he said, "but not by those who come to you on behalf of their fellow citizens. Rather, they have been committed by those who seek to overthrow the constitution." Adams paused. "The troops are quartered here illegally, and the meeting demands they be removed."

Hutchinson stared back at him. "You may adjourn to the other room to await our decision."

Molineux snuffed out the light in his lantern as the committee entered the meetinghouse. He had never seen Adams this ecstatic. Hutchinson had at last succumbed to their demands. Even the lieutenant governor's continuous advice against the removal of the troops to the castle did not dampen the spirits at Old South. The entire council, which had been divided in the forenoon, now stood as one for the removal of both regiments—for the peace of the province. The two commanding officers had agreed. Dalrymple had given his word that he would begin preparations in the morning and the regiments would be removed without any unnecessary delay.

In the meantime, the people voted to provide a night watch over the town. They gratefully accepted the offer of those who had delivered the last message to the governor to now act as its committee of safety.

Only one task remained. Molineux was sure Adams would not let it pass by without a good amount of fanfare.

Two days later, Molineux joined the multitude who followed the hearses through King Street and down to the Liberty Tree. There must have been ten or twelve thousand—Adams would be pleased. The funeral for little Christopher Seider ten days before paled in comparison to that of the four victims. Shops closed and bells tolled. Late afternoon sunbeams created shadows from the grave markers in the Granary Burying Grounds where the four bodies were lowered into a common grave. Everyone expected a fifth to succumb to the clutches of the grim reaper within days and join his fallen comrades deep within earth's soil.

With Hutchinson's promise to remove the troops, this chapter of the town's history would be closed, and life could return to normal.

So went the townsfolk's prayer.

CHAPTER NINETEEN

Regroup
March 10–April 21, 1770

Molineux stood at the top of King Street in a borrowed blue-and-red uniform. The frustration of another battle with Hutchinson that morning had dissipated with the sight of four companies of the Twenty-ninth prepared to board awaiting ships. Hundreds of jubilant townsfolk lined the way to the wharf.

The merchant placed a hand on his cocked hat and raised his nose toward the late winter sun. Today he would make any court jester proud.

Drums rolled, and Molineux nodded at Lieutenant Colonel Dalrymple then, with arms flailing, pranced to the front of the troops' procession.

"Do you not think," one of the spectators said to Molineux with a smile, "the lobsters can find their own way back to the sea?"

Molineux lifted his hat. "Perhaps, but someone must protect them from the harm that might befall them along the way." He gave an energetic bow.

The crowd cheered.

Molineux performed a jig then tumbled several feet down the street.

They roared as he ran back for his hat then joined the commander and marched alongside him.

Molineux lingered until the last of the troops had boarded the ships. As he watched them sail toward the castle, months of tension eased. Soon the Fourteenth would join them, and a full measure of tranquility could return to the town.

Molineux stood in front of the King Street coffeehouse with Revere. The buttons of their coats glimmered beneath the waning moon. Winter's grip on the town would soon give way to spring's thaw.

"Peace at last," Molineux said.

"Thanks to you." Revere extended one hand in Molineux's direction.

"Ah, so many had a part."

"Yet your meeting with Dalrymple this morning provided the final shove he needed to remove the Fourteenth."

"It did no harm, did it?" Molineux turned to face the harbor. "Care to join me for a stroll to my store? I need to retrieve something before heading home."

"Happy to."

The men started toward Molineux's shop.

"With need for the night watch gone," Molineux said, "what will you do with—"

The sound of shattering glass came from behind them.

"What the . . ."

The men glanced at each other then turned and ran up the street. The noise came again—and again.

Molineux's breathing grew heavy. "What do you think . . ."

"I cannot imagine," Revere said, keeping pace with him.

Molineux held out his arm. Both men stopped. "Listen."

Revere tilted his head. "Singing?"

"Come join hand in hand," the man in the darkness mumbled. "Brave Amer-i-cans, aaaall."

Another crash of glass.

"And rouse your bold hearts to fair liberty's caaaall."

"Pretty awful, if you ask me." Molineux moved toward the racket with Revere by his side.

Molineux squinted. "Mr. Otis?"

The two men drew closer.

Otis swaggered toward them and sputtered. "All ages shall speak with amaze and applauuuuse, of the courage we'll shew in support of our laaaaws."

Revere took two steps back. "Phew, do you smell that?"

Molineux grabbed Otis's arm. "He is a bit tipsy."

"To say the least," Revere said.

"Grab the stone," Molineux said as he wrestled with Otis.

"Whoa." Revere reached for Otis's hand. "Don't let him tumble onto me."

The rock fell to the ground. "Mr. Otis, what are we going to do with you?"

"Apparently he has not received word his nemesis departed for England today."

"Mr. Robinson?"

Revere nodded. "With his new bride. The other commissioners scattered as well."

"I guess I was too busy with meetings to have heard," Molineux said. "Good news, nonetheless."

"With both the troops and commissioners gone," Revere said, "we haven't a care in the world."

Molineux pulled one of Otis's arms around his own neck. "I believe you have forgotten one thing, my friend—we still need to convict those responsible for shedding blood on King Street."

Molineux stood beside the fireplace in Hancock's parlor. The smoldering embers furnished just enough warmth for this first day of spring. Molineux surveyed the men who had gathered. Hancock,

Samuel Adams, and a few others had gained traction against the young attorney's arguments—the ones he used against his defending those accused of the bloodshed on King Street.

"If you accept," Adams said to Quincy, "someday people will rejoice over your willingness to be an advocate for these men."

"The reputation of our town is at stake," Hancock added. "If they do not receive a fair trial, we will forever be known as a lawless people."

"The murderers must be brought to justice," Molineux said.

Quincy glared at Molineux. "Until they are proven guilty in a court of law, they remain innocent men."

Adams shifted in his chair. "We desire nothing less than a trial based upon the facts. Now that it is upon us, we must act swiftly."

Quincy leaned forward in his chair. "Your tactics of intimidation against the court were less than respectable."

Molineux picked up the fire iron and waved it around with a grin. "They needed a bit of encouragement."

"Otherwise," Adams said, "they would have delayed the trials indefinitely."

"Lawyers for the prosecution are already in place," Molineux said. "I sent the narrative of the massacre, along with eighty affidavits, to Mr. Paine ten days ago."

"I hear my brother will also represent the Crown."

"'Tis true," Adams said. "We need someone to be his equal."

"You are already well versed in the facts," Hancock said.

Quincy stared out the window. "So is Mr. Adams's cousin."

Molineux glanced at Adams who lifted both of his trembling hands a few inches from his lap, palms down. Everyone remained silent.

Then Quincy spoke. "I will act in their defense on one condition. John Adams must assist me."

Samuel Adams lowered his hands. "I believe that can be arranged. He believes council should be the last thing an accused man should lack in a free country, especially for those whose lives are at stake."

Molineux scanned the room. Tension had vanished from every face.

Adams stood and walked to the exit. "You will not regret your decision, Mr. Quincy."

Quincy rose and joined him.

"You are free to leave," Adams said. "I will send word once my cousin's acceptance has been confirmed."

"As for the rest of you," Adams said, "roll up your sleeves. We have work to do."

Molineux wiped the perspiration from his brow then walked to the bow of his ship. Sweat in late March? This was young man's work. He leaned against the boat's edge and scanned the shoreline.

"Mr. Molineux?" The voice came from outside the boat.

The merchant sauntered to the entryway. "Ah, Mr. Dennie, come aboard."

"They told me I might find you here." Dennie glanced around. "What are you doing?"

"Preparing my ship in case it is called upon to race the Tories' lies across the high seas."

"Where are your laborers?"

"All taken ill," Molineux said. "I made them go home to rest. If they are needed, they must be in top form."

"I see," Dennie said. "But I thought the patriots' account of the killings had already been shipped to England."

"The short version." Molineux motioned for them to sit on the deck. "Several of us sent our version to the former governor."

"But—"

"Not Governor Bernard," Molineux said, "but an earlier one who tends to see things as we do. We asked him to help prevent unflattering reports from casting us in a bad light—at least until we could provide a more detailed account."

"When will your ship depart?" Dennie asked.

"I am not certain it will be the one," Molineux said, "but the town asked me and a couple others to find a suitable vessel to carry the packet of materials, once it is ready."

"Er," Dennie uttered as he unbuttoned his jacket. "I almost forgot." He pulled out a newspaper. "I came to ask your opinion of Mr. Revere's engraving."

"Help me up, lad, and we can examine it together."

Dennie stood then helped the merchant to his feet. Molineux directed Dennie to an area where they could spread out the paper.

Dennie pointed to the clock in the picture. "Did you notice the time?"

"Pre-curfew." Molineux gave a lopsided grin. "How convenient."

"And the soldiers' guns are pointed squarely at unarmed civilians."

"I was not present when the guns fired," Molineux said, "but this is how many are telling the story of what happened."

"The *Chronicle* referred to it as a most unfortunate affair," Dennie said. "Others are calling it the horrid massacre."

"The letter we sent to England"—Molineux motioned toward the horizon—"explained how the soldiers' intimidation prevented our complaints to local officials from being addressed."

"The town is pleased that the troops are now at the castle."

"I have reason to believe they will be sent out of the province entirely. And soon."

"Did you not hear of the sixty or more soldiers who returned to Wheelwright's Wharf a couple days ago—with their baggage?"

Molineux nodded. "We have alerted the selectmen to be prepared to call another town meeting if additional unwanted guests arrive."

Molineux continued to study the image. "The captain's sword is clearly raised with a command to fire." He moved his hand over a portion of the depiction. "And here, smoke is coming from the Custom House. How interesting."

"You may keep this copy, if you like," Dennie said.

"Thank you, Mr. Dennie," Molineux said. "I would like to study it further, and my copy is at home."

Molineux stared at the Custom House. Smoke. Smoke from guns. Dennie was speaking.

"Huh?"

"Any more news as to the trial of Mr. Richardson and his friend?" Dennie asked.

Molineux looked up. "They keep postponing the court date but claim it will be soon."

"Not soon enough for anyone I have spoken to."

"The whole town is pretty frustrated, but his day will come." Molineux returned his gaze to the paper. "His day will come."

Molineux leaned against the back wall of the courtroom. Weeks of delay had produced a pent-up desire for justice. A thousand people from all walks of life filled every seat. Light from lamps flickered against an array of expressions—somber, concerned, angry. And with the evening's eleventh hour approaching, tired.

Molineux's body ached. Three days of wrangling with those whose vessels had arrived from London with a spring shipment of saleable goods had taken its toll. Would the work to convince the importers of the error of their ways never end? He had been in and out of the courtroom all day dealing with them. Grateful to be back, Molineux shook his head and focused on the scene playing out in front of him.

Each side rested its case.

The judges scanned the crowd then faced the jury.

"Evidence has been presented," one of the justices said, "that would lead one to believe that Mr. Richardson was attacked in his own home. It is a man's right to practice self-defense—no matter the age of the attackers."

Molineux had arrived in time. Words of the judges to the jury would provide clues. Molineux's weariness forgotten, he stood straight, careful to catch every word.

The judge leaned forward in his chair then sent a piercing stare through Molineux. A few heads turned. "Those responsible for encouraging the actions that warranted the response of the defendants are the ones on whose hands the child's blood rests. They, not the prisoners, are guilty of murder."

Molineux did not dare glance around yet felt several looking in his direction.

The judge sat back and continued to speak to the jury. "You have heard from the defendant's own children as to the intensity of the attack upon their home."

The crowd hissed.

"Guilty," someone said.

The judge did not flinch. "Cases of self-defense allow for a verdict of manslaughter, not murder, for the defendants."

Another judge rose. "Let it be clear. Some of us doubt there is even enough evidence for manslaughter." He glanced at the audience. "And, yes, those who drew the tumultuous assemblies are guilty of the greater crime. Perhaps the newly erected gallows would be better suited for them."

"The ones whom we have tried today," another judge said to the jury, "are guilty of no more than justifiable homicide."

From the back of the room, one of the rabble jumped up. "Let me at 'em."

Unmoved, the judges concluded their charge to the jury. The twelve men stood and fell in behind the clerk. As they filed out of the courtroom, shouts went up from the crowd.

"Remember you are upon oath. Blood requires blood."

"Hang the dog."

"Murder—not manslaughter."

Several from the crowd moved toward the door. One held a hangman's noose.

The sheriff stood and raised his voice above the commotion. "No prisoner will be transported back to the gaol until it is safe to do so. You should return to your homes to await the verdict."

Molineux stepped aside for those who wanted to pass. The thought of the journey home drained him, but his weary bones pleaded for the comfort his bed would bring. If the jurymen's expressions had been a true indicator, they would debate through the night, without food, drink, or slumber until they had settled upon the verdict. A few hours of sleep would allow him the ability to return in time to hear the fate of the two men whose actions had haunted the town for weeks.

The next morning produced another full house. Molineux stood in the back of the courtroom surveying the spectators. Both fatigue and anticipation filled each face. A few nervously mumbled to those seated around them. Others sat in silence with hands folded in their laps.

Judges took their seats. They exuded confidence.

The jury filed in.

A stillness settled over the crowd.

The clerk rose and addressed the foreman of the jury. "How say you?"

"Wilmot, not guilty."

No one moved. It was Richardson's verdict they wanted to hear.

"Richardson," the foreman said, "guilty of murder."

The crowd burst into applause.

"Huzzah!"

Some jumped from their seats and did a jig in the aisle.

Another man stood and raised both hands. "For shame," he said. "For shame, gentlemen."

Several slinked back to their chairs, and a hush returned.

Molineux studied the faces of the judges. They had not considered murder as a possible verdict.

"We will deliberate," one of the judges said, "and set the sentence at the appropriate time."

Those in the crowd could hardly contain themselves.

"Meanwhile," the judge said, "the prisoner will remain committed to the gaol. As for this gathering, the verdict is in and this court is dismissed."

Murmurs of affirmation rippled throughout the room. Molineux dodged those who pressed toward the exit, then he slipped into an available seat. Every part of him drooped, inside and out. The question he had refused to ask finally surfaced. Had Richardson's bullet been intended for him?

A few minutes passed, then a small boy approached.

"Mr. Molineux?"

"Yes?"

The lad dropped a piece of paper into Molineux's lap. "Someone told me to give this to you."

Before the merchant could respond, the boy ran off.

Molineux stared at the page and forced his weary eyes to concentrate. A poem?

> *Young Seider's fate we ought to bemoan,*
> *And drop a tear on his unhappy tomb.*
> *He was the first that fell in a just cause,*
> *His murd'rer now must die by heaven's laws.*
>
> *Justice demands, and vengeance loud doth cry,*
> *Come forth, O Richardson, for thou must die.*
> *You acted then against the laws of God,*
> *And now must feel the scourges of his rod.*

No matter Richardson's intent, he would be the one to pay for the life that had been lost.

In the meantime, there was work to be done. While attorneys prepared for the massacre trial, Molineux would tend to other matters. His financial mess would be a good place to begin. He crinkled his nose. Why do today what can be put off until tomorrow? Today, he needed inspiration, and the newspaper could provide it. He put his shoulders back and started home. He had read it so many times he could quote it by heart, but he wanted to see it again with his own eyes. It would provide stimulus he needed for the work that lay ahead.

CHAPTER TWENTY

Highs and Lows
March–October 1770

The chairs and table in Molineux's parlor had been pushed aside. Two spinning wheels stood in their place, each with a lassie hard at work.

Elizabeth held up the yarn she had spun. "What do you think, Papa?"

"Very good," Molineux said. "Very good, indeed. Your teacher must be amazing."

Elizabeth giggled.

"What about my spinning?" Deborah Revere said.

From behind Molineux came the clicking of shoes on the hardwood floor. Maryann appeared in the parlor doorway. Molineux walked to Deborah's spinning wheel. "My, oh, my. You have both learned so quickly. Before long, the entire town will once again hum with the sound of spinning."

"Spring has a way of inspiring activity." Maryann walked over and put her arm around her husband. "Of course, the success is primarily due to the indefatigable pains of Mr. Molineux." She smiled at him. "Did I quote the newspaper correctly?"

He smiled. "If we can get spinning back to pre-winter levels, we will be doing just fine."

Elizabeth jumped up. "Oh, Papa, I have been practicing a play—taken from the *Boston News-Letter*. You and Momma must see it. Stay here and I will get John."

Molineux extended his hand toward the rocking chair. "Mrs. Molineux, will you join me for a performance I am sure we will not soon forget?"

Maryann took a seat, and Elizabeth returned with John.

"Please join us, Deborah," Molineux said.

The girl slid to the floor in front of her hosts.

Elizabeth stood erect and held out her hand to her brother. "I present to you the shopkeeper, Mr. Well Disposed. And his customer"—she put her hand to her chest—"a tailor."

John rolled his eyes. Molineux cleared his throat and cast a stern look in his direction.

"Da, da, da." Elizabeth singsongy voice confirmed her excitement. She parted the imaginary curtains then faced her brother.

"Pray, sir, have you any broadcloth to sell?" Elizabeth asked, doing her best to look the part.

"No," John said. "But I have very good duffels which I dare say will suit you."

"Duffels will not do. That type of cloth is too coarse for my needs. I want broadcloth imported from England. Can you inform me where I may get some?"

"As my duffels are of an extraordinary kind, you had better examine them before you decide." John held out an English broadcloth for inspection.

Elizabeth bit her lip to prevent a giggle from escaping. "Really, sir, I never saw such fine duffel cloth as this—so smooth and soft. I believe it would do if the price were not too high."

"It is very reasonable."

Elizabeth pulled out imaginary money and handed it to John then pranced to the window with the fabric. She held it up, gaped at it, then turned back to her audience. "What a scoundrel. A Pharisee. Cheating, with the devil as my witness."

Producing the most grownup voice she could muster, she continued. "I hope these times do not last long. If they do"—she waved her hand in dramatic fashion—"Lord, have mercy on my poor soul."

Elizabeth curtsied and signaled for John to take a bow. Then she grabbed her stomach and laughed as her admirers applauded.

"Bravo! Bravo!" Molineux sent a quick glance to John to let him know not to ruin her fun. "Now if we could simply lock up those who import these forbidden wares, it will open the door for us to provide the homespun variety." He picked up a cloth near one of the spinning wheels and placed it around Elizabeth's shoulders. "This will set you apart and make you one of the most patriotic ladies in town."

Elizabeth provided another curtsy then spread wide the homemade shawl.

John made a face. "May I leave, Pa?"

"You may go," Molineux said. "And, Deborah, shouldn't you be heading home soon?"

"Oh, Papa," Elizabeth said, "may I walk with her at least part of the way?"

"Run along, but be home in time for supper."

"And bundle up," Maryann said. "There is still a nip in the air." She turned back to her husband with a sad smile. "They grow up too fast."

Molineux began putting their parlor back in order.

Maryann walked to the window. "Are you expecting someone? A young boy is running up the hill."

"Perhaps he has word from the court about my petition." Molineux picked up the wingback chair. "If they would provide me with what I need to get the Manufactory House back up and running, the province would reap benefits beyond what it can imagine."

"Do you believe the counterpetition of the current occupants will hurt—" A rap at the front door interrupted her.

Molineux set down the chair. He strode to the hall and returned to the parlor a few minutes later. "We have our answer."

"Oh?" Maryann asked.

"It was indeed a messenger from the court," Molineux said. "They will allow us use of the factory." He bit his lip.

"Wonderful." Maryann's forehead wrinkled. "Are you not pleased?"

"They denied my request for funds," Molineux said.

Maryann walked to her husband and put her hand on his arm. "I am sorry. Perhaps you can—"

Molineux pulled away. "No, it was final."

"Maybe—"

"There is more," Molineux said. "Mr. Hutchinson will not let me oversee the project."

"What?"

"The House voted to turn it over to Samuel Adams and Mr. Hancock and one of the other representatives."

"But—"

"I know," Molineux said. "I have given it my life's blood—not to mention the toll it has taken on our pocketbook over the past year." He walked to the window. "Mr. Adams is busy trying to get the troops removed from the province and get the massacre trial underway. And Mr. Hancock has his hands full dealing with Mr. Mein's creditors."

"The program will die, won't it?"

Molineux nodded. "Unless someone is available to give it his all, it could. I had convinced myself Mr. Hutchinson's influence had diminished in recent weeks."

"I had heard the same."

It was as if someone had punched him in the gut. Did all of his hard work matter? Were the powers that be always going to get the upper hand? "If we cannot produce our own goods," Molineux said, "we will be forced to buy them from Britain and accept their power to control us. Not only that, the poor of our town will continue to suffer."

He took a deep breath. Even if the results were not to his liking, he would go on. Maybe the battle had been lost, but there was still a war to fight, and people were counting on him to lead the charge.

Molineux tilted his nose into the air. "But no matter." He marched to the middle of the room. "Word came a few days ago Parliament has repealed all but the tax on tea."

Maryann's brow wrinkled.

"Do you not see?" Molineux said. "There could be another tug of war among the merchants."

"What does Hutchinson's decision have to do with that?"

"Without the Manufactory House to think about, I will be available to encourage potential dissenters from going down the wrong path," Molineux said with a smirk. "I can hardly wait."

Beads of sweat formed on Molineux's brow beneath late July's sun. He kept pace with the three men in front of him who each carried a flag, grateful for the draft of air they produced. "Liberty and No Importation" one declared. Drums and a horn completed the trappings, and Dr. Young led the procession. The small army of merchants and their supporters hissed as they marched past the British Coffee House where the defectors were meeting.

A few hundred yards later, they ascended the stairs to Faneuil Hall. Once inside, Molineux followed Dr. Young and Samuel Adams to the front of the room. He shifted the clammy piece of paper from one hand to the other as he and the others took their seats.

Dr. Young made his way to the podium. His written words were often more powerful than those that came out of his mouth, but everyone waited expectantly for what he had to say. "My dear merchants," he began, "as you know, word has arrived that Parliament ended its session without repealing the duty on tea." He pointed to Molineux who waved the document.

Several in the crowd hissed. Others snarled.

"Earlier in the month," Dr. Young said, "you and your colleagues voted to continue nonimportation."

"Hurray!"

"Friends on the other side of the water have encouraged us to continue with both our boycott and the manufacturing of goods—as a final push to receive a total repeal. Some even believe if Parliament does not bend to our demands, independence from the Motherland would be in order."

Quietness settled over the assembly. Molineux dared not look around, but he jumped to his feet and joined Dr. Young on the stage.

Dr. Young took two steps back. Molineux gritted his teeth then addressed the crowd. "Those now meeting at the coffeehouse are rebels and usurpers."

"Huzzah!"

"We invited every Tom, Dick, and Harry to attend this meeting," Molineux said, "for we have nothing to hide." He grabbed the podium with both hands. "Our British allies tell us we still have friends in Parliament who argued on our behalf—for total repeal of the act."

Molineux held up the letter. "Once they realize the suffering we have endured under the guns of their soldiers, reason will find them—and they will grant us our request. But we must stand united in our efforts, lest it all be for naught."

Dr. Young stepped back toward the audience. "What do you say? Will you stay true to your agreement? Yea or nay?"

"Yea!"

"And what of Parliament's refusal to provide a total repeal?"

"Tear it up!"

"Is it worthy of our feeblest attention?" Dr. Young asked.

"Nay!"

"Shall I destroy it and throw it to the wind?"

"Yea!"

Molineux handed the document to Dr. Young who moved to an open area of the stage.

"Then so be it." Dr. Young lifted the paper and tore it into tiny pieces, which he threw into the air.

"Huzzah!"

Molineux hurried from the stage to join the celebration. He spent several minutes exchanging words of elation with his comrades. "Where is Samuel Adams?"

Someone pointed toward the exit where Adams stood.

Molineux walked over to him as he was bidding farewell to one of the merchants. Adams's mouth twitched.

"Is all well?" Molineux asked.

"Several of the younger merchants left the meeting. They desire to restore a general importation."

"But why?"

"Fear," Adams said. There was a weariness in his eyes.

Molineux took in a breath and tightened his lips. "They should be afraid of those in their own backyard who have the power to bring them harm, not those on the other side of the Big Pond."

"They do fear you. Nonetheless, the number of defectors among us is increasing," Adams said. "But we have bigger concerns."

Molineux lowered his head and squinted one eye.

"News has come from ports to our north and south," Adams said. "Rumors indicate merchants there have begun to break the agreement."

"What would you suggest?" Molineux asked.

"It is time to send a delegation to investigate. I will arrange for another meeting to make it official, but I would suggest you begin packing your bags."

"Right away, sir," Molineux said with a salute.

"Mr. Molineux, rumors are simply that," Adams said. "We do not know what to expect. I want you to be in charge of those we send. Be ready for anything."

Molineux grinned. "I will look forward to the adventure."

Molineux lay on the bed in an unfamiliar room. Moonbeams cast eerie shadows against the walls. Commotion from the tavern below had ceased. The four men who had joined him on the mission tossed and turned in the other beds scattered around the chamber. One snored.

Salem was different. Really different. His reputation had preceded him—agitator . . . a nuisance . . . raising disturbances wherever he went. Yet he had come despite personal threats of tar and feathers. He didn't care for the people of Salem either.

"What was that?" one of the men asked.

"Your imagination," Molineux said. "Go back to sleep."

Thud.

Molineux and the other man jumped up and raced to the door. Molineux arrived first and swung it open. Someone was exiting the entryway at the foot of the stairs.

Molineux ran down a handful of steps. "Come back, ye scoundrel." He slammed a fist against the wall. "Confound it," he said, then returned to the bedroom.

The other man stooped at the window. "No need to go after him. He is gone, and I see no one else." He turned to Molineux, who stood in the doorway. "What is that?"

"What?"

"Tacked to the door."

Molineux snarled and ripped the paper from its place.

The man walked over and stood beside Molineux. "I assume it is not a 'Thank you for coming' note."

Molineux shoved the document at him.

He tilted it toward the moonlight. "Ah, but it is addressed to you, General Molineux."

One of the other men stirred in his bed. "What is going on?"

"We had a visit from a midnight messenger." Molineux motioned for the other man to read the note.

"They advise us to depart or suffer the consequences—it says thirty or forty are standing by."

"To harm us?" the man in the bed asked.

"Read into it what you will." Molineux slumped back into his bed. "The courier was alone. Everyone else is at home in bed."

The man holding the note nodded. "Where we should be."

"The note does not reflect the sentiment we received earlier today," Molineux said. "We will check with the merchants again tomorrow, return to Boston with our report, then head south to Rhode Island."

The man set the paper on the dresser and walked back to his bed.

"We must keep the coalition together," Molineux said, "or many years of effort will have been wasted."

The snoring returned. Molineux fell back on his bed and put his hands over his ears. "Good night, gentlemen," he said, and rolled over.

Molineux's shoulders drooped. He barely noticed the autumn colors outside the coffeehouse window.

Adams sat across the table. "You have returned all the stored goods to their owners?"

Molineux nodded.

"It has been a tough year, Mr. Molineux, but we have also had a number of successes," Adams said.

"Such as?"

"Your neighbor shipped fifteen thousand pounds' worth of goods back to England for us."

Molineux managed a faint smile. "Must you go back so far in order to find good?" He extended both hands and shrugged.

"The Twenty-ninth went to Providence, and the *Chronicle* is no more."

"Both good, I will agree."

"You helped run two Scots out of town without having to use tar and feathers."

"Quite a ruckus, wasn't it? They learned a lesson from the one who did not get away." Molineux half smiled. "My threats alone were enough to kill one of them. Maybe I should have been more receptive to his pleas to be restored to our good graces."

"It is for good reason Mr. Rowe refers to you as the leader in dirty matters," Adams said.

"Ah, yes, Mr. Rowe," Molineux said. "Another of our defectors."

Adams sat back in his chair. "I admit, it has been a tough year and you are fatigued."

"Your year has also been less than magnificent—losing many from the council who are of like mind. Then Hutchinson not allowing Mr. Hancock to serve as speaker. And losing Mr. Otis to—well, you know. His body is still with us, but his mind is less predictable."

Adams's eyes welled up with tears. "We have lost a true patriot, yet others are attempting to fill the void. I am happy your other neighbor, Mr. Bowdoin, joined the council. And my cousin now sits beside me in the House in Mr. Otis's stead." Adams smiled. "And I was pleased the two houses chose to observe a day of solemn prayer and humiliation."

"But you lost your reverend," Molineux said.

"Whitefield?"

Molineux nodded.

"A great loss indeed," Adams said. "We were blessed to have him dine with us under the Liberty Tree. Who would have imagined he would be in glory a few weeks later?"

"The whole town remembers how he helped us after the great fire."

Adams sat up straight. "Back to you, Mr. Molineux. Your attempt at Salem was valiant."

Molineux chuckled. "I almost left town with the taste of feathers in my mouth." He stared at the table for a few moments then back at Adams. "If I decide to stay on board, where do we go from here?"

Adams looked down then turned his gaze to Molineux. "We need to get back to the heart of the matter."

"If sacrificing my business and time with my family isn't giving you, the town, and all the colonies my heart, I do not know what is."

"Mr. Molineux, you have sacrificed much, and I feel sure Mr. Hutchinson's belief that you are still smuggling does not help." Adams paused. "You are not still smuggling tea from Holland, are you?"

"Would it matter either way?"

Adams placed both hands on the table. "The nonimportation agreement continued beyond my expectation."

Molineux shot him a quizzical look.

"It took a year for the propaganda left behind by Mr. Mein to take full effect. Most of the merchants stayed united largely due to your efforts."

Molineux provided another half-smile.

"You have been amazing. Rallying the laborers, artisans, and any others who care to come along. Even your enemies recognize you as the commander of our troops—great William their commander."

"The song has made the rounds," Molineux gave a feeble attempt to tap out the jingle on the table. "And do not forget, I am also the bully in disguise and magazine of lies."

"The chorus also mentions your more positive attributes," Adams said. "You are a truly patriotic man."

"Who bellows day and night," Molineux chanted.

"Our troops follow your bellows—they love you for it."

The thought delighted Molineux's soul.

Adams shut his eyes. "We must not forget about the *why* of what we are doing."

"The why?"

Adams opened his eyes and leaned in. "You want to be the master of your own destiny, do you not?"

Molineux's tired eyes became serious.

"Our forefathers came to this great land to shake off the grip of tyranny. We must not let them make slaves of us once again. We have rights—unalienable rights that must not be trampled upon. Stay the course, Mr. Molineux, and unborn millions will rise up and call you blessed."

CHAPTER TWENTY-ONE

The Massacre Trials
Late October—December 5, 1770

Molineux glared at the prisoner through the bars of the jail cell. He thumped the British newspaper lying in his lap. "So you do not deny penning your account of the massacre for publication in England?"

Captain Preston sat with hands folded in front of him. "The foundation of the story is mine, but it must have been altered after it left my sight in order to create the version you have before you."

Molineux jumped up and slammed the paper on the back of the chair.

Preston flinched. "I understand the *Gazette* has misrepresented my intentions by printing the revised piece beside my earlier letter of thanks to the town."

Molineux jerked. "And what exactly were your intentions in that message?"

The captain blinked. "For truth and justice to prevail in light of the unhappy affair."

"An unhappy affair indeed," Molineux said.

"I hear the paper declared I am guilty unless I am able to prove otherwise."

"The facts speak for themselves." Molineux began to pace back and forth. "You should know several of us have written to Dr. Franklin in London to convey the true state of our town."

Preston rose and moved toward the bars separating them. "My dear sir, you are a resident here and must know of the good reputation I carried with me until that cursed night. Should a man not be given the opportunity to present his case before he is judged?"

Molineux's eyes narrowed. "They say Mr. Hutchinson will seek your pardon from the king if a jury convicts you. Is that proper justice?"

"I desire for the truth to be told," the captain said, "and will leave the outcome to the hands of the Almighty God."

Molineux stared at the prisoner for a moment. "If the verdict is less than satisfactory, the Almighty may need to contend with a throng of unruly citizens. We want justice too—something which seems to have departed our shores the day your soldiers arrived. We will keep that in mind as we push forward for your trial. Your day will come, and rest assured, justice will be served."

Autumn leaves crinkled beneath Molineux's feet outside the courthouse on Queen Street. The justices had used every possible delay tactic, but tempers had quieted, and the captain's case had finally gone to trial. Molineux glanced at the door to the building for the hundredth time. Where was Adams with an update?

Several men stood nearby, chatting to pass the time.

"Do you believe Mr. Hutchinson's action will affect the ruling?" one of them asked.

Another replied. "What, his allowing someone else to serve as chief justice for this case?"

Molineux heaved another sigh. What was taking so long? The case had dragged on for nearly a week—longer than any previous criminal case—but what did it mean? At last report the jury—

A screech from a second-story window turned everyone's eyes toward it.

"Not guilty," the man shouted down to them. "The jury found the captain not guilty."

Some cheered while others looked astonished. Molineux returned his gaze to the door. A few dozen military men filed out—then Samuel Adams.

Molineux ran to him. "What happened?"

"My cousin and Mr. Quincy were better prepared than the prosecution," Adams said.

"But all those depositions..."

"The ones for which we allowed no cross-examination?" Adams said.

"Those would be the ones."

"They crumbled under scrutiny." Adams reached out his palsied hand. "The verdict is not necessarily a bad thing. John placed our town in the best light, and a conviction of the captain might have made us appear as savages."

"Now what?"

A rustle rippled through the crowd. Molineux and Adams pivoted to see Preston being escorted to a waiting carriage.

"There is little doubt," Adams said, "he will hide out at the castle until arrangements can be made to transport him to England. As for your question, we will redouble our efforts and be better prepared for the soldiers' trial."

"How soon?"

"A few weeks," Adams said. "Ministers have reminded their congregations blood requires blood. Someone must pay for the lives which were lost." Adams focused on the ground for a moment then looked up at Molineux. "If you can remain calm, I would like you to join me inside when the court reconvenes."

"I will be ready," Molineux said.

At eight o'clock on the Monday morning after Thanksgiving, Molineux glanced around the packed courtroom. Samuel Adams sat beside him with quill and paper poised for action.

Four justices, in their full-bottomed wigs and scarlet robes, filed in and took their seats at the long bench in front of the hearth. The fire crackled behind them. Once again, no Hutchinson.

The attorneys sat at tables several feet in front of the red robes. Josiah Quincy had demonstrated his lesser experience in the previous trial, but John Adams appeared wiser than his thirty-five years. A third man who had assisted with the case completed the trio. At the table representing the Crown sat Josiah's brother Samuel Quincy and Robert Treat Paine.

A rustle came from one of the doors, and everyone turned. The eight soldiers, donning their bright red coats, marched until they stood facing the four justices.

The clerk stood and read the indictment: guilty of the murder of five civilians. Each man answered with "Not guilty."

"God send you a good deliverance," the clerk said, then all took their seats.

The attorneys selected twelve men to form the jury. Molineux and Samuel Adams exchanged knowing looks—not one juryman was from Boston.

Then a parade of witnesses took to the stand. Dozens of them. Day after day. After day.

As testimonies droned on, Molineux kept track of the key points.

Many witnesses testified about the same two soldiers now before them—saying they had fired into the crowd on the fifth of March. The same men had also participated in the scuffle at the ropewalk in early March.

On Thursday, the Crown rested its case, and the defense took over.

Was the firing justified?

Should blame rest at the feet of the town for provoking it?

Throw out preconceived ideas, the attorneys argued. Instead, focus on the facts.

Then, late Saturday afternoon, the defense called their last witness, a doctor who had tended to the man who had held onto life for several days after receiving wounds during the massacre.

"He heard many voices cry out to kill them," the doctor said from the stand.

"Did you ask him whether he believed it was in self-defense?" the attorney asked.

"He believed they fired to defend themselves," the doctor said, "and he did not blame whoever shot him."

Josiah Quincy glanced at the jury then back to the witness. "Was he aware of his imminent death?"

"He was told of it."

Quincy returned his gaze to the jury. "It has been said no man who is about to meet his Maker will do so with a lie upon his lips." Quincy faced the judges. "We rest, Your Honors."

The court adjourned, and Molineux let out a sigh. "Six long days," he said to Samuel Adams. "My constitution has been taxed in every way imaginable."

"I agree—we sat for way too long," Adams said. "Tomorrow we must kneel."

Molineux stood and stretched.

"The case will wrap up soon," Adams said. "Unfortunately, today ended on the wrong note." Adams stood, and the men made their way to the door. "Find some refreshment in the Sabbath, and I will see you back here next week."

Monday and Tuesday found Molineux and Adams in the courtroom listening to each side's closing arguments.

Josiah Quincy paced before the jury. "Commotions in various parts of town that night"—Molineux perked up—"represented indiscreet conduct on the part of the town's inhabitants."

Molineux held his breath and leaned forward. The defense had protected the identity of Joyce Junior. Would their restraint hold? Samuel Adams placed his trembling hand on Molineux's arm. Quincy moved on to other aspects of the defense, and Molineux slumped back into his chair.

Quincy returned to his seat, and John Adams took to the floor and explained the various types of homicide.

"Manslaughter," John said, "is killing a man on a sudden provocation. The soldiers were provoked, but only by a small portion of the town's population."

Molineux caught a glimpse of Samuel Adams's faint smile as he observed his cousin's skillful presentation. Defending the soldiers, while protecting Boston's reputation, was no easy task.

"Facts are stubborn things," John said, "and whatever may be our wish, our inclination, or the dictates of our passions, they cannot alter the state of the evidence." He took two steps closer to the jury. "To your candor and justice, I submit the prisoners and their cause." He bowed his head toward the judges and returned to his seat.

Mr. Paine rose to provide closing arguments for the Crown. Tuesday faded into Wednesday morning, and the Crown concluded.

The clock struck ten. Molineux shifted in his seat and scanned the crowd. Weary faces reflected his own sentiments, but they paled in comparison to Mr. Paine's slight cough and bags under his eyes.

One by one, the judges stood and gave their charge to the jury.

Then Justice Peter Oliver rose and peered out over the crowd before shifting his attention to the jury. "During this trial we have heard testimony that, on the night in question, a tall man with a red cloak and white wig talked to possibly two hundred people in Dock Square."

Molineux sat motionless, but his mind was a whirl.

"I cannot but make this observation," Oliver said. "Whoever he was, if the huzzahing for the main guard and attack on the soldiers was the consequence of his speech to the people, that man is guilty in the sight of God of the murder of the five people mentioned in the indictment." The judge pivoted back to the people. "And although he may never be brought to a court of justice here, yet, unless he speedily flies to the city of refuge, the Supreme Avenger of innocent blood will surely overtake him."

Oliver sat down, and Molineux stared straight ahead while the judges concluded their comments and sent the jury to deliberate.

Samuel Adams pulled out his watch and tilted it toward Molineux. One thirty.

An hour passed. Then two.

At four o'clock, the jury returned to the courtroom.

The foreman stood and read the names of six of the soldiers. "Not guilty," he said.

The courtroom waited. What of the other two—those who had been at the ropewalk?

He read their names then pronounced the verdict. "Not guilty of murder, but guilty of manslaughter."

The remaining formalities passed before Molineux in a blur. As people rose to leave, Molineux felt a nudge.

Samuel Adams gestured toward his cousin who sat lifeless at the counsel table. "No greater weight has ever been carried," he said, "nor greater burden lifted from any other man in this country."

"True," Molineux said.

"His work is done for now," Adams said. "But we have much to do." He lifted the notes he had taken during the trial. "I will get with Edes and Gill, and I believe you have your work cut out for you elsewhere."

"The commissioners?" Molineux asked.

Adams nodded. "They also need to stand trial—wouldn't you agree?"

Molineux smirked. "I believe that can be arranged."

CHAPTER TWENTY-TWO

The Rise and Fall of Power
January–December 1771

Hutchinson surveyed the scene inside the concert hall. Music and dancing—what a delightful way to spend the queen's birthday. Light from candles sparkled against the ladies' jewelry and ball gowns, adding to the general merriment of the crowd. Provincial and military leaders mingled with likeminded guests.

"Governor Hutchinson?"

Hutchinson turned to see Mr. Rowe. "Lieutenant Governor, if you please," he said with a smile.

"I beg your pardon, sir," Rowe said. "You have served so long in Governor Bernard's stead, it only seemed natural—"

"No harm done." Hutchinson returned his gaze to the celebration. "Does this not warm your soul?"

"To be sure. It is a far cry from all we experienced last year," Rowe said.

"I am hopeful that the way the year ended," Hutchinson said, "is a sign of things to come."

"The way the year ended, sir? You refer to the trial of the commissioners?"

Hutchinson nodded. "It was mayhem."

"I believe the attorney referred to it as a windmill adventure."

Hutchinson smiled. "A weak case from the beginning—and he knew it."

"Mr. Molineux's fingerprints were all over it," Rowe said.

The lieutenant governor bristled at the mention of the name.

"He pressed hard for the trial," Rowe said. "His son was in the balcony with one of the witnesses who claimed shots came from the Custom House on that dreadful night."

"Do you believe Mr. Molineux influenced the French boy's testimony?" Hutchinson asked.

"Something, or someone, must have pressured him to change it," Rowe said. "Mr. Molineux certainly has the gift of persuasion."

"He does indeed."

"I am grateful the boy eventually admitted to his lies."

"And sits in the gaol to await his just punishment," Hutchinson said.

"You must be relieved the jury found the commissioners innocent of any involvement."

"The charges should not have been brought against them in the first place," Hutchinson said. "An acquittal without the jury even going from their seats to deliberate testifies to the absurdity of the entire sham."

"Yet, if I may be so bold as to mention it," Rowe said, "rumors continue to circulate as to the evidence. Some say the angle of the bullets prove shots came from the upper windows of the Custom House rather than from the street." Rowe took a glass of punch from a passing tray.

"The hearsay will die, and things will return to a new normal." A faint smile spread across Hutchinson's face at the thought of the letter he had sent to London. Power must be removed from the people, he had suggested, but in a way that they would not detect the criminality of it. After all, he had explained, the change was designed to break up their union and prevent a greater mischief.

"Would you agree?" Rowe said.

Hutchinson blinked. "With what?"

"Peace, harmony, and friendship will once again be established in Boston." Rowe took a sip of his punch.

"I would," Hutchinson said. "My desire is that 1770 will forever be forgotten."

Rowe grimaced and wiped his mouth. "I suggest we toast to it, but not with this punch. It is awful. If you will excuse me, Governor—er, Lieutenant Governor, I will see if anything better can be found."

Hutchinson waved him off and returned to his own concerns. Nearly a year had passed since he hinted to London of his wish to be replaced. With the changing of the tide, perhaps it would not be needed—or even desired.

Rowe returned with two glasses and handed one to Hutchinson. "I believe you will find this better suited for our tastes."

"May I ask your opinion on a matter, Mr. Rowe?" Hutchinson said.

"Certainly."

"What are your thoughts regarding the newspapers' attacks on my family?"

"They are not pleased that so many in your family hold high positions of power." Rowe shifted his weight. "Yet censorship may concern them more. In countries where a man cannot call his tongue his own—and I merely quote what others have said—can anyone expect him to lay claim to any of his other possessions?"

"But no one should be permitted to print lies this freely," Hutchinson said.

Rowe shrugged. "If your council's lawsuit succeeds, your wish may come true."

"Do you see the irony?" Hutchinson asked. "Those who for several years have advocated the liberty of the press are the very ones who saw to the demise of the *Chronicle*."

"Point well taken," Rowe said.

The orchestra commenced a lively tune, and the two men listened as they finished their punch. Hutchinson stared at his empty glass. The commissioners and their wives often lingered too long at the taverns.

Oh that—rather than his good friends—it were the likes of Adams, Otis, Molineux, and a few dozen others who suffered the ill effects that came from those visits. And if the radicals would simply let bygones be bygones, peace would return to his beloved town.

Molineux walked beside Samuel Adams, keeping a watchful eye in case he needed an arm to lean on amid the crowd. The near full moon and carefully placed lanterns led the way to Revere's North End home.

Molineux tugged at his own jacket to ward off the late winter chill. "Despite Mr. Otis's lack of ability to assist, you have done well to keep the press supplied these last few months. And you have skillfully protected the identity of Joyce Junior."

"Some things we must keep secret. Others we must keep alive in the minds of the people, such as Britain's atrocities, until they have addressed our complaints." Adams motioned he needed to rest. "Never has there been a time when the politics of America were in a more dangerous state."

"To set aside this day for reflection was brilliant," Molineux said.

"Had it not been for the atrocities of the fifth of March," Adams said, "it would have been Christopher's death we mourned."

Molineux remained silent, and the two resumed their walk.

"Dr. Young provided an excellent oration to a full house," Adams said. "And I felt you would appreciate the venue."

"Yes," Molineux said, "but why the Manufactory House?"

"Its tie to the regulars upon their arrival," Adams said, "made it a logical place for our first commemoration." He stopped, and Molineux followed his eyes to the small obelisk that stood in front of them.

"My vision fails me in this light," Adams said, "but is that writing on the pedestal?"

Molineux grabbed a nearby lantern then knelt. "It is the names of the massacre victims." He rubbed his fingers into the inscription. "And there is more."

"What does it say?"

"Seider's pale ghost, fresh-bleeding stands," Molineux read, "and vengeance for his death demands."

Adams took two steps toward another object that sat in front of the monument. "This bust must be of the boy." Then Adams pointed upward. "Mr. Revere has outdone himself."

Molineux pushed up with a grunt, wiped himself off, and scanned over to the patriot's two-story home. "Oh, my. He has." Suddenly his voice seemed too loud. Hundreds, perhaps thousands, stood in solemn silence outside the engraver's home gazing up at his masterful artwork.

The glow from the home's three upper windows revealed outlines for the artist's story. In the first window, Christopher Seider's ghost pressed a finger into his bleeding wound. Alongside him stood his weeping friends. The middle window displayed the King Street massacre with soldiers firing into the crowd, the dead lying on the ground, and the wounded falling around them with blood running from their wounds. In the last window, a woman representing America sat on a stump with staff in hand and the cap of liberty on her head. She pointed to the tragedy as a grenadier lay beneath her foot.

Time slipped by, and at nine o'clock Revere removed the exhibit, church bells tolled, and the townsfolk headed home.

"Mr. Molineux." Adams's tone indicated he needed the merchant's undivided attention. "There are a few things you should know— rumors I have heard, which may soon come to fruition."

The two men found a spot among the crowd where others were engrossed in their own conversations, then Adams began. "Word came that London has appointed Mr. Hutchinson as our new governor."

Molineux stopped to let it sink in.

"But that is not the worst of it," Adams said. "We will no longer pay the governor's salary directly. Instead, London will pay him from the duties they collect from us. The duties on tea."

"What? Should I assume his brother-in-law will slip into Hutchinson's current role?"

"Yes. Neither are good." They resumed their walk, and Adams continued. "The financial relief it brings is little consolation for those of us who prefer unrestrained freedom, but I am fearful not everyone will see it as we do."

"I assume you will fight against it in the papers," Molineux said.

"Of course," Adams said.

They walked in silence for a few moments. Adams took a deep breath. "I also hear other whispers."

Molineux tilted his head.

"Some believe our new governor will ask London to make it treasonous for anyone to declare acts of Parliament as invalid."

"Which we—you, me, and a handful of others—have all done."

Adams turned to Molineux as if expecting more.

Molineux's jaw tightened. "And will continue to do—so help me God."

"You do know the penalty it carries," Adams said.

Molineux nodded. "Death."

Four . . . five . . . six. The church bell tolled.

Molineux paused in the parlor doorway. Consoling was not his area of expertise. He took a deep breath then strode over, put his hand on his wife's shoulder, and gave it a gentle squeeze. Maryann sat motionless in the rocking chair, staring at the fireplace. The smoldering wood provided ample heat for the late March day.

"Your mother was a strong soul," Molineux said. "Being married to a merchant is not easy."

Maryann looked up at him and offered a faint smile. The gleam in her eyes and nod of her head assured him she had caught the double meaning.

"I was always happy to see Papa come home from a long journey," Maryann said. "Now, after all these years, mother's journey has taken her to him. I'm glad your extended travels are behind us."

"Me too," Molineux said. "As a young man, I thought little about how those trips would have affected you and the children. But now I realize how hard they must have been for all of you."

Maryann began to rock. Over the years, Molineux had learned there was a time for everything. Even silence. A lone tear trickled down Maryann's cheek.

After what seemed like an eternity, Molineux spoke. "I will prepare the carriage."

Maryann nodded.

The path they would take played out in Molineux's mind. He would avoid the route by the pillory, for the French boy would be meeting his punishment for perjury there today. He pushed other cares from his mind. Today he would give his attention to his wife and family.

Sufficient unto the day is the evil thereof.

Indeed.

Attendance had waned at the so-called merchant meetings. A couple dozen sat around the tables at the British Coffee House. Molineux brought a second cup of the black liquid to his mouth. Putting something hot into his body during the summer months never made sense to him, but maybe it would help unmuddle his mind. There had been too many sleepless nights of late.

The town had pressed him to pay back the loan.

A local paper had taken a veiled swipe at his integrity, claiming money he had collected for Seider's monument was being mishandled.

And, most disturbing of all, Anne had eloped. Eloped with Benjamin Hallowell's son. A Tory.

"Mr. Molineux?"

He stirred at the mention of his name.

"Do you agree we should hold the annual feast tomorrow as usual, Mr. Molineux?" Samuel Adams asked.

Molineux set down his cup. "Of course," he said, unsure if anyone knew his attention had been elsewhere. "We must keep memories alive."

"My sentiments exactly," Dr. Warren said.

"No," a red-faced merchant said. "It is high time you radicals admit your fight is over and get back to life as we once knew it."

"Minus the smuggling of Dutch tea," another merchant said. He glared at a few of them who sat around the tables. "We need a level playing field or we will never reunite."

"What are you implying?" Molineux asked.

The man leaned onto the table in front of him and squinted. "I think you know."

"If the seizures continue," Molineux said, "you will not need to worry about it, will you?"

"Gentlemen," John Adams said. "Back to the question at hand. I returned to Boston from my peaceful farm in anticipation of tomorrow's celebration, not for this bickering."

"And how do you expect to pay for the festivities," one of the merchants asked with a smirk, "if there is disunity? We all know Mr. Hancock has cut off his funds to the cause."

Molineux glanced at Samuel Adams.

"Mr. Hancock's health has been poor," someone said. "And his funds are going to support his brother's new business."

"Simply an excuse," another said. "I hear he intends to back out of all public affairs soon."

Samuel Adams stood and placed his fingertips on the table. All eyes shifted to him. "We will find a way to pay for tomorrow's feast," he said. "As for this meeting, I believe our years at the British Coffee House have come to an end."

Several exchanged questioning looks.

"Those who continue to believe in our cause," Adams said, "may journey with me to the Bunch of Grapes' more Whig-friendly atmosphere."

Silence. Then John stood and walked over to his cousin. Josiah Quincy, Dr. Warren, and a few others followed suit. Molineux joined them. Then, as if a migrating flock of geese, the group moved toward the exit.

Change was in the air, and each man had chosen the pack with which he would associate. Molineux already felt the world caving in— and now this. He was unsure how much more he could bear.

A few friends and colleagues had gathered at the smoke-filled coffeehouse for the evening meal. Molineux was relieved to see Otis's continued bouts with insanity had not kept him away.

Molineux set down his fork. "That a man who has given so much should be treated as I am is intolerable."

Otis, with a twinkle in his eye, rose from the table. "Come, come, Will, quit this subject, and let us enjoy ourselves. I also have a list of grievances. Will you hear it?"

"Aye! Aye!" John Adams said, in an apparent attempt to lighten the mood. "Let us hear your list."

"I have lost a hundred friends," Otis said, "among whom were men of first rank, fortune, and power. At what price will you estimate them?"

"You are better off without them," Molineux said, starting to play into Otis's hands.

A hearty laugh went up from the group.

"To add to my discomfort," Otis said, "you know I love pleasure, but I have renounced all amusement for the better part of ten years."

"But you have made politics your amusement," Molineux said.

More laughter.

Otis straightened to full stature and placed both hands on his waist. "In the next place, I have ruined as fine health and as good a constitution of body as nature ever gave to man." Then Otis bent his head toward Molineux. "Look upon this head. My friends think I have a monstrous crack in my skull."

Molineux winced. "This is melancholy indeed, and there is nothing to be said on that point."

"Now, Willy," Otis said with a smile, "my advice to you is say no more about your grievances. You and I had better put up our accounts of profits and loss in our pockets and then remain quiet, lest the world should laugh at us."

Molineux stood and raised his glass. "Then I propose a toast to all the pleasant things in life, especially to my good friend Mr. Otis, who has done more for us than we could ever repay."

"Hear! Hear!" Those sitting around the table clinked their glasses together and spent the remainder of the evening in joyous celebration. Molineux resolved to enjoy the occasion with his friend—for who knew how many more times they would have together.

Molineux stoked the fire in his shop and returned to his chair. Junior flung part of the fishing net over his pa's lap. Molineux picked up his knife and cut away at the damaged portion while his son did the same.

"With numerous years of discord between them," Molineux said, "I am not surprised Mr. Hutchinson would be the one to declare Mr. Otis a lunatic."

Junior looked up from his work. "You should have seen him, Pa. He was in rare form, even for Mr. Otis."

"What happened?"

"Well, I was testifying," Junior said, "and a crashing noise came from one of the courtroom doors."

"Mr. Otis?"

Junior nodded. "I'm not sure if he was intoxicated, but he kind of stumbled to the front of the room."

"What did John Adams do?"

"He did the same thing as the judge—stared at Mr. Otis with wide eyes and an open jaw."

Molineux chuckled. "Sad but funny."

"Mr. Otis started to wax eloquent—or tried to." Junior grabbed the ball of fresh cord and cut off the pieces they would need to repair the net.

"He loves the classics, doesn't he?"

Junior smiled as he threaded the oversized needle. "Maybe all the learning is what made him crazy."

"Nice try, but I don't think so."

"Anyway, he went on about some man who dressed up like a woman in order to gain access to Caesar's wife."

"Clodius of Rome?" Molineux asked.

"I think so." Junior adjusted the netting and wove the needle through it. "Since the trial I was part of was about a boy who dressed up like a girl, I guess Mr. Otis's brain made a connection."

"Making each a pretty strange episode," Molineux said.

"Sure did," Junior said.

"Then what happened?"

"Someone must have sent word to Mr. Hutchinson as to what was going on," Junior said. "In no time, a couple of men showed up and bound Mr. Otis hand and foot and carried him off."

"Mr. Otis was on a committee several years back," Molineux said. "Its purpose was to raise funds for a bedlam."

"A bedlam?"

"A place for people who have lost their minds," Molineux said. "Mr. Hancock's surrogate father left money for the cause, but it never materialized." Molineux lifted the net from his lap and stood. "I believe Uncle Michael will be pleased."

"The way I smell," Junior said, "one would think I am the fisherman. I hope he appreciates all our hard work."

Molineux grinned. "He will. He simply did not have time to deal with repairs right now."

"When will he return from Nova Scotia?"

"Soon," Molineux said. "He knows the path well." Molineux's mind reviewed the three decades since they had settled in Boston.

"Are you all right, Pa?"

"Uh?" Molineux said.

"You kind of faded out."

"I was thinking." Molineux stared into the fire. "Mr. Otis led us for nearly a decade. It started with a trial in which I was one of the plaintiffs and has ended with one in which you were a witness." He faced Junior. "It seems significant."

"Mr. Otis's brother says it is a great loss to both his family and to the world."

"Indeed it is," Molineux said. "And Mr. Otis is as good as his word."

"His word?" Junior asked.

"Years ago, Mr. Otis said he would set the province in a flame and perish in the attempt." Molineux put his hand on his son's shoulder. "And he has done just that."

"We must carry on where he has left off," Junior said.

"If we don't," Molineux said, "I am not sure who will. Even Mr. Hancock continues to grow cold to the cause."

CHAPTER TWENTY-THREE

Reignite the Fire
Summer 1772–May 26, 1773

*M*olineux pounded on the door of Hancock's home. Sweat from the summer's heat burned his eyes. The door swung open, and the uninvited merchant hurried past the servant.

Molineux spun around. "Where is he? Where is Mr. Hancock?"

"In the parlor," the servant said, nodding toward it.

Molineux rushed toward it and began speaking before he entered the room. "Mr. Hancock, I need a word with you." He stepped into the parlor to find Hancock wide-eyed and with both hands extended toward the door.

"Mr. Molineux," Hancock said. "Take it easy, or you will destroy a masterpiece."

Molineux stopped in his tracks. John Singleton Copley stood at a canvas with paintbrush raised. Miss Quincy, covered in pink and lace, sat poised at a table, albeit with a pained expression from the sudden interruption.

"I beg your pardon, Miss Quincy," Molineux said. "I did not know—"

She offered a cordial smile.

"And Mr. Copley," Molineux said, "I did not realize you had returned from New York."

"Well, he has," Hancock said. "Perhaps—"

Molineux marched over to Hancock and put both hands on his own waist. "Why will you selectmen not honor the town's request for a meeting?"

Hancock took a deep breath. "The people requested a meeting to discuss a rumor that has no foundation in reality."

"You do not believe the Fourteenth intends to return to town?" Molineux asked.

Copley cleared his throat and cast a pleading look in Hancock's direction.

Hancock turned to Molineux. "Shall we take this matter into the hall?"

Once outside the parlor, Hancock spoke. "If I did not know better, Mr. Molineux, I would think you were twenty years my junior and not the other way around."

Molineux grinned.

"As you know," Hancock said, "Mr. Copley prefers to stay out of matters of controversy, especially if they are political in nature."

"The selectmen need to call a meeting so we can discuss the soldiers."

Hancock drew his index finger to his lips.

Molineux gritted his teeth and lowered his voice. "What are you going to do about the regulars?"

"I have been busy with unrelated matters the past few days, but the other selectmen made inquiries and assured me the Fourteenth have no intention of leaving the castle to come here."

Molineux huffed. "If the authorities can sneak Mr. Richardson out of town, they could also have secretive plans regarding the soldiers. How can we know you are not simply covering for them?"

Hancock's face softened. "Let me show you something—you may have missed it before." He led Molineux back into the parlor then pointed to one of the walls.

Two portraits, one of Hancock and the other of Samuel Adams, hung there. Molineux blinked at the pictures then at Hancock. "Those are recent."

"Mr. Adams and I have worked out our differences. And, as you would say, I am back in the fold."

Words refused to escape from Molineux's mouth. "When—"

"Recently."

"But the recipe—"

Hancock smiled. "The recipe for a modern patriot the newspaper printed awhile back?"

"That's the one."

"I was not on the list of ingredients, was I?"

The merchant shook his head.

"I suppose my inconsistencies may have ruined an otherwise delectable stew," Hancock said. "Maybe someday I will be considered as true a patriot as you and Messrs. Adams and Otis."

Molineux found his voice. "What changed your mind?"

"Many things. Certainly some of the statements Dr. Warren made at the massacre's commemoration a few months ago gave me a lot to ponder."

Hancock tilted his head toward the door, and the two men returned to the hall.

"As you may recall," Hancock said, "he reminded us if we can be taxed without our consent, we can ultimately be deprived of everything we possess." His eyes became distant. "He spoke of our forefathers coming to this great land in order to preserve liberty—and of the hardships they endured and the weapons they clutched onto as they sought to protect her."

"I remember," Molineux said.

Hancock faced Molineux. "And I believe they left us a portion of their noble spirit and courage, which we can use to preserve their legacy."

"Well said." A shadow passed over Molineux, and he glanced at the parlor door where a Miss Quincy now stood. "She must also agree."

Hancock smiled at her. "God has been good to me."

Molineux moved toward the exit. Three was a crowd.

"I missed the recent selectmen meetings," Hancock said, "because I was tending to the furniture and other items I purchased for the new meetinghouse. I want to share with others what I have been given." Hancock walked Molineux to the door. "The calmness we have experienced since the so-called massacre has allowed me to turn my attention to purchasing gifts for the town I love."

Molineux opened the door and stepped onto the porch. "You are indeed a generous man."

"I think you will find my next gift rather fascinating."

"Oh?"

"I expect it to arrive any day," Hancock said. "Drop by my wharf and you can be among the first to see it in action."

October colors dotted the town. A gust of harbor wind blew across Molineux's face as he patted the new fire engine at Hancock's Wharf. "A fine piece of machinery, if ever there was one."

Hancock grabbed the lever and pointed with his head. "Grab the other end, Mr. Molineux." Once he was in place, Hancock pushed his end down. "Now you do the same."

"Keep pumping and water will come through the pipe." Hancock jumped onto the engine's bed, grabbed the hose, and pointed it toward the harbor.

Molineux chuckled as a stream of water came through the pipe. "Amazing."

"It has two cylinders and can reach up to one hundred fifty feet."

"It must have cost a fortune."

"Worth every pence for the protection of the town. And as Mr. Adams likes to remind us, natural law allows us to spend our fortunes as we please."

"Whew." Molineux stopped pumping, took a deep breath, and glanced toward the town. "Talk of the devil." Molineux waved his arms at Samuel Adams who began walking toward them. Then Molineux shifted his attention back to Hancock.

"It is too bad," Hancock said, "all the writing Mr. Adams has done for the *Gazette* has been for naught."

"Indifference does prevail," Molineux said, "despite all his efforts to reignite the flame."

Adams neared the two men. "Good day, gentlemen."

"Mr. Adams." Hancock gave a respectful nod.

"Testing the new engine, I see," Adams said.

"Would you like to give it a try?" Molineux asked.

"No, thank you," Adams said. "The gift is much appreciated, Mr. Hancock, but I have other things on my mind today."

"Then what gives us the pleasure of your visit?"

"I bring both good and bad news," Adams said. "And one may result in the other."

Molineux took his hands off the lever.

Adams eyes narrowed. "News has arrived of an attack on a British schooner, His Majesty's Ship *Gaspee*."

"Good news, indeed," Molineux said, "if the ship had been used to seize smugglers' ships. Begging your pardon, I mean, ships they *believe* are used to smuggle."

"Where did this take place?" Hancock asked.

"Rhode Island," Adams said. "People there burned the ship and attacked one of its officers. They say the protesters may have killed one of the schooner's officers. England may ship the suspected colonists to the Motherland for trial."

Hancock cleared his throat. "I assume the attack is the bad news. How will it turn into good?"

"The people of our town have been complacent far too long," Adams said.

"Very true," Molineux said.

"Our people have been sleeping," Adams said, "while many seek to change our government in ways that will have far-reaching consequences."

"How so?" Hancock asked.

"For one, the Crown would like to pay our superior court judges directly," Adams said. "Doing so would essentially set up tyranny over us."

Molineux turned to Hancock. "And you have probably heard about the latest attacks on the press."

"If the press is not free," Adams said, "they may as well place padlocks on our lips and fetters on our feet. Judges tend to obey those who pay them, rather than those they are sworn to serve."

Molineux leaned against the fire engine. "Using money as their means of control, the government will have the power to silence those who speak against them."

Hancock rubbed his chin. "The event in Rhode Island could be a wakeup call—it will get people to finally listen to your concerns. Is that your thinking?"

Adams nodded. "When I spoke to townsfolk in the taverns earlier, I saw a renewed gleam in their eyes."

"That *is* good news," Molineux said.

"Mr. Hancock," Adams said, "expect a written request to the selectmen soon for a town meeting so we can discuss our concerns."

Molineux did a quick jig. "I see a flicker."

"We must renew the patriotic fire in Massachusetts Bay. And where there is a spark, we will rekindle it." Adams placed his hand on the fire engine. "This would be the wrong apparatus to bring to the meeting." He turned to Molineux. "Instead, a fireplace bellows is what we will need."

Molineux pumped an imaginary bellows in his hands and puffed air. "Get the matches ready, for I shall have mine there."

Molineux thrummed his fingers on the table in the Faneuil Hall meeting room. Curtains from an open window fluttered in the spring breeze. Convincing the province of the danger of a change to the judges' salaries had been tougher than anticipated.

Adams, the only other one in the room, sat two chairs down. "I still believe it was a good thing for Boston to put you on the committee. The people of Barnstable only know the part of you that seeks a fight, not the jovial character many of us have come to appreciate. Besides, that town was already divided before you came along."

Molineux let out a long sigh. "But those of our *own* town used my reputation to convince members of the House to change their votes."

Adams placed both hands on the table. "It is true your approach has had some negative effects, but good has also come from your activities on the committee." Adams picked up a piece of paper lying in front of him. "I have here one of the replies we received from another of the towns."

Molineux's ears perked up, and Adams began to read. "'It is better to risk our lives and our fortunes,' they say, 'in the defense of our rights—civil and religious—than to die by piecemeal in slavery.'"

Molineux smiled.

"You see," Adams said, "your efforts, along with the twenty others on the Committee of Correspondence, are making an impact."

Molineux leaned back in his chair. "But we sent the pamphlets to six hundred towns."

"It will take time before we hear from everyone," Adams said. "But there are many more of these, and the general consensus is positive. If our governor refuses to call the General Assembly back into session to hear our grievances, we must stay in touch with the people of our province directly. We must keep them informed of what their government is doing."

"All right. I will reconnect with Drs. Warren and Young," Molineux said. "We can—"

Movement at the doorway caught his eye. "Mr. Dennie, we were just talking about the committee."

"You are panting," Adams said.

"Yes." Dennie held up one hand until his breathing slowed a bit. "I wanted to get the news to you as quickly as possible."

"News?" Adams asked.

"From Virginia." Dennie laid a document on the table.

Adams picked it up and began to scan.

"Their House of Burgesses," Dennie said, "has formed its own Committee of Correspondence."

Adams beamed. "This says they want to help their sister colonies stay informed of any intelligence they receive about Parliament." He stood. "I must get this to the *Gazette*. The support of our largest colony will sway many of those who previously refused to get behind us."

Molineux grinned at the new energy in the room.

Adams's eyes darted around. "And we must do what we can to get the House back in session." He returned his gaze to Dennie and Molineux. "Make sure your committee stays in touch with the towns in our province." He walked to the door. "And I will see to it the House forms a similar one to correspond with the other colonies."

"Do not worry about us," Molineux said. "Mr. Dennie and I will do our part to keep things aflame here."

Adams scampered away.

Molineux took in a deep breath. "Mr. Dennie, Mr. Adams has his way of doing things, and I have mine. I have had a lot on my mind lately which I believe will interest you. If you have a few minutes, I will be happy to share with you my latest scheme."

Molineux leaned against the outside wall of the concert hall. The rough brick against his back mirrored his demeanor. Music from inside hummed behind him. "Better not light anything," he said to Revere, "or it might give us away."

"It is good the streetlamps have not yet arrived," Revere said. "Are you sure the others will know where to find us?"

"I told them the east side of the building." Molineux beat the stick he held into his free hand. "You sure you can handle this?"

"It will be a good outlet. The house has felt empty these last three weeks without Sarah."

"And the baby?"

"The other children have tended to her as best they can," Revere said, "but she does not appear to be well."

"Is that you?" The whisper came from their left.

Molineux squinted into the darkness. "Mr. Dennie?"

"I found them," the voice said.

Within a minute, Mr. Dennie and a few other men had joined them. The nervous energy was palpable.

Noise from a lone carriage on the street caused everyone to freeze in place. Once it had passed, Molineux surveyed the scene. "Everybody have their weapon of choice?"

"My fists," Dennie said.

"There are guards at the door," another man said.

"Three of you take care of them," Molineux said, "and three of us will handle the commissioners."

"Would you like us to leave Mr. Hallowell for you?" Dennie asked.

"That would be much appreciated," Molineux said. "Are we ready?"

"Let's go."

The men hugged the wall as they crept toward the front of the building. When they reached the corner, Molineux motioned for them to swing around.

Molineux looked at Revere who seemed to have the best view, yet enough darkness to keep him undetected. Revere shook his head and held his palms toward the others. Molineux became aware of his own breathing. He kept his eyes on Revere. Several minutes passed. Then Revere gave the signal.

The men emerged from their hideaway, took a moment to gain their bearings, then rushed toward their respective targets with a whoop.

Molineux got in a good blow to Hallowell's back before he could ascertain what was happening. "Who invited you to this banquet?" Molineux asked.

Hallowell spun around and sucked in his breath.

"Ah, yes," Molineux growled, "our dear governor—that's who." Molineux dodged a blow from the only other commissioner who had emerged from the building. With his heart pounding wildly, Molineux turned back to Hallowell and stalked toward him. "The town told you to stay away."

Molineux took another swipe, but Hallowell grabbed the end of his club. Molineux shook him loose.

"Argh." Hallowell clasped his hands then glared at Molineux. "All you people want is independence." He hunched over and mirrored Molineux's steps but in the opposite direction.

"Freedom from you slugs who want to control us." Molineux caught sight of Dennie inching closer to Hallowell from behind. "I believe—"

Hallowell spun around to make his escape—only to find Dennie.

Molineux threw down his stick then grabbed both of Hallowell's arms from behind. Molineux motioned with his head. "Would you like to do the honors, Mr. Dennie?"

"Gladly." Dennie punched Hallowell in the stomach.

Molineux slung Hallowell around then pushed him to the ground. The commissioner pulled himself up with his elbows then used them to crawl a few inches away. "Your financial troubles have made you mad." Hallowell spit in Molineux's direction. "And our governor is twice the man you'll ever be."

"He seeks unrestrained power," Molineux said, picking up his stick.

Dennie took two steps toward Hallowell. "Mr. Hutchinson's letters are all the proof we need."

"We will hang him," Molineux said, "with his own words." He strutted toward Hallowell and hovered over his heaving chest. "And as for the East India Company"—Molineux beat the stick in his own hand—"rest assured, we will find a way to deal with them as well."

Molineux scanned the area. The other men had scared away their prey and had clustered a few yards away. "One more thing, Mr. Hallowell," Molineux said. "This is on behalf of my wife." Molineux kicked Hallowell in the side. "Since our children married, she has shed more tears than I care to count."

Molineux rejoined his comrades then shouted back at the wounded. "Mark my words," he said. "If things do not change, we will find additional ways to help you see the error of your ways. And, another thing, you may want to give more thought to those you call your friends—our governor should not be one of them."

CHAPTER TWENTY-FOUR

The Coming Plague
September–November 19, 1773

Hutchinson sat at the head of the table in the Province House. Although he had not moved into the home Massachusetts Bay provided for their royal governor, he enjoyed the rich wood and fine tapestry it afforded. It often provided a more serene environment than his Town House office, yet with a close enough proximity to keep abreast of any important developments.

Had the years of filling the appropriate roles at the proper times been worth it? The summer months had been some of the most difficult of his life, yet as the season had turned to fall, efforts of the radicals had fallen flat. Remote parts of the province had cooled to their efforts to set them ablaze with fury by using Hutchinson's own words against him.

A rap at the door interrupted his thoughts, and a few minutes later, Hallowell stood before him in the large reception room.

"Have you heard the news?" Hallowell asked.

Hutchinson's mind raced. "News?"

"The East India Company plans to ship tea to several ports along our coast."

"Oh? Which ones?" Hutchinson asked.

"New York, Philadelphia, Charleston—and Boston."

"I see. Please, have a seat."

Hallowell obliged. "Of course, we will require duties to be paid on the tea once it has been landed."

"In the minds of the people," Hutchinson said, "to pay the tax would be an admission of Parliament's authority over them. Something they will not do without a fight." He sat in silence for a moment then looked at Hallowell. "What if they refuse to unload the tea?"

"A ship cannot leave our port with the cargo it brought in," Hallowell said. "Once unloaded, the taxes must be paid." Hallowell took a deep breath. "If the people refuse to unload the tea, I will have no choice but to confiscate the entire vessel."

"How long will they have to remove the goods?"

"Once a ship has come into the harbor, they will have twenty days before I would take action," Hallowell said. "Merchants on the other side of the Big Pond asked me to help prevent the tea's landing." Hallowell fixed his eyes on the governor. "But I will not."

The governor laced his fingers and placed his hands in his lap. "Mr. Hallowell, there is something you should know. I have sent a request to England, asking them to relieve me of my duties as governor."

"What?"

"As much as it pains me to admit it, my usefulness to the Crown has come to an end."

"But—"

"The patriots' misrepresentation of my letters to the Motherland has destroyed any confidence the people of Boston ever had in me." Hutchinson said. "I wished only good for this colony when I sought to restrain their liberty. And although I expect London to vindicate me with regards to the charges our own House sent to them, Mr. Adams's skillful pen and the *Gazette*'s willingness to publish what he produces is more than I can overcome."

Hallowell jumped up. "The paper—I almost forgot." He pulled a newspaper from his jacket and handed it to Hutchinson. "They published the names of those the East India Company has assigned to receive the tea."

Hutchinson opened it and Hallowell pointed to the list.

"Richard Clarke & Sons, Benjamin Faneuil," Hutchinson read.

Hallowell stepped back. "And your two sons, Thomas and Elisha."

"Boston will not be happy, but the consignees must stand firm." Hutchinson stood and returned the paper to Hallowell. "It is too late in the year for London to call me home. Until they do, I am still the governor and will fulfill my duty as best I know how. If the people refuse to submit to Parliament's demands, I will fight them with every ounce of my being."

Molineux surveyed the men at his table in the Green Dragon Tavern—Adams, Dennie, and Drs. Warren and Young—those with whom he worked on the Committee of Correspondence. They, along with a few dozen others who sat at the remaining tables, made up the North End Caucus.

"Their being on the verge of bankruptcy does not give the East India Company the right to dip into my pockets," Molineux said. "I rose by my own power and will also fall by it. I will not require anyone to rescue me from the peril of my own making and refuse to be pressured into doing the same for anyone else."

"I may go down with you," Dennie said. "Haven't I heard you say, 'It is better to be a free man who is poor than to be a slave of any sort, rich or otherwise?'"

"Ah," Molineux said. "I was simply passing along what Mr. Adams has taught me. Parliament's attempt to control me is of greater concern than the havoc they are wreaking on Boston's number-one commodity. The monopoly they have allowed will eventually destroy us all."

"Just one more means of control," Adams said. "I am grateful our governor has not convinced you the advantages of the Tea Act outweigh the harm it will cause."

"I read Hutchinson's piece carefully," Dennie said, "and he did not even address our most basic concerns."

Dr. Young pushed his empty plate away. "Enough with the merchant talk. I want to know how Joyce Junior fared in delivering the messages to the consignees last night?"

"You mean this morning." Molineux yawned. "Early this morning. Very early."

"Um. And amid the chill of early November," Dr. Warren said. "How is your knee?"

Molineux rubbed the joint. "To be sure, it has seen better days."

Dennie grinned. "I hear Mr. Clarke was not too pleased to receive visitors at one in the morning."

Adams leaned back in his chair. "Two other couriers did the honors of delivering the note to him."

"Do you believe," Dr. Young asked, "the consignees will respond favorably to our invitation and show up at the Liberty Tree tomorrow?"

Adams shrugged. "If things go as planned, we will gain the support of other colonies as a result of the circular we sent to them two days ago. And there is power in unity—perhaps enough power to encourage the consignees to resign."

The sound of clanking from one of the other tables interrupted the conversation. "Gentlemen, may I have your attention?" The moderator walked to the front of the room. "We can wait no longer for Mr. Hancock or others from the Committee of Correspondence to arrive."

"I am certain," Adams said, "they will agree with what we have already discussed. I will be happy to pass along any pertinent information to them as soon as possible."

"Very well," the moderator said. "Does anyone desire to make any additional comments before we take a vote?"

Molineux stood up, and all eyes turned to him. "It is no secret I am not the most patient man on earth." He ignored the knowing looks. "Yet for more than ten years I—we—have sought redress. And for what? To have tea shipped to us against our wishes—tea for which London requires duties to be paid."

Several hissed.

"The weight of our country is behind us," Molineux said. "We must not fail them."

"Hear, hear," someone said.

The moderator smiled. "Those of you who attended Saturday's meeting know Mr. Molineux was among those who went on record as opposing the sale of the East India Company tea."

"Oppose it with my life and my fortunes," Molineux said. "Dr. Warren and Mr. Revere also pledged the same." Solemn faces assured him he had gotten through, so he had a seat.

"Mr. Adams," the moderator said. "Is there anything you would like to say before our vote?"

Adams glanced at the table then up at the men who had gathered. He rose from his chair. "I would remind you of but two things."

Molineux sensed both concern and resolve welling up inside Adams—as well as the tears he held back.

Adams took one step away from the table. "First, our brothers in Philadelphia have recently reminded us of the dangers of the Tea Act—dangers that far exceed those of the Stamp Act." Adams paused. "The Stamp Act was felt by all ranks of people, and therefore, quickly rejected. The tax placed upon the tea, however—once blended with its normal price—will eventually pass unnoticed and, therefore, receive no objection."

Adams scanned the room. "Second, we must remind everyone who will listen that the cheaper price of tea afforded to us by the Tea Act should not tempt them to surrender their liberties. Doing so will someday cost us more than we can ever imagine." He returned to his chair.

Without moving his head, Molineux examined nearby faces. Serious and solemn.

"Thank you, Mr. Adams," the moderator said. "Gentlemen, I present to you the matter we discussed earlier today. Are we determined that tea the East India Company has shipped to us shall not be landed?"

A round of "ayes" went up from around the room.

"Opposed?"

A few men glanced around at the others in the group as an expected silence filled the room.

The moderator nodded to the secretary then shifted his attention to Molineux's table. "Dr. Warren, could you please remind us of the core points of the report your committee gave earlier?"

"Certainly." Dr. Warren stood. "Dr. Young, Dr. Church, and myself believe we should be prepared to declare the consignees as enemies of our country if they do not resign their commission. Furthermore, we believe they should not fail to feel the weight of just resentment."

"Thank you, Dr. Warren," the moderator said. "If there is nothing further, we are adjourned. Tomorrow promises to be a long day for all of us. I will see you at the Liberty Tree at high noon."

Church bells rang for an hour, summoning people to the Liberty Tree. A large flag swayed in its branches while Dr. Young provided a rousing speech.

Molineux scanned the crowd, satisfied. A mix of high and low ranks was present, including Hancock. Molineux leaned over to Adams. "How many do you suppose are here?"

"At least five hundred." Adams pulled out his watch and glanced at it. "Quarter 'til one. It is time." Adams turned to Molineux. "Are you ready?"

Molineux nodded.

Adams placed a piece of paper into Molineux's hand then walked to the stage.

Dr. Young wrapped up his thoughts then motioned toward Adams. "It is without any further delay I present to you our fearless leader, Mr. Samuel Adams."

"Huzzah!"

Despite Adams's ailing body, he offered a hearty smile as he walked to the center of the platform. "I thank you all for coming, especially those who traveled from the surrounding towns. Your support is much appreciated."

Adams raised both arms slightly. "Did we not request the tea consignees to come here today and deliver their resignations?"

Sentiments of agreement arose from the assembly.

"Did we not tell them it would be to their own peril to refuse our invitation?" He lowered his hands. "Nearly an hour has passed since the appointed time. Word has arrived that at least five of the seven consignees are holed up at Mr. Clarke's warehouse on King Street, and they have no intention of heeding our call."

The crowd hissed.

"In anticipation of this possibility," Adams said, "the Sons of Liberty selected nine men to pay the consignees a visit. The Sons will reiterate our desire for them to return the tea expected to arrive in our port at any time." Adams motioned for Molineux to come forward. "If agreeable with you, Mr. Molineux will lead the delegation."

"Huzzah!"

"In addition, Dr. Warren, Dr. Church, Mr. Dennie, and several others will make up the committee," Adams said. "I encourage you to join them in order to demonstrate the strength of our appeal." Adams nodded to Molineux.

The merchant jolted over to the street that led to Clarke's warehouse. He waved for the people to follow. "This way, everyone. We have a job to do."

To keep the throng entertained as they followed him, Molineux performed a spirited march all the way to King Street. He slowed as he passed the Town House. If Hutchinson were there, he needed to see the parade of protesters. Molineux led the group down the street until they reached Clarke's warehouse, then the merchant spun around. "Everyone from my committee here?"

Several nodded.

Molineux raised a hand. "Everyone else wait here."

The door to the building stood open. Strange. Molineux stepped in, and the committee followed. No one.

"Maybe they are in the counting room," Dr. Warren said.

"Mr. Dennie," Molineux asked, "would you care to check it out?"

Dennie ran up the stairwell then called back. "They are here."

Molineux and the others ascended the narrow staircase and entered the counting room.

While the committee filed in, Molineux scanned the room. About a dozen friends had joined the consignees. Several sat and others stood. Several faces revealed a nervous anticipation. Others indicated resistance.

With the delegation surrounding the traitors, Molineux began. "Gentlemen," he said to the consignees, "you have insulted the people by refusing to appear at the appointed time and place in order to provide your resignation."

Molineux reached for the message in his jacket's pocket and unfolded it. "Here are the demands of those who have sent me." He read from the paper. "We request you not land nor pay duty on any tea sent to you by the East India Company." Molineux sucked in his upper lip then continued. "Instead, we ask you to return the tea to England in the same vessels in which it arrives." Molineux folded the document and returned it to his pocket.

Clarke glared at Molineux. "We shall have nothing to do with you—any of you."

Molineux took a step toward Clarke and rose to full stature. "Then since you have refused our most reasonable demands, you should expect to feel the utmost weight of the people's resentment." He looked at the committee. "Gentlemen, our job here is done."

He spun around to face the exit then led his eight comrades down the stairs and to his band of followers. "Back to the tree," Molineux said with a wave to the crowd. Then he ran to the upper end of the group and began the journey up the slope toward the Town House. Halfway up King Street, Dennie nudged Molineux. "I believe we have lost a good number of our following."

Molineux turned around. A few hundred people were rushing back toward the warehouse. Molineux took in a breath. "Let them do their work," he said. "Once it is done, the rest of us will pressure the consignees by our own means."

Hancock stood beside the platform in Faneuil Hall chatting with Adams while awaiting the return of the four hundred merchants meeting outside. Others scattered around the large room had found various ways to pass the time.

"Do you believe Mr. Hutchinson will find a way to prosecute the rioters?" Hancock asked Adams.

"A door torn from its hinges is fairly minor," Adams said. "Besides, I doubt anyone other than Mr. Clarke would be willing to identify them."

"After reading the letter one of the consignees received last night," Hancock said, "even he may be hesitant. I heard it was quite menacing."

"It did mention our restraint for spilling human blood may be coming to an end."

Noise from the back of the hall and the cool air from the opening doors ended the meeting with Adams. Merchants filed back into the hall, and Hancock returned to the stage.

Once everyone had settled into a seat, Hancock resumed the role of moderator. "May we hear a report from the merchants' meeting?"

Molineux jumped to his feet. "We found the handbills one of the commissioners distributed yesterday in support of the tea consignees to be false and scandalous. There is no evidence those who supported the nonimportation agreement have set a trap with regards to the tea we expect to arrive in our port."

"Very well," Hancock said. "While one purpose of this meeting was to address concerns over the threat to trade, it is time to move on to the more primary matter—the potential for the loss of our liberties. Specifically, those liberties which would be lost to not only us, but to our posterity as well."

Hancock took a step back from the podium. "Many, if not all, of you have read the resolutions produced by Philadelphia last month. Those resolves deny Parliament's right to tax us without representation. In addition, they affirm the duty of every American to oppose those who attempt to send us tea on which such duties would be required. Anyone who aids the receiving of the tea would be considered an enemy to America."

"As you may have heard," Hancock said, "the consignees received yet another message last evening asking them to resign their assignment to receive the tea. The notice indicated it would be the last warning they would receive." Hancock scanned the crowd. "I would like to propose, however, that we provide one more opportunity for them to respond to our numerous requests. If you wish, I would be happy to lead a delegation to obtain their reply."

Those gathered accepted his proposal then adjourned until three o'clock to give the delegation time to make the visits.

Hancock sat in a chair on the platform in Faneuil Hall awaiting word from the second committee. He let out a faint sigh. His moderate approach had not produced the desired effect, so the people had commissioned a less congenial group to try to persuade the consignees. Would even they be able to—

A rustle in the back of the hall caught his attention. Dr. Warren, Adams, and Molineux had returned. Hancock met Adams at the edge of the stage, received the message, then stepped to the lectern.

A hush fell over the audience.

"As you know, Messrs. Clarke and Faneuil are the only consignees we could find in town," Hancock said. "This second delegation reports these men will provide us with a response to our request within a half hour. In the meantime—"

One of the men in the auditorium stood. "In the meantime, I propose we select yet a third group of men to send to Milton to speak with the Hutchinson boys. We do not know exactly when the tea will arrive and cannot wait until Monday to know their thoughts on this matter."

Murmurs of affirmation went up around the room. The gathering selected Hancock, Adams, Dr. Warren, and four others to leave for Milton once the meeting freed them to do so, then they moved on to other matters.

A squeak from the backdoor followed by the pounding of boots down the aisle commanded everyone's attention. A messenger had arrived.

Hancock scanned the note and walked back to the podium. "We have received word from Messrs. Clarke and Faneuil. They claim they are unable to comply with our request until instructions arrive from the East India Company."

Several groaned.

"Is this a satisfactory reply?" Hancock asked.

"Nay," the crowd said.

"Then we shall adjourn until eleven o'clock tomorrow morning," Hancock said. "By then the committee you have selected to go to Milton should have an answer from Governor Hutchinson's sons. I will see you here tomorrow morning."

Governor Hutchinson sat at the table in the Province House surrounded by six of the seven men assigned to receive the tea. A mid-November fire crackled nearby.

"Two weeks have come and gone," Hutchinson said, "since my sons and the rest of you told the town you could not provide an answer until you received instructions from the company. Still, no word has arrived."

"But the people will assume some sort of guidance came on Mr. Hancock's ship yesterday," Mr. Clarke said, "especially since one of my sons was onboard."

"Until his welcome home party last night," Elisha said, "things had been relatively calm."

"The mobs are never far beneath the surface," Hutchinson said. "Given an opportunity, they will take it." He faced the senior Clarke. "I am truly sorry for any pain you may have suffered as a result of the attack on your home."

Mr. Clarke blinked back tears. "Several windows were shattered, and a pistol discharged before Mr. Molineux and Dr. Young arrived to squelch the violence."

Hutchinson shook eight-year-old memories from his mind. He pulled out his watch. "We told the committee to expect our reply by three o'clock."

All eyes looked to him.

"If no orders have arrived from the East India Company," Hutchinson said, "then it is out of your power to reply to the town's request."

"All we know is those in England entered into agreements on our behalf," Elisha said.

"Then that is what we will tell them," one of the Clarke sons said. "And we should add we have yet to receive instructions from the company, leaving us with no change in our ability to provide additional information to the town."

"Please address it to the moderator, Mr. Hancock," Hutchinson said to the scribe. "He has rejoined their ranks, and we should document it accordingly."

The reply complete, the courier left with the message.

"Governor, there is another matter we would like to discuss with you," the senior Clarke said. "What of the increased violence? Not all of us feel safe."

"I have called a meeting of my council for tomorrow morning," Hutchinson said. "I plan to review it with them then."

Hutchinson sighed. Only eight of the council members sat in the chamber. The remaining twenty had refused to come. The suddenness with which the town had dissolved the previous day's meeting had struck terror in the hearts of the consignees. Council members did not seem to be immune.

Hutchinson called the meeting to order. "I have sought without success to collect information regarding the inflammatory speeches being given at Faneuil Hall. Nonetheless, I did receive one report that a call to arms was made in at least one of the meetings."

One of the men leaned forward. "I have also heard the selectmen have begun to inspect the town's arms."

"And to call in those they had lent out," another said.

Hutchinson spoke. "As you may know, a week ago, I ordered one of the selectmen—Mr. Hancock—to prepare his company of cadets to appear in arms in order to preserve the peace. He refused so I directed one of the military companies to hold themselves in readiness."

Several of the men glanced around.

Hutchinson continued. "They need to be prepared to suppress any riotous assemblies the people may have."

"The only way to prevent violence," one of the council members said, "is to have the tea consignees resign their commission."

A knock came on the chamber door.

Hutchinson pivoted. "Come in."

The secretary of the province stepped in and held up several papers. "The consignees have made an official request for protection." The man looked around at those who had gathered. "Protection not only for themselves, but also for the tea which is to come."

"Protection for the tea?" one of the men asked.

"Yes. They are asking for the governor and his council to relieve them of their responsibilities and, instead, have you all take charge of it once it arrives."

Eyes turned to the one who had suggested that the consignees resign.

The man held up both hands. "I in no way meant for them to turn over the responsibility of the tea to us."

Hutchinson dismissed the secretary and shifted his attention back to the men at the table. "Those on yesterday's ship indicated vessels carrying the tea departed from England on the same day—four of them bound for Boston. I will call another meeting of the council for next Tuesday in hopes we will have a quorum."

"Governor Hutchinson," one of the councilmen said, "may I remind you if the tea ships come into the harbor, they will not be allowed to pass by the cannons stationed at Castle William again without a written permit from you."

Hutchinson smiled. "'Tis true and quite unfortunate for the radicals among us, is it not?" He paused to ensure he had everyone's attention. "Gentlemen, there is very little time to prepare."

CHAPTER TWENTY-FIVE

The Final Plea

November 28–30, 1773

Molineux's knee bounced underneath the table in the selectmen's chambers at Faneuil Hall. Late afternoon sun filtered in through the windows. Others of the Committee of Correspondence sat around the table, with Adams at the head.

"The ship is currently making its way from the castle to the docks," Adams said. "Dr. Warren and Dr. Church will get the word out regarding tomorrow's meeting."

"You want us to inform both the locals and people of Boston's surrounding towns, correct?" Dr. Warren asked.

"Yes," Adams said. "What happens to the *Dartmouth* and the other three ships expected to arrive will have far-reaching effects. Everyone will want to be here."

Movement outside the door caught Molineux's eye. "I believe Francis Rotch has arrived."

"Thank you again, gentlemen, for coming," Adams said. "I never imagined the first tea ship would arrive on a Sunday. It has been a trying Sabbath, but the ox is in the ditch and we must pull it out."

The committee members scattered to carry out various tasks while Molineux and two others stayed behind.

"Please come in, Mr. Rotch," Molineux said.

Rotch entered and took a seat.

"How old are you, lad?" Molineux asked.

"Twenty-three," Rotch said. "Your son Junior and I are about the same age."

Molineux said. "Do you know why we called you here?"

"To inquire about the ship, I suppose."

"That's right. More specifically, to discuss its cargo."

"As part owner of the vessel," another of the committee said, "you will need to work with us to determine what happens to the taxable goods it carries."

"How many crates of tea are on board?" Molineux asked.

"One hundred and fourteen." Rotch provided a nervous smile.

"Did the captain land the cargo on Cape Cod?"

Rotch straightened. "No, sir. I assure you that is simply a rumor."

Molineux rose from his chair. "Then we need to ask you to delay entering it at the Custom House. This will leave open the possibility of returning the tea to London."

"I can only delay a short time. As you know, forty-eight hours is generally acceptable—but no longer."

"I understand," Molineux said. "That will give us until Tuesday to weigh our options."

Hancock appeared in the doorway. "We are here for our five o'clock meeting. I simply wanted to let you know."

"Unless anyone has additional questions or comments," Molineux said, "we are finished here."

Everyone stood. "Mr. Rotch"—Molineux stared square into the eyes of the young man—"we will likely call on you during tomorrow's meeting. Please make sure you are available."

Rotch nodded and left.

"Mr. Hancock," Molineux said, "the room is yours."

Hancock and a few other selectmen entered.

"We met with the Clarke brothers yesterday," Hancock said to Molineux. "The one recently arrived from England was surprised at the town's unfavorable opinion of him."

"He does not know us very well, does he?" Molineux said.

"Apparently not, but he was willing to negotiate until we told him returning the tea to England would be the only thing that would bring Boston satisfaction."

"Why did they refuse?"

"If they return the cargo, it would risk confiscation."

"How did the meeting end?"

"They indicated they would provide the town with a proposal once instructions arrive from the East India Company."

"Which I assume came on today's ship," Molineux said.

"Exactly," Hancock said. "We sent word for them to meet with us at noon today, but they never showed up—so here we are again."

"What about their father?"

"He is a bit battleworn. Hence he has retired to the country."

"Leaving his sons to determine the fate of them all?"

"That appears to be the case," Hancock said.

"Then I will wish you luck," Molineux said. "And will look forward to receiving a report at tomorrow's meeting."

"If we do not secure a response from the consignees this evening," Hancock said, "the selectmen cannot technically call for a town meeting."

Molineux lowered his head and raised his eyebrows. "Do you really think that will stop us? I will see you tomorrow."

Molineux pulled the sweaty shirt away from his body. He had just delivered the most passionate speech of his life. Hancock and Drs. Warren and Young had also made their pleas.

Bells had rung on that Monday morning as a thousand people streamed into Faneuil Hall. The overflow had forced a change of venue to Old South Church. Today it welcomed people from all walks of life, from both inside and outside Boston.

Molineux scanned the audience once more for any sign of the Clarkes. They had not shown up at the previous evening's meeting, so there was no additional information regarding the plans of those to whom tea had been assigned.

Adams stood behind the podium. "We must impress upon the minds of our friends, neighbors, and fellow townsmen the necessity of exerting ourselves in the most zealous and determined manner. For the tea which has come to our shores should be dreaded more than plague or pestilence. These can only destroy our bodies, but what has arrived seeks to crush our very souls."

"Even our own governor has refused to ask for the resignation of those assigned to receive the tea," Adams said. "Instead, as Mr. Hancock can attest, Mr. Hutchinson preferred to call for the sword." Adams took a step back and scanned the auditorium. "We must choose. Will we sit down as good-natured slaves, or will we rise and resist this and every other plan our enemies laid out for our destruction? Choose you this day, but as for me and my house . . ." Adams returned to his seat, and the moderator walked to the lectern.

"We have heard the arguments," the moderator said. "Now I will review the timeline. As you know, the first of the tea ships arrived before midnight two days ago. If a ship's cargo is landed, taxes must be paid—which none of us wants to happen, since it would indicate to Britain our willingness to submit to anything she desires to do to us. If not landed within twenty days, customs officers may confiscate it and demand that we pay the related taxes."

Molineux looked around. No one moved.

"There are conflicting reports as to which day is considered the first of the twenty," the moderator said. "Assuming the strictest constraints, we have until midnight on the sixteenth to come up with an alternative plan. If we do not, ten years' worth of resistance will be lost. And, as we have been reminded, we will be forced to submit to lives filled with tyranny."

"With the stakes so high," the moderator said, "I propose we give the consignees one last chance to agree with our request that they return the tea to England. Since this is a meeting of The Body rather than an official town meeting, I will allow anyone to vote, regardless of age, estate, or town of residence."

Molineux smiled.

"All in favor of providing one more opportunity to the tea consignees let it be known by saying 'Aye.'"

"Aye," the people said.

"Opposed?"

Silence.

"Then I will get word to them, and we will reconvene at three o'clock this afternoon to hear their reply."

Molineux turned around from his front row seat in the Old South Church. Attendance had doubled since the morning meeting.

The moderator stepped to the podium, and a quiet settled over the assembly. "I am sure you will be as disappointed as I am," he said, "but the consignees have not responded to our request."

Several groaned.

"Then I propose we reaffirm our earlier vote." The voice from near the front was unmistakably Adams's. "The vote demanding the tea be returned to England on the same vessel that brought it—returned as soon as possible."

"Hear, hear," someone said.

The moderator raised a hand to encourage calm. "Mr. Rotch, would you care to address this?"

Mr. Rotch? Molineux whirled around. The ship's partial owner and its captain sat on the other side of the room.

"Please come to the stage," the moderator said, "so you may be heard by all."

Rotch walked to the platform with his head down. He ascended the stairs then looked to the moderator who tilted his head toward the auditorium.

Rotch turned to face the assembly. "Although I understand Mr. Adams's concerns," he said, "I am unable to comply with his request to return the tea to London. For you see, to do so would require an official pass from Governor Hutchinson."

"And can you not ask for a pass?" the moderator asked.

"The governor is only allowed to provide me with clearance if my ship has been cleared at the Custom House." Rotch glanced at Molineux. "And without a proper clearance, I may not make it safely past the guns at the castle. If I did, the freight would be seized upon its return to London." Rotch stared at the floor. "The loss would be my ruin."

Mr. Adams stood, and the moderator gave him the floor.

"Mr. Rotch claims it would be a hardship to return the tea to England," Adams said. "Have not other merchants made protests at the Custom House for reasons of much less consequence, such as the loss of goods due to unforeseen forces of nature?" Adams shifted his weight. "Do we not now have a political storm upon us that should require Mr. Rotch to do as much?" He turned to the crowd. "Can he not honestly protest that, for the safety of his person, a mob of several thousand compelled him to send the tea back?"

Adams faced the man at the center of the debate. "Mr. Rotch, would it not be in your best interest to comply with the will of The Body gathered here?"

"I will enter a protest," Rotch said, "but it will be one that is against the desires of these proceedings."

"Do as you wish," the moderator said. "But if you suffer the tea to be landed, it will be at your own peril. We would be happy to provide your ship with twenty-five men to protect the tea until arrangements can be made to return it to its proper place." He looked to the back of the room. "I believe Mr. Hancock has additional information to share."

Hancock approached the front. "Thank you, sir." He turned to address those assembled. "I have been informed our governor desires to suppress any riot that may occur due to the situation with the tea. He also recommended to his council they take the tea and its consignees under their own protection—which, to their credit, they readily refused." Hancock took a deep breath. "I believe our governor's conduct is calculated to serve the views of the administration, and not our own. I move, therefore, that we make this a matter of record."

Hancock remained near the platform while the people voted unanimously to document their view of the governor's intent.

"Mr. Hancock," the moderator said, "do you have additional thoughts to share with this body?"

"I do. Word has come from Mr. Copley that the consignees have received letters containing instructions from the East India Company."

The crowd gasped.

"I was also informed most of them have removed to the castle and will provide their proposals after they have had time to consider the matter."

Dr. Young jumped up, shouting, "Throw the tea overboard."

The moderator motioned for calm. "We desire to bring this matter to a peaceful end so will grant the consignees the additional time they have requested. Until they provide us with a proposal, there is little we can do. We stand adjourned until tomorrow morning."

Tuesday morning produced another good turnout at Old South. Heat had crawled up Molineux's neck as one of the selectmen read the letter he had received from the consignees.

The moderator stepped back to the lectern. "Thank you for providing us with that communication." He turned to the audience. "As you heard, the consignees claim it is beyond their power to send the tea back until they hear from their constituents in England. Anyone care to comment?"

Molineux leapt to his feet and faced the crowd. "Their proposal will not work. We have tried to store tea in the past but to no avail." The merchant paused. The sheriff had entered the building and was making his way to the stage. Molineux pulled his mind back to what he was saying. "Their plan simply will not work," he said then threw himself back into his chair.

"Thank you, Mr. Molineux," the moderator said. "Those in favor of declaring the consignees' reply unsatisfactory, please indicate by saying 'Aye.'"

"Aye," the audience said.

The crowd watched as the sheriff and moderator spoke quietly over a piece of paper the officer had brought with him.

The moderator stepped to the lectern and spoke. "The sheriff has brought another matter to our attention by way of a letter from our governor."

Several jumped to their feet in protest.

"I object."

"We do not want to hear it."

Hancock stood and raised his hand until order returned. "I believe the message should be read. We cannot offer a proper response until we know what he has to say."

"I agree," Adams said.

Molineux scowled. Like the consignees, the governor had already proven he had nothing left to say that would be of interest to the people.

The moderator motioned to the sheriff who stepped to the lectern and began to read. "Yesterday's meeting openly violated and defied the good and wholesome province under which you live. I warn, exhort, and require you—since you are unlawfully assembled—to disperse and refrain from all further proceedings."

The crowd hissed.

The sheriff returned control of the podium to the moderator and left the platform.

Molineux caught movement to his right. Adams, with lips pressed together, was walking to the stage. His eyes screamed of frustration.

The moderator took two steps back, and Adams stepped to the podium. "Mr. Hutchinson declares those gathered here have an unlawful purpose and are unlawfully assembled. I am so provoked I can hardly bear to hear these repeated insults cast upon such a respectable body."

His frame shook beyond the disease that plagued him. "Our governor says he is the Majesty's representative. He? He is the shadow of a man, scarcely able to support his withered carcass or his hoary head. Is *he* a representation of majesty?" Adams's eyes filled with tears. "Has not a free and sensible people, who felt themselves to be injured, always had the right to meet together and consult for their own safety? We are far from riotous and do, indeed, have this right." Adams raised one fist. "Do not let him tell you otherwise."

The group clapped and cheered.

"Huzzah!"

Adams made his way back to the top of the stairs where Dr. Warren met him and assisted him to his seat.

Dr. Young stood and addressed the assembly. Fury spewed from his eyes. "The law, dating back to the Magna Carta, does indeed give us this right."

"Will we disperse?" the moderator asked.

"Nay!"

"Then what shall be our next order of business?"

A rustling came from another part of the room. Molineux pivoted to see Mr. Copley.

"You have something for us, Mr. Copley?" the moderator asked.

Mr. Copley stood and addressed the moderator. "If the Clarke brothers should come to this meeting, could you ensure their safety until they returned to the castle?"

Whispers of affirmation rippled through the auditorium.

"Would you be so kind as to bring them to us?" the moderator asked.

"I will do my best," Copley said. "It is all I can offer."

"Then we will grant you two hours and stand adjourned until two o'clock."

The people began gathering their coats. Molineux caught Hancock's eye. "Mr. Copley?" Molineux mouthed as he made an ocean's wave motion with his hand. Not only did Copley despise politics, but he was terrified at the thought of being on the water.

The trip to the castle would involve more than two miles each way in a small boat. Even if Copley survived the trip, would he be able to accomplish his mission?

Molineux shifted in his chair and rubbed his neck. Two o'clock had come and gone without any sign of Copley. Rotch and his ship's captain walked back to their seats while the moderator summarized their statements.

"Both Mr. Rotch and his captain," the moderator said, "have agreed to return the tea on the vessel in which it came, but Mr. Rotch will file a formal protest regarding the matter." The moderator motioned to the back of the room. "Mr. Rowe and his ship's agent have arrived. Please come to the platform so I may ask you a few questions."

The two men came forward, and the interrogation began.

"As you know," the moderator said, "*Dartmouth* came to us a few days ago carrying an item that has become the focus of the controversy we now face. There are rumors that, of the three ships still expected to arrive carrying the tea, one of them belongs to you."

Rowe shuffled his feet then looked up. "It is true. The detestable and obnoxious commodity will come on one of my ships, the *Eleanor*. I am very sorry. It has caused me great uneasiness."

The crowd broke into applause.

Rowe provided a faint smile. "Would not a little saltwater do the tea some good?"

Rumbles of laughter stirred the room.

A whisper came from behind Molineux. "A good Tory has been brought over to our side. Taxes cannot be collected on something that has been destroyed."

"I have already purchased cargo for *Eleanor*'s trip back to England," Rowe said. "But under the circumstances, I may try to make other arrangements."

"A wise idea," the moderator said.

"Upon its arrival, I will notify the town officials and see that the tea is returned to England."

"Thank you, Mr. Rowe. I believe that will be all of our questions for today."

The two men descended from the stage and found seats among those gathered.

"As we have been talking," the moderator said, "Mr. Copley has returned from his mission."

Everyone turned to see Copley walking down the aisle toward the front.

"You seem to be alone," the moderator said as Copley walked up the steps.

"'Tis true."

"Do you have a message for us?"

Copley nodded. "Rest assured the consignees have a tender regard for their families and a great desire to help return peace to the town. They want to do their utmost to provide their fellow citizens with satisfaction."

Molineux's eyes narrowed. Copley's words sounded good, but something was amiss.

"They understand," Copley said, "nothing short of reshipping the tea will be satisfactory. They deem that to be impossible, however, so did not believe it would be of any value to appear at this meeting."

Molineux raised a fist. "This is Mr. Hutchinson's doing."

"Indeed," Dr. Young said. "He desires to place blame for the fate of the tea on this town rather than on those who sent it to us."

Copley shook his head. "To my knowledge, the consignees have not seen nor spoken with our governor. The Clarkes, however, have offered a proposal. They will consent to storing the tea anywhere the people desire and would submit it to constant inspection. Anything beyond that, they believe, would be to their ruin."

Molineux clenched his teeth.

Copley continued. "They understand this body desires to return the tea to England. Since the consignees were not active in introducing the tea, they ask to be excused from being instruments in sending it back. They do, however, give this body the freedom to send it back amid the political storm you say now exists."

Molineux's muscles relaxed a bit.

The moderator returned his gaze to the audience. "Do we find either of these proposals satisfactory?"

"Nay!" the crowd said.

"Mr. Copley," the moderator said, "thank you for your willingness to be the mediator. You may inform the Clarkes and others of our decision."

The moderator turned to those who had gathered. "Mr. Adams, would you care to read the resolves that have been prepared?"

Adams came to the podium. "'Be it resolved,'" he read, "'until the unrighteous act shall be repealed, if any person shall import tea from Great Britain, he shall be deemed by this body an enemy to his country. We will prevent its landing and payment of any duty thereon. And we will bring about its return to the place from whence it comes. We will do so at the risk of our lives and properties.'" Adams returned to his seat.

The moderator walked back to the lectern. "Those in favor of accepting these resolves?"

"Aye."

"Those opposed?"

Silence.

Attendees began gathering their things, but Hancock ascended the stairs, and a hush fell over the crowd.

"Mr. Hancock, do you have a parting message for us?"

Hancock faced the assembly. "My fellow countrymen, we have put our hands to the plough, and woe be to him who shrinks or looks back."

"Thank you, Mr. Hancock," the moderator said. "In closing, I will remind you of Mr. Adams's admonition to keep your arms in order. And you may want to do as he does—keep them at your bedside during the overnight hours. I will also remind the Committee of

Correspondence of the responsibility we have given them to make provisions for the continued watch over the ships. And for the rest of us, should any issue arise for which they need our help, they will ring the bells by day or toll them by night. No further meetings are scheduled at this time, but stay alert as that will likely change."

CHAPTER TWENTY-SIX

The Tea Party

December 13–16, 1773

*M*olineux leaned against the inside of the ship and squinted at the night sky. "Is that Orion?" he asked Revere.

"I think so."

The half dozen lanterns scattered around *Dartmouth*'s deck barely flickered. A couple men snored.

Molineux pulled his blanket tighter. "Boston really appreciates your carrying its message to the other port towns."

"Someone needed to warn them not to let the tea ships unload there," Revere said. "Besides, my new wife is as apprehensive as the other ladies that if the tea is landed, it will be crammed down her throat."

"Do you think the fourth vessel will arrive in time?"

"In time for Thursday's deadline? It is hard to say. Has Mr. Hancock said anything about when the *Beaver* will be released from quarantine?"

"No." Molineux let out a puff of air. "It has three more days there. With the way our luck has gone, I was not surprised it arrived with sickness onboard."

"I like how the *Gazette* put it," Revere said. "It arrived not only with the plague onboard, but also with smallpox."

"The tea has certainly become a curse." Molineux pulled his hat over his ears. "It would be helpful if all four ships could anchor at this wharf."

"Are you going to tell me the plan?" Revere asked.

"Mr. Adams would have my hide if I revealed anything. Discussions from today's meeting must be kept secret."

"But how can I help if I am in the dark?" Revere chuckled. "No pun intended."

"We will inform you in plenty of time. You are probably wise enough to keep your schedule open for the sixteenth." Molineux blew into his hands and rubbed them together. "At least they brought *Eleanor* to dock here at Griffin's Wharf. Having these two ships together will make it easier. Not easy, but at least easier. Do you know how much a crate of tea weights? A whole lot more than either one of us."

"I heard that Mr. Hutchinson ordered the officer at the castle do whatever necessary to prevent unauthorized ships from leaving the harbor."

"We heard the same," Molineux said.

"Any progress as a result of your meetings with Mr. Rotch and Mr. Rowe?"

"We will find out tomorrow." Molineux rearranged his sack of hay then settled his head onto it. "In the meantime, I need to get some rest."

"Too bad they were allowed to unload the other cargo," Revere said. "The ship rocks more with less weight."

"All the better to sleep by," Molineux said. "Do you mind keeping one eye open for a while?"

"Not at all. All right if I wake you in a couple hours so I can take a turn?"

Molineux shut his eyes and grinned. "Good idea. We both need to stay awake during tomorrow's meeting." He rolled over. "Good night."

Molineux arrived at Old South a little late so took a seat in the back. The side galleries—and presumably the one above him—were full, meaning several thousand in attendance. Once settled, he turned his attention to the stage. A new moderator presided. A non-Bostonian, Adams had declared, would demonstrate their concerns went beyond their own town.

"We have received word from Philadelphia," the moderator said. "Their tea consignees have resigned, and New York has confirmed its commitment to refuse their tea to be landed."

The crowd burst into cheers.

The moderator motioned for quiet. "As you know, those assigned to receive the tea here have refused to send the detestable weed back to England. As a result, we have been speaking directly with the owners and captains of the ships in order to reach a resolution."

"If an answer is not found within the next three days—by midnight on Thursday—the customs officials will have legal authority to confiscate the cargo and demand that we pay the taxes. We have gathered today to get a status regarding two of the vessels."

"The captain of *Eleanor* has joined me on the platform." The moderator faced the man. "Have you secured clearance for your ship to depart?"

The captain scanned the audience. "I have not but planned to do so once the non-offensive cargo has been unloaded."

"You are probably aware," the moderator said, "the people expect you to depart for England even if clearance is denied."

"I am," the captain said, "but have concerns about the thirty-two pounders at Castle William I would need to sail past in order to do so. Those cannons would do great damage to my ship and possibly to its crew."

"Then we ask you to seek permission for clearance," the moderator said, "and will discuss alternatives after you determine if they are needed."

The captain departed, and the moderator called Rotch to the stage.

"Have you made preparations," the moderator asked, "to comply with the resolutions of the people?"

"Since our last meeting," Rotch said, "I have sought counsel. To allow my ship to depart without proper clearance would ruin me. The promise I made earlier to send my ship back to England was a result of fear. I no longer believe I should be held to a promise made under duress."

Rotch's eyes begged for mercy. "I desire to go as far as any reasonable man ought for the sake of his country, yet I cannot see the justice or patriotism of my being put at the front of the battle. Everyone in this room is aware of the impossibility of my getting the tea back to England and that I would be ruined if I attempted to do so."

Faces of those sitting around Molineux softened.

"I am willing to bear my portion of the loss, if the vessel is destroyed," Rotch said. "But would it not be reasonable for those involved in its destruction to do the same?"

Quincy rose from his seat and faced the bulk of the group. "Mr. Rotch has made a fair case, and I will put fifty guineas toward the cost of sending his ship back to Britain."

"You speak very finely, sir"—the voice came from the gallery— "but you do not show your money."

Quincy addressed the heckler. "I have not taken any money from Mr. Rotch to say what I have said. Anyone who would suggest so is a scoundrel." The attorney sat down.

Mr. Rotch cleared his throat, and the audience turned back to him. "What Mr. Quincy has stated is true. And I am surprised no merchant or any other citizen, until now, has offered to share in the damages I might sustain."

The moderator stood in silence for a moment. "If we can arrange for a committee to accompany you to the customs officials to seek clearance, would you agree?"

Rotch nodded. "As you know, Mr. Harrison and Mr. Hallowell— or their close relatives—still have scars they suffered during the *Liberty* episode several years ago. I am not sure how receptive they might be to my request."

"We understand," the moderator said, "but have no choice but to ask. We will form a committee to accompany you and give you until Thursday morning to complete your mission."

Cool air from the back of the room hit Molineux's neck. A messenger walked to the front and handed a note to the moderator who scanned it then returned to the podium. "You will be happy to hear the *Beaver* has been released from quarantine and is making its way to Griffin's Wharf to join the other tea-laden ships. The fourth ship has run aground amid a gale on the back of Cape Cod."

He looked up from the note. "I will see you back here Thursday morning at ten o'clock. At that time, we expect to receive an account of Mr. Rotch's inquiry to the customs officials."

Molineux stood in the doorway of Old South and brushed the drizzle from the blanket someone had thrown over his shoulders. Thursday morning's cold rain had not deterred the crowds. No hand-bills nor ringing bells were needed. With the deadline hours away, everyone wanted to see for themselves how the drama would unfold.

Thousands inside and more outside had held their collective breath only to learn the customs officials had denied Rotch's request for clearance. The meeting asked Rotch to make one final plea to their governor. They had given him until three o'clock to make the seven-mile trip to and from Hutchinson's country estate.

Three o'clock had come and gone with no signs of Rotch.

Adams, Hancock, Dr. Young, and others had appeased the gathering with speeches while Molineux remained in the shadows. Light from the candles flickered across weary faces. Molineux pulled out his watch and tilted it toward the glow. Twenty 'til six. He placed the watch back into his pocket and returned his attention to the stage. Quincy had been at the podium for a while.

"Let us look to the end," Quincy said. "Let us weigh and consider before we advance to those measures that must bring on the most trying and terrific struggle this country ever saw."

The lawyer took two steps back, gazed upward, and raised one hand. "I see the clouds, which now rise thick and fast upon our horizon. The thunder and lightning play." Quincy lowered his head and hand. "And to God who rides the whirlwind and directs the storm I commit my country."

The moderator returned to the podium. "Next we will hear from—"

"We have waited long enough," someone from The Body said.

"He is not coming back," added another.

"Some of us have traveled many miles. I say we give him until six o'clock to return."

Molineux felt a tug at the blanket and turned to see Rotch. The group parted, and a wet and muddy Rotch made his way to the stage. All eyes focused on him.

"Has our governor given you permission to pass safely beyond the castle?" the moderator asked.

No one breathed.

Rotch shook his head. "He has not."

"A mob! A mob!" someone said.

Dr. Young rose from his seat. "Mr. Rotch has done all in his power to comply with our demands. We do not need to harm him or his property."

Molineux glanced at the seat where Adams had been sitting. Empty. He was making his way to the platform.

The moderator faced Rotch. "Will you attempt to send your vessel back to England with its tea?"

"I cannot, for it would be my ruin."

"Do you intend to land the tea?"

"If called upon by the proper authorities, I would do so."

Adams ascended the stairs and walked toward the podium. The moderator stepped back.

"Who knows how tea will mingle with saltwater tonight?" someone said.

A hush settled over the crowd. All eyes were on Adams.

"The authorities of whom Mr. Rotch speaks," Adams said, "have refused our repeated requests and have placed us at the end of a very long journey."

Molineux waited for the signal.

"This meeting can do nothing more to save the country," Adams said.

Molineux grabbed the edge of his blanket and whirled it in the air, then he let out a war whoop. Others in the meetinghouse gallery and in the street answered with the same.

The time had come, and the assembly erupted.

"Boston Harbor a teapot tonight!"

"Hurrah for Griffin's Wharf!"

"The Mohawks are come!"

The rain had ceased, and Molineux ran into the street to join the Mohawks making their way to the wharf for a tea party.

Thin moon. Gusty winds. Low tide.

Lamps and torches.

Axes and hatchets.

Plans from three days before played themselves out.

A hundred men, most less than one score and ten. Molineux, at fifty-seven, the eldest.

Hundreds watched from the shore in silent awe.

Quietly. Methodically. And without harm to the ships, their captains or crew.

Three ships. Three hours.

Three hundred forty-two chests of tea now in the harbor.

The die cast.

CHAPTER TWENTY-SEVEN

All In

December 31, 1773–October 24, 1774

The bonfire crackled as hundreds celebrated New Year's Eve on the Common.

Molineux picked up another bundle of tea and heaved it into the flames. "How inconsiderate for the tide to carry the tea right back to us—and for someone to smuggle it home for his own use."

Revere slid onto the ground. "I hope this will take care of it once and for all. I'm exhausted."

Molineux laughed. "You are simply worn out from all the traveling you have done."

"I suppose. But it was worth it to see the glee on their faces. I wish you could have heard the bells ringing in New York and Philadelphia. You would have thought we had crowned a new king."

"Mr. Adams is almost giddy with delight," Molineux said.

"His cousin says the destruction of the tea was so important and bold, he considers it an epoch in history."

"Interesting." Molineux shook the tea leaves from his hands. "Did you read about the renewed call for a congress in the papers a few days ago?"

Revere nodded, stood up, and grabbed another bundle of tea.

"I tend to agree with it," Molineux said. "The consequences of failure can't be worse than what would happen without the attempt."

"At least the event in our harbor went off without a hitch—logistically, I mean. Politically, it may be another cup of tea."

Molineux chuckled and picked up more of the despicable weed.

"You laugh now, but when word reaches London, they may send over a hangman with his noose," Revere said. "You, Adams, and Hancock will be among the first he seeks out."

Dr. Young emerged from the crowd. "Have I missed anything?"

Molineux threw his batch of tea into the fire. "Only Mr. Revere's prediction as to how Britain might punish us for our misbehavior."

Revere let out a weighty breath of air. "Dr. Young will likely hang with the rest of you."

"All the more reason to enjoy what we can while we can, right?" Molineux winked.

Dr. Young rubbed his hands toward the fire. "They had better send their best ship over for us. I would welcome the all-expense-paid opportunity to display our political talents before the British legislature."

"Please tell the king we refuse to pay any more taxes," Revere said.

Molineux began to sway his arms back and forth then burst into song. "Rally, Mohawks! Bring out your axes, and tell King George we'll pay no taxes." He motioned for those nearby to join in.

"On his foreign tea!" they sang.

Molineux sauntered through the crowd and continued the now-familiar tune. "His threats are vain and vain to think, to force our girls and wives to drink."

The crowd responded. "His vile Bohea tea!"

Molineux scurried back toward the fire for the grand finale. "Our country's 'braves' and firm defenders shall ne'er be left by true North Enders."

He swung his hands toward the ensemble.

"Fighting freedom's cause!" they sang.

Molineux threw up his arms in victory. England might very well punish them, but no matter what came, Boston would stand firm. He was sure of it.

Molineux leaned on the handrails of his front porch as he watched the newly arrived red coats march onto the Common. Spring had brought news of London's response to the dumping of the tea, and in the early days of June, their plans had begun to unfold.

"Can you believe Mr. Hutchinson is gone?" Molineux asked Dennie.

"It is hard to imagine," Dennie replied.

"The day I watched his ship pull away," Molineux said, "is one I will not soon forget."

"He will be happy in England. It is as if he lived there in his mind while his body was here."

The sound of rolling drums drifted up the hill.

"As difficult as he was to deal with"—Dennie made a sweeping motion toward the Common—"I am not sure *this* is an improvement."

"General Gage will likely rule us with a rod of iron," Molineux said.

"At least Mr. Hancock was able to get in a few words to the townsfolk before the troops rolled back in."

Molineux smiled. "He gave quite the fiery speech, didn't he?"

"Who knew he had so much fire in his belly?" Dennie said.

"His flame flickered for years," Molineux said, "but the massacre anniversary provided him with the opportunity to pull it out from under the bushel."

"He certainly gave us a lot to think about."

"Yes, he did." Molineux took a step back and raised his head and a hand toward the sky. "They have usurped the right to rule us, in all cases whatsoever, by arbitrary laws." Molineux looked at Dennie. "Is that how it went?"

Dennie nodded.

Molineux reset his pose and wrinkled his brow. "Let our misfortunes instruct posterity to guard against these evils."

"Am I posterity?" Dennie asked.

Molineux relaxed. "You are someone's posterity. It also includes those yet to come—those we can only imagine who will one day make this great land their home." Molineux surveyed the scene before him. "If only we can keep this land great until they arrive."

"A standing army is not part of a great country, is it?"

"Not an army who seeks to suppress the freedoms of a righteous people," Molineux said.

"Samuel Adams is also concerned about other ways the king is taking charge of our affairs," Dennie said.

"And so he should be. The king already took over paying the judges, and with his new ability to appoint the governor's council, it provides one person with way too much power than is safe."

"And what about the juries?"

"They are going to be closely monitored," Molineux said. "Again, it is all about power—the ability of someone to control us."

"And to control our port," Dennie said.

"Parliament closing our port is where we will feel it most, but sometimes the true danger is more difficult to see. And often we do not recognize it until it is too late."

"Does it not seem a bit extreme to you?" Dennie asked. "All of this for throwing tea into the harbor? I heard John Adams ask if the killing of a child or the slaughter of a half dozen citizens by a party of soldiers was not as bad as drowning a cargo of tea."

"I see his point, but dumping the tea was a statement," Molineux said. "A huge statement against the tyranny Britain has tried to force upon us these past ten years."

"What are we going to do?"

"Well," Molineux said, "our Committee of Correspondence is drafting a letter to send the other colonies. We believe, with their help, we will be able to survive whatever else comes our way. Virginia declared a day of prayer and fasting, and Boston has done the same."

"And I heard all the colonies may come together for a meeting."

"The idea has been out there for years," Molineux said. "And Mr. Adams believes the time is finally ripe. Our desire remains redress, not independence. If the Motherland will hear our grievances, we believe there is still hope."

"In the meantime, we have this to contend with," he said, pointing to the troops. Molineux stretched to full height. "What Mr. Adams doesn't know is I plan to engage the mob to help me destroy the king's troops. Otherwise, left unchecked, there is no telling what they might do."

Steam rose from the steps of the Cambridge courthouse as sweat rolled down Molineux's back. September had brought no relief from the heat, and the troops' seizure of the provincial gunpowder had pushed the town over the edge. A predawn call for help had set Boston's Committee of Correspondence into action. Throughout the day, several had spoken to the well-armed crowd, which had grown to four thousand strong.

Dr. Warren now stood on the stairs addressing them. "There was a time when some good men among us were insensible to the danger and preferred obscurity to action. But the late maneuvers of tyranny have roused them from their lethargy, and they now pant for the field in which the fate of our country is to be decided. The treatment we have received from the soldiery makes us think they regard us as enemies rather than fellow subjects."

Dr. Warren wiped the perspiration from his brow. "Some of you have come through the night in order to assist your brothers in need. As my colleagues and I traveled here this morning, we saw incredible numbers along the way, with arms in hand, who were determined to die if they could not live free. We commend you all, yet at least two things prompt me to ask for calm amid recent events."

"First, Boston has suffered a great deal as a result of the latest measures taken by Parliament. Yet the generous spirit of our ancestors has been revived among our fellow colonists who have shared with us during our time of need."

"Second, as I have written to Samuel Adams in Philadelphia, we must continue to seek milder plans—such as nonimportation—until they have been exhausted."

Molineux perked up.

"Have no fear, my friends," Dr. Warren said. "If and when prudence demands it, you will be called upon to defend your country with every piece of artillery within your means. But until that time comes—"

"Mr. Hallowell!" someone in the crowd cried.

Everyone's attention shifted to the street. There, a carriage followed by a servant mounted upon a horse came to a halt. A red-faced Hallowell emerged onto the step of the chaise with a pistol at his hip.

"You people should know better than this," Hallowell said. "Have you not received word from our new governor these meetings are forbidden?" Hallowell jumped down and tramped toward the gathering. "But what should I expect from such a despicable collection of people?"

One of the men in the group charged toward him. Hallowell pulled out his gun.

The crowd gasped.

The pistol refused to fire, and Hallowell darted toward the back of his carriage, pulled the servant from the horse, and jumped on. He spun around. "You lowlifes will never learn."

"We will have your guts out," one of the men shouted as he mounted his own horse.

Hallowell and his horse galloped away, and within minutes, more than a hundred were in pursuit.

Dr. Warren cast a helpless glance toward Molineux.

Several minutes passed before many of the impromptu cavalry returned.

"We scared him," one of them said. "That's satisfaction enough— at least for now."

The meeting wrapped up, and Molineux chatted with Dr. Young while awaiting the others to join him for the trip back to Boston.

"Did you hear?" Dr. Young said. "General Gage has sent a cannon to Boston's Neck."

"He what?" Molineux said.

"He apparently wants to cut us off from anyone who seeks to bring us aid."

Molineux spit. "And from any shipments of supplies making their way to us through other ports."

"Unfortunate for us all," Dr. Young said. "By the way, how is Junior doing? I haven't seen him since he was attacked by the soldiers."

"Shaken up at first," Molineux said. "But now he is madder than a hornets' nest and ready to fight back."

Dr. Young let out a long sigh. "My wife thinks we should join the caravan of those leaving Boston—and very soon. She, like so many others, believes it has become too dangerous for us to stay."

Molineux's eyes widened. "Oh?"

"We will see," Dr. Young said. "Maybe Mr. Revere will bring us good news from Philadelphia on his next trip."

"The way things are going," Molineux said, "I would not set my heart on it."

"I'm coming. I'm coming." Molineux hurried to the front door of his Beacon Hill home. "Who would be calling at this hour?"

Molineux opened the door. "Mr. Revere."

"My apologies for the lateness of the hour," Revere said, "but there was a light in your window, so I assumed you were up. I have just returned from Philadelphia and thought you would want to hear the news."

Molineux stepped aside. "Please, come in. The parlor should be comfortable amid the October chill. Speaking of news, did you hear of Dr. Young's removal to Newport?"

Revere nodded.

Molineux stoked the smoldering embers, then the two men took a seat. "Now for your report. You have piqued my curiosity."

Revere unbuttoned his jacket. "A portion of what I want to tell you will be in the newspaper in a couple days, but I wanted you to receive it firsthand—and provide you with additional information. Congress has approved our province's opposition to the late acts of Parliament."

"Very good news, indeed."

"They have also prepared a petition to the king stating our grievances," Revere said. "What I thought you might find particularly encouraging is the talk surrounding a possible continental association."

"Oh?"

"They want to encourage manufacturing in this country," Revere said.

Molineux leaned forward.

"There is more," Revere said. "If goods reach our shores contrary to any nonimportation agreement, the profits would go to relieve and employ those who suffer the most as a result of the Port Act."

Molineux's spirit danced within him.

"There are many other topics being discussed," Revere said, "including freedoms for which you have fought long and hard."

Molineux reached for his head with one hand and grabbed the armrest of his chair with the other.

"Are you all right?" Revere asked.

"All of a sudden, I do not feel well," Molineux said.

"Would you like me to fetch Dr. Warren?"

"No, I will be fine." The room blurred as Molineux attempted to put together his thoughts. "British soldiers visited me last evening. I believe they brought with them some bad wine." He strained to focus on Revere. "There is more. What are you not telling me?"

Revere glanced down then back at Molineux. "If you're not feeling well—"

"What is it?"

"Congress has confirmed Britain's desire to transport several Bostonians to England to stand trial for treason."

"Did I make it onto the list?"

Revere nodded. "Along with Samuel Adams, Dr. Warren, and a few others."

"Then I am in good company."

"Has it been worth it? If they make you stand trial, that is. If they find you guilty, the cost is high."

"Ten years ago, I might not have thought it worth the price." Molineux sat back in his chair. "But now I understand more of what is at stake. So, yes, it has been worth it." The room whirled about him. Then everything went dark.

A damp pillow rested beneath Molineux's head. The ceiling of his bedroom faded in and out. Dr. Warren had come and gone—and conveyed enough information to leave no doubt. Molineux knew he was dying.

Resisting the temptation to swoon, he forced his mind to reflect on what his death might mean for those who remained. Samuel Adams and the others would be able to carry on certain aspects of the fight, but with his own impending death and Dr. Young's recent move, who would be left to incite the crowds to action? While other men of Boston intentionally avoided rabble-rousing, Molineux had embraced it.

He pushed the bed linens away from his clammy body as other unorthodox distinctions floated through his mind. Molineux's most notable trait, at least to his fellow patriots, was his lack of judgment in choosing colleagues. Other revolutionaries preferred to remain aloof from the Tories with whom he chose to associate, both at Sunday vespers and in weekday commerce. Neither Boston-born nor Harvard-bred, Molineux considered himself fortunate to have been accepted at all. Yet, in time, even those who distanced themselves from his more radical ways had come to appreciate the importance of ungentleman-like tasks.

As for his relationship with the British, had his prominent role leading up to the destruction of the tea been the final straw? No doubt they would mount a counteroffensive and claim Molineux's struggling business and mishandling of Mr. Apthorp's funds had brought him to the brink of despair. Whispers of suicide would find their way into gossip already circulating throughout the local taverns.

Muted conversations drifted up the stairs. Molineux's sons had dropped by to get an update on their father's condition. The echo of footsteps came then faded away. Had he fallen asleep? A soft hand gently brushed the back of his own. Maryann was at his bedside, keeping vigil.

His thoughts muddled, yet he managed a tired smile as the sun and wind danced with falling leaves outside his window. He would not live to see it, but spring would come again. Would others continue to fight for American liberties? Or would his efforts have been in vain?

Hancock surveyed those who had gathered at Old Granary Burying Grounds—people as far as the eye could see. "When did he die?" Hancock asked Dr. Warren.

"Six o'clock Saturday morning," Dr. Warren said. "The suddenness with which illness invaded his body has given rise to rumors the British used poison to silence him."

"Did you hear? Some of the soldiers have requested Trinity Church make arrangements for them to begin attending Sunday services."

"Really?" Dr. Warren said. "How ironic they would seek penance in the very place Mr. Molineux's children were baptized."

"Speaking of places of worship," Hancock said, "the bell I ordered for my church finally arrived."

Dr. Warren cast a questioning glance.

"It came through the port in Salem," Hancock said. "The inscription on it seems timely: 'I to the church the living call, and to the grave I summon all.'"

"Indeed it is."

Townsfolk continued to pour into the graveyard. "What do you think of this crowd?" Hancock asked.

"It does not surprise me. Mr. Molineux was one of the most well-known Sons of Liberty," Dr. Warren said. "His death will leave a great hole."

"And be lamented by patriots far and wide," Hancock said. "I am sure Mr. Revere will carry the news of his death to the other colonies during his next trip—certainly to Philadelphia."

"Do you regret not being part of our delegation to the congress?"

Hancock shook his head. "My efforts have been needed here."

"Even more so with the passing of our friend and fellow patriot," Dr. Warren said.

Hancock watched as they lowered Molineux's body into the grave.

"His mantle has passed to us," Dr. Warren said, "and we must not disappoint him." The doctor pulled a paper from his jacket. "I included his dying words in the obituary I provided to the newspaper—a final plea to us all."

"In all the rush," Hancock said, "I have not had time to read it. Would you be so kind?"

Dr. Warren lifted the paper and began to read aloud.

On Saturday morning last, after three days' illness, departed this life Mr. William Molineux in the fifty-eighth year of his age. A noted merchant of this town.

But what rendered this gentleman more eminently conspicuous was his inflexible attachment to the liberties of America. 'Tis not to be wondered that Mr. Molineux—who was unappalled at danger and inaccessible to bribe or corruption—should become obnoxious to those in power and their informants for his enthusiastic zeal in so noble a cause.

His time and his labor were with unremitted ardor applied to the public service. It was his pride to confront the power and malice of his country's foes. It was his constant wish and relentless effort to defeat them.

It may with truth be said of this friend of mankind that he died a martyr to the interests of America. His watchfulness, labor, distresses, and exertions to promote the general interest produced an inflammation in his bowels. The disease was rapid and poignant, but in the severest pangs, he rose superior to complaint. He felt no distresses but for the public.

"O save my country, Heaven!" he said and died.

Epilogue
October 26, 1774, and Beyond

Two days after Molineux was laid to rest, delegates of the Continental Congress departed Philadelphia. They planned to reconvene the following May, if Britain did not redress their grievances. In November 1774, King George wrote of the New England colonies that "blows must decide whether they are to be subject to this country or independent."

In March 1775, Dr. Warren gave the oration at the annual event commemorating the massacre. Several weeks later, the first shots of the Revolutionary War were fired at Lexington. Hours before, Dr. Warren had dispatched two horsemen, including Revere, to warn the countryside of the danger at hand. They also warned Samuel Adams and John Hancock who were already in hiding. Dr. Warren wrote to General Gage, "I think I have done my duty."

In June, the Provincial Congress of Massachusetts Bay commissioned Dr. Warren as a major general of its militia. General Warren died three days later at what would become known as the Battle of Bunker Hill. Boston fell to General Gage and his troops, and patriots surrendered nearly two thousand muskets then left the city. Loyalists poured into Boston from the countryside.

Eleven months later, Americans utilized cannons retrieved from Ticonderoga, New York, to reclaim their town. One thousand British troops, along with a thousand women and children, sailed for Nova Scotia. Colonists took charge of property left behind by the Loyalists, including that of the Hallowells and the Hutchinson brothers. Bostonians replaced the less popular word "British" with "American" on the sign in front of the King Street coffeehouse. Most who had fought for nonimportation would become patriots, while those who fought against it became Loyalists.

While General Gage had the upper hand, he offered to pardon everyone except Samuel Adams and John Hancock "whose offences were too flagrant in nature" to go unpunished. A year later, both men signed the Declaration of Independence while serving in the Second Continental Congress, which Hancock oversaw as president.

Hancock married his Aunt Lydia's houseguest in 1775. They named their daughter after his Aunt Lydia and their son after George Washington. Neither survived childhood.

After the war, Massachusetts elected Hancock as its first and third governor, and Samuel Adams as its fourth.

Adams, Hancock, and Molineux died years apart, yet all in the month of October.

John Hancock died in 1793 and was laid to rest at the Old Granary Burying Ground, a few feet from Molineux. Neighbors both in life and in death.

Christopher Seider and the five massacre victims lay in the same cemetery. Many of Molineux's other patriot friends were also interred there: Samuel Adams, Paul Revere, Drs. Young and Warren, and James Otis. Otis had received the means of death he had wished for when, in the spring of 1783, a bolt of lightning struck him down.

Molineux "has been famous among the Sons of Liberty," Rowe mentioned in his diary on the day of his burial. "A great concourse of people attended his funeral," he added before listing the half dozen pallbearers.

The first pallbearer was Molineux's neighbor to the east, James Bowdoin, who would have been in Philadelphia with the delegates had it not been for his wife's poor health. His presence in Boston, however, enabled him to help get Molineux's body to its grave. Bowdoin served as Massachusetts's second governor.

Another pallbearer, William Dennie, came into the patriot fold a bit late. Once he did, he often found himself at Molineux's side. Dennie served on the Committee of Correspondence with a fellow merchant and pallbearer, Captain John Bradford. After bloodshed at Lexington, however, Dennie fell away from the patriots' cause. He died soon after the war ended.

"Mr. Pitts" mentioned in Rowe's diary may refer to Lendall, an officer in Hancock's cadets and a Son of Liberty who had commanded one of the three divisions of "Mohawks" who dump the tea into Boston's harbor ten months before. Lendall's brother served with Molineux on the Committee of Correspondence and with Hancock as a selectman. Lendall's father was a member of the governor's council.

"Old Mr. Erving" also helped with Molineux's interment. Some of Erving's family had joined Molineux for at least two decades in upholding merchants' rights. Another part of the family sided with the Loyalists and provided temporary headquarters for General Gage. They eventually left Boston with the British army.

The remaining pallbearer, Thomas Boylston, had served with Molineux in various capacities, including going to Rhode Island in 1770 to get cities there back on track with the nonimportation agreement. Like Erving, Boylston had experienced the pain of being on the opposite side of the debate from a family member. Thomas's Tory brother and business partner, Nicholas, died in 1771, leaving his fortune to their nephew who immediately eloped with Molineux's daughter, Anne. In order to receive his uncle's estate, Ward Hallowell was required to take on the name of his childless benefactor. Thus, the marriage of the offspring of the patriot William Molineux and the Tory Benjamin Hallowell, made Thomas a relative of the one he helped place into the ground on that October day.

After Molineux's death, his children lived out their lives in a variety of ways.

Anne led a difficult life after her marriage to Ward Nicholas Boylston (Ward Hallowell). Two years after their elopement, Ward left for an extended trip to Italy then to ports beyond—including Turkey, Egypt, Syria, and Palestine. As the war in America heated up, Anne sailed for London where Ward and their son, Nicky, had settled. But Ward wanted nothing to do with her, and Anne died on her voyage back to America in 1779.

Their eight-year-old son survived the trip and was placed into the custody of his uncle, Captain Benjamin Hallowell, who put him to sea on one of the Royal Navy ships over which he had some charge. In 1794, Nicky married Mary Bentham in Charleston, South Carolina. The senior Boylston made it clear in his Last Will and Testament his son was only to receive an inheritance upon the condition he never return to Massachusetts. When the will was written, Nicky was "in the service of the East India Company in the City of London." He died in 1839 and was buried in Savoy, London.

While Anne was in London working to reconcile with Ward, her brother Junior helped support her.

In mid-April 1775—less than six months after his father's demise and mere days before shots were fired at Lexington—Junior witnessed the seize of most of the munitions at Fort Pownal in what later became Maine. By this time, the Molineux brothers had property-related dealings—which eventually turned into lawsuits—in the Beauchamp Neck area of Camden. At the time of the seizure, Junior may have been at the fort doing business with the fort's storekeeper, who was also from

Boston. Less than two weeks before, Boston had voted Junior as one of the clerks of its market.

Junior, commissioned by Major General John Hancock, served in the colonial militia in various capacities from 1776 to 1779.

In 1780, Junior and John followed in their father's footsteps when they established a general wholesale store on King Street, renamed State Street after the war. The shop included "a beautiful assortment of English goods" and accepted "hard or paper money, French, Spanish or Dutch bills." The siblings' relationship was less than ideal, as John accused Junior of using "indelicate language" toward him as an "effect of high passion." In the days following the war, the brothers bought and sold property that the Loyalists had deserted.

In 1794, Junior took up residence in Camden, Maine, where he married and built grist and saw mills. He drowned in the lake in front of his home in 1801. No documents have surfaced to indicate whether the "good drink" of which Junior wrote in 1774 or the "strong drink" for which he was permitted to sell in 1782 played a role in his death.

In 1805, John returned to his deepest roots by partnering with a Mr. Cook to start a hardware business on Union Street. In 1810, he began a brass foundry, eventually focusing on andirons, which graced the fireplaces in many a Boston parlor. John was "celebrated for his superior work" in that field as late as the twentieth century. A few years before his death, he became a member of the popular Massachusetts Charitable Mechanics Association of which Paul Revere was the first president. John died in Boston in 1826.

At the time of this publication, nothing had been uncovered regarding the destiny of William Molineux's youngest daughter, Elizabeth.

Hutchinson lived out the remainder of his days in England where he received an honorary degree of Doctor of Civil Law on the fourth of July 1776. He died in 1780, a few months before the tide of the war turned in the Americans' favor. While in exile, Hutchinson wrote, "It may be questioned whether any persons engaged in this cause could hope for a separation of the colonies and a total independency upon the Parliament of Great Britain during their lives."

Molineux did not live to see his desire for liberty fulfilled, but his widow, Maryann, did. On the third of September 1783, the United States of America and Great Britain signed the Treaty of Paris. On November 12 of the same year, Maryann succumbed to her aged body.

Upon the death of William Molineux Sr. in 1774, his estate passed to Loyalist Charles Ward Apthorp—likely his biggest creditor. As fate would have it, however, under a 1777 act pertaining to estates of absentees, Apthorp's properties were confiscated in 1781, and Molineux's former lands and dwelling sold on the fourth of July 1782. Thirteen years later to the day, Revere presided over a cornerstone ceremony for the erection of the Massachusetts State House. The grounds on which it would be built included the property where Hancock's and Molineux's homes once stood.

A nineteenth-century historian claimed, "With the exception of Samuel Adams, no name is oftener found in connection with the public acts of the day, than that of William Molineux, and his death . . . was a great loss to the patriot cause." In the early part of the twenty-first century, an expert on Revolutionary Boston declared that "between 1768 and 1774, Molineux was behind only Samuel Adams in importance as a Boston organizer."

Although his name eventually passed into obscurity outside academia, Molineux was instrumental in the years leading up to the Revolutionary War.

During the writs case of the early 1760s, Otis had mesmerized a twenty-five-year-old attorney and future president, John Adams, who later stated, "American independence was born. Then and there was the first scene of the first act of opposition to the arbitrary claims of Great Britain."

Molineux was a plaintiff in the case.

Several years later, John Adams claimed neither the Battle of Lexington nor Bunker Hill, nor the surrender of Cornwallis, "were more important events in American history than the Battle of King Street, on the fifth of March 1770." For it was on that night, which his cousin referred to as the massacre, "the foundation of American independence was laid."

A British officer dubbed Molineux as the event's author.

In the 1830s, the dumping of the tea into Boston's harbor became known as the Boston Tea Party. John Adams exclaimed the 1773 event was the grandest since the controversy with Britain had begun.

Molineux was among the handful of those everyone agrees was there.

In 1772, Molineux joined twenty others to form the Boston Committee of Correspondence. A few months after Molineux's death, a Tory spoke harshly against the group. "It is the foulest, subtlest, and most venomous serpent that ever issued from the eggs of sedition. It is the source of the rebellion."

Shots had been fired at Lexington, thrusting the colonies into war with the homeland, and Molineux was to blame.

Although Molineux did not live to see America's official Declaration of Independence, he was involved from the beginning—and died believing in all for which it stood.

I trust your journey into prerevolutionary Boston has inspired you in ways I can only imagine. If it has, I would appreciate your considering any or all of the following:

- Writing an online review—or multiples.
- Recommending this novel to friends, family, book clubs, home/private schools, special-interest groups, etc.
- Purchasing additional copies to use as gifts.

For bonus material, announcements about future publications, etc., please visit:

cammolineux.com.

Acknowledgments

Writing and publishing a book is a mammoth undertaking and is rarely accomplished alone. For those who have been part of my journey, I will be forever grateful.

Those who aided in my formal research:

- J. L. Bell, whose online journal (Boston1775.blogspot.com)—and enjoyable lunch together at the Boston Public Library during one of my research trips there—confirmed William Molineux had a story worth telling.
- The man who portrayed William Molineux at the Boston Tea Party Ships and Museum in the fall of 2015. I enjoyed a delightful conversation with him about the extraordinary rabble-rouser he sought to depict.
- Gary Gregory, executive director and print master of The Print Office of Edes & Gill, which is along Boston's Freedom Trail, who afforded me a few minutes of his time during my unexpected visit so that I might pick his brain.
- Staff at the New England Historic Genealogical Society (NEHGS) in Boston who directed me to insights about Molineux and his family.
- Staff at the Boston Public Library who provided resources, including newspapers from Molineux's time that contained priceless accounts of events for this story.
- Christian Higgins, archivist and library manager at the Independence National Historical Park in Philadelphia, who introduced me to a wealth of information about the Continental Congress.

Professionals and friends who gave of their time and talents to turn my research into something people would want to ingest:

- Betty Hassler, the first to lay a professional pen to the initial pages of my work.
- Yolanda Smith, whose editor's eye transformed my three hundred pages of facts into a novel.
- Christine Boatwright who graciously took one last look—actually, two looks—at my manuscript before the publisher transformed it into the finished product.
- Beta readers who added their precious input to help make my manuscript shine.
- Those at Redemption Press who contributed their amazing expertise to this project in order to turn the dream into reality. I especially want to thank:

  - Athena Dean Holtz, cofounder of Redemption Press, whose enthusiasm is contagious.
  - Hannah McKenzie, senior project manager, who skillfully guided me through the maze to publication.
  - Tisha Martin, editor, who went beyond the call of duty with her suggestions so readers would enjoy their journey through the sea of historical facts.
  - Dori Harrell, managing editor, who oversaw the editing process.
  - Cathy Sanders, cover designer, who captured the essence of this book in ways I only thought possible in my dreams.

Authors and others in the industry who had already achieved a level of success yet took time to spur me along and, dare I say, accept me as their friend:

- Eva Marie Everson, president of Word Weavers International, who provided the venue for me to learn what it meant to be a writer and who caused jaws to drop with her compliments of my initial attempts.

- James L. Rubart, best-selling and multi-award-winning author, who took the initiative to find the person behind my written words.
- Edie Melson, codirector of the Blue Ridge Mountains Christian Writers Conference (BRMCWC), who provided me with the opportunity to attend the largest Christian writers conference in the southeastern United States.
- Yvonne Lehman, founder of the BRMCWC and director of the Blue Ridge Christian Novelist Retreat, where I enjoyed honing my craft in a more intimate environment.
- Diana Flegal, literary agent with Hartline, whose encouraging words were among the first to let me know I could do this.
- Other professionals who poured into me in so many ways.

Authors and author wannabes who have climbed the mountain with me and elevated my writing to a whole new level:

- Members of the Word Weavers International chapters of which I was a part, especially Jean Wilund and Lori Hatcher, whose prayers kept me plugging along.
- Members of my Word Weavers International narrative subgroup, notably, Linda Summerford, Mary Reynolds, and Ron Gremore.
- Members of the American Christian Fiction Writers chapter where I periodically poked my head into their meetings.
- Other writing friends who have been part of this amazing adventure.

Distant cousins at the International Molyneux Family Association who joined me in piecing together my family tree:

- Its faithful leaders—Marie Mullenneix Spearman, Betty Molyneux Brown, Wayne Straight, Steve Mullinax, and Jim Molineux—whose labor of love have allowed so many the joy of discovering their Mx (Molineux, etc.) ancestors.

- Eldred and Sarah Mullinnix, whose years of research made it possible for me to climb my own tree more quickly.
- George Mollineaux, who joined me for several hours of research at the NEHGS.
- Donna Ripley, whose genealogical ties to William Molineux appear to go deeper than anyone else I know.
- Julie Mullinax Crawford who journeyed with me to the Old World in search of pieces to our family's puzzle.
- Antony Molyneux-Steele who, although fate left his Mx line on the other side of the Big Pond, graciously guided Julie and me through old graveyards where our common Mx relatives are buried.
- Russell Molyneux-Johnson, genealogist extraordinaire, with whom Julie and I were privileged to share a lunch in London.
- Charles Molineaux IV, whose amazing intellect keeps me inspired.

Most importantly, I want to thank my husband, who cheered me on every step of the way. Early on in this venture, a literary agent told me, "The writer whose spouse is on board is the one who will make it." I am fortunate to be married to one of the best encouragers in the world. Without his willingness to join me in this calling, I doubt this novel would have ever set sail.

Huzzah!

ORDER INFORMATION

MOUNTAIN VIEW PRESS

To order additional copies of this book, please visit
www.redemption-press.com.
Also available on Amazon.com and BarnesandNoble.com
or by calling toll-free 1-844-2REDEEM.

CPSIA information can be obtained
at www.ICGtesting.com
Printed in the USA
BVHW030959210821
614138BV00002B/7